RICANNESS

Ricanness

Enduring Time in Anticolonial Performance

Sandra Ruiz

NEW YORK UNIVERSITY PRESS

New York

NEW YORK UNIVERSITY PRESS
New York
www.nyupress.org

References to Internet websites (URLs) were accurate at the time of writing. Neither the author nor New York University Press is responsible for URLs that may have expired or changed since the manuscript was prepared.

Library of Congress Cataloging-in-Publication Data
Names: Ruiz, Sandra, author.
Title: Ricanness : enduring time in anticolonial performance / Sandra Ruiz.
Description: New York : New York University Press, 2019. |
Includes bibliographical references and index.
Identifiers: LCCN 2018041762| ISBN 9781479888740 (cl : alk. paper) |
ISBN 9781479825684 (pb : alk. paper)
Subjects: LCSH: Postcolonialism and the arts—Puerto Rico. | Time and art—Puerto Rico. |
Arts, Puerto Rican—Themes, motives. | Group identity in art.
Classification: LCC NX180.P67 R85 2019 | DDC 700.68/7295—dc23
LC record available at https://lccn.loc.gov/2018041762

New York University Press books are printed on acid-free paper, and their binding materials are chosen for strength and durability. We strive to use environmentally responsible suppliers and materials to the greatest extent possible in publishing our books.

Manufactured in the United States of America

10 9 8 7 6 5 4 3 2 1

Also available as an ebook

For all of the victims of Hurricane Maria

Listen real tight for a whimper,

Or perhaps a delicate address from the dead,

because even the hushed,

those unwanted,

those unrecorded

carry essence.

For my mentors dreaming elsewhere

Randy Martin

José Esteban Muñoz

For my father, que siempre le dio tiempo al tiempo

Juan Carrion Ruiz

CONTENTS

FIGURES

Introduction

A Living Colonialism, or Simply, the Aesthetic Life of Ricanness

I came into the world imbued with the will to find a meaning in things, my spirit filled with the desire to attain to the
source of the world, and then I found that I was an object in
the midst of other objects.
—Frantz Fanon, *Black Skin, White Masks*

Puerto Rico is the most important place in the world.
—Laura Briggs, *Reproducing Empire*

It's the sense of denial of self-determination . . . that feeling
you get from not being in control of your own life . . . not having a voice, feeling impotent inside of your own condition.
—ADÁL, interviewed by Jhoni Jackson

If "Puerto Rico is the most important place in the world," that is, the
perfect site to detangle the threads of modern globalization and the
incessant desires of colonialism, how do we critically reorganize the significance of the Rican being in a larger analysis of existence?[1] At the
apex of the Rican colonizer/colonized dialectic exists a subject that is
continually hunted and unwanted, and is equal parts needed and ines-
sential. This book, then, tells the story of the most important people in
the world through a series of aesthetic sites, disclosing this ambivalent
interplay between being dispensable and demanding to be wanted.

Almost fifteen years after Briggs's bold claim, Puerto Rico continues
to reveal how imperial methods sustain nations and dismantle bodies.
September 2017's Hurricane Maria is a chief instance of how the Rican
body, in particular, continuously enacts permanent endurance practices
to cultivate an existence under colonial time.[2] Ricans, then, not just the

1

island, are the infinite example of that perennial subject of the world, always already working against their own life at the cost of perpetual death, while simultaneously revealing how practices of Empire surpass the annexation of land. The colonial figures into every corporeal, performative, and psychical contour of the subject, at the pinnacle of their essence, regardless of where they build ground. In this book, the aesthetic directs our understanding of politics and Ricanness, leading us through the most painful but promising inquiries of subjugation at the scene of the enduring body.

The history of Ricanness embodies colonialism's global desires—an everlasting conquest of land, resources, cultural and social practices, and native peoples themselves—that began even before it started in 1492.[3] The Rican body—always indigenous, African, by consequence European—is marked by a common ongoing endurance and death that infiltrates the center of the subject's call to life, whether on or off the island. In colonialism's abiding assault against the present, then, we are forced to contend with its future at the very limit of its historical past. As we wait for colonialism's eternal death, its enterprise is invigorated by the violent friction both sustaining and destroying subjects; its violence is the most common thread in and constant pulse of the human. Of such violent acts, anticolonial theorist, philosopher, and psychoanalyst Frantz Fanon shares, "National liberation, national renaissance, the restoration of nationhood to the people, commonwealth: whatever may be the headings used or the new formulas introduced, decolonization is always a violent phenomenon."[4] Regardless of prefix, there is no getaway plan that erases the historical intensity and discursive practices of colonialism's aggressive force. Such force is also a psychological illness that manifests itself in material life—the material, here, is the physical body, the national body, the body of discourse, and the legal body. In the case of Ricans, we can randomly turn to any US/PR historical moment and notice the perpetual interplay of too much time and timelessness as an internal Rican phenomenon. For instance, during the Spanish-American War of 1898, one colonizer's demise became another colonizer's surplus through different laws, policies, and procedures. From Spain to the United States, Puerto Rico became a recurrent colony in different manifestations—from the Foraker Act of 1900 to the Jones Act of 1917,[5] from the sterilization policies of the 1930s to the pre-1947 English-only instruction policies,[6] from the gag laws of 1948 to the revised colonial project of the Commonwealth, or US territory, or Estado Libre Asociado, of the 1950s.[7] In our turn to new decolonial language to meet the demands of an emerging historical moment, the colonial refuses its own disappearance. It remains a living enterprise.

Following the largest migration of Puerto Ricans to the United States in the late 1940s, political tensions between the island and mainland reignited, and the 1950s rehearsed opposing nationalisms from both the colony and the colonizer.[8] As Puerto Rican freedom fighters staged an attack on President Truman's life in 1950, organized vigorously against imperialism, and were imprisoned and tortured for these actions, the United States responded with the Commonwealth of Puerto Rico, and a larger call against global insurgency.[9] Since 1952, this has been one version of the political, cultural, and economic interarticulation between the *us/them* dialectic through the Estado Libre Asociado. However, a Free Associated State, or a Commonwealth, as a national designation is filled with biting irony: for whom is the wealth common, or whose *common wealth* is implicitly denied in economic exchanges? The current debt crisis on the island points us in the direction of surplus labor and dead time—both in which Ricans are always unpaid in their endless fight for existence. It is difficult to ignore how the colonial history of Puerto Rico and the United States is always beginning again—it's an infinite project that forces one to contend with the future, even in spaces of present and foreseeable violence. It is also a project in temporal looping whereby actions to redress the past lead us into the future and back again to something prior; this is the affective consequence of colonialism—an active state in the here and now, looping forward and back into itself as if time never started or stopped ticking.

This eternal looping exposes what is done to the material, national, and discursive body in the name of historical expansionism. Puerto Rico is that colony that sustains the global and refuses to surrender local indignations. It's the Empire's response to the violence of its very own modernity, in which the people learn repeatedly how to disperse new ways of being and becoming in their acts of survival. But what does a historical tale about colonialism impart on the aesthetic life of Ricanness? How does the story of this book, in which the aesthetic reshifts the political contours of existence, get us closer to the temporal demands of Ricanness?

Ricanness under Water/*Los Ahogados*: The Aesthetic's Refusal of Submersion

ADÁL, Puerto Rican photographer and seminal figure of the Rican avant-garde, takes up these very questions in his 2016 photographic series, *Puerto Ricans Underwater/Los ahogados*.[10] In conversation with the current economic crisis in Puerto Rico—specifically the impact of the Puerto Rico Oversight, Management, and Economic Stability Act and the imposition of a federal Fiscal Control Board, which goes hand in hand with the massive migration of almost five hundred thousand Puerto Ricans to states across the United States, like Florida, in the last ten years alone—ADÁL reveals how Puerto Rican subjectivity, Ricanness, is the ultimate testament to this colonial nondeparture.[11] He maps out those spaces of negation, imbuing death and dread, dangerous migration, and national debt at the site of the drowning Rican body. Hitting against narratives of progress and economic development, ADÁL illustrates how the Rican situation is always already postcolonial, neocolonial, decolonial, settler colonial—none able to outrun their own temporal designation or destination, for the colonial alone harbors the ontological sustenance of Ricanness. In staging a dramatically painful encounter between colonialism and the island's debt crisis, ADÁL creates a series of one hundred photographs of Puerto Ricans, some friends of the artist and others strangers, from different professions and backgrounds. Individually submerged under water with objects/props of their choice and profession, each subject lays resolutely still in the bathtub, as the photographer captures what appears to be that last moment of tireless breath.

Each model contributes to their individual portrait through different performative acts that relate to their profession or personal likes and habits. Through the fine art of posing under water, detailed costuming, and deliberate use of props like play money, pill bottles, books, cigarette holders, instruments, and sometimes *plátanos* and *papayas*, all models reveal a sense of themselves in quotidian life, against the current of portending death. Whether as a Rican novelist, musician, chef, educator, poet, or dancer, each subject performs their vocation against their own mortality, through these acts of everyday labor, while also holding their breath underwater. The artist re-creates the deadly scene between the

United States and Puerto Rico in which labor and economic exploitation sit at the center of existence and national insolvency. Shot after shot, ADÁL's bathtub serves as that relational object between the territory and sovereign, in which the water flowing to its top is the metaphorical reality. Although a foreshadowing of impending disaster, it is the "very big ocean,"[12] symbolized in ADÁL's natatory bathtub, that remains a fixture of Ricanness—in between cultures, nations, and a colony and colonizer, water persists as a weapon, a situation of warfare, and an all-encompassing deathtrap between worlds.

These images foreshadow a colony soon to be indisputably underwater. In illustrating the elliptical and looping nature of the colonial circuits of Ricanness, the artist's images expose every social and psychical dynamic of daily life, even in the narrow space of a tub, doubling as a symbolic ocean. In the aftermath of Hurricane Maria, one notices how ADÁL prefigures Rican endurance, each subject breathing against the national current of death, disease, and debt. These photographs leave the viewer in a state of suspension: in seeing this breathless subject, we, too, are left without breath. In capturing the quotidian life of Ricans struggling to stay afloat under imperial rule, the artist unveils the perceived "debris" of those unwanted lives given scant attention in dominant visual narratives. ADÁL grants us lasting breath—even if belabored—in shots of engulfed portraiture. As historiography neatly conceals certain lives while vividly displaying others, ADÁL compels us to confront the unwanted by committing them to print, in water, against the brink of mortality, at the edge of communal breath. Let us remember that breathing is a shared endeavor. We intimately breathe together, feeling—even if unconsciously—the plural right to life. Perhaps ADÁL moves us to respire communally against the colonial current, for how else might we sense the inhale/exhale of an always drowning subjectivity?[13]

As a major innovator shaping the Rican experimental scene, ADÁL has regularly turned to visual culture and performance to reorganize singular constructions of subjectivity. For the past forty years, the artist has offered variant answers to the question of Rican identification through the scope of the aesthetic. For instance, with good friend Reverend Pedro Pietri, he collaborated on *El Puerto Rican Embassy*, "an imaginary world" that had its own passport and national anthem.[14] He also cocreated the performance piece *Mondo Mambo: A Mambo Rap Sodi*

Figure 1.1. Underwater Puerto Rican, ADÁL, 2016. Jeannette Betancourt. From series *Puerto Ricans Underwater/Los ahogados.* Strange Cargo Press, San Juan, PR, 2017. Courtesy of the artist.

Figure 1.2. Underwater Puerto Rican, ADÁL, 2016. Nelson Rivera. From series *Puerto Ricans Underwater/Los ahogados.* Strange Cargo Press, San Juan, PR, 2017. Courtesy of the artist.

with Pietri, Tito Puente, and Eddie Torre. Other works include musicals (*La Mambopera, Coconauts in Space*), a novel (*Mambo Madness*), a salsa opera (*Delito Cha Cha Cha*), and a film (*Nuyorican Zombies Ate My Baby*), as well as a poetry, music, and visual art festival in Vieques ("Viequethon 2002: Poetry and Concert for Peace"). But ADÁL is largely known for his ironic and evocative self-portraits, photo novellas, and portraiture of famous Puerto Rican figures.[15] Of his photographic travels with identity, ADÁL himself conveys, "From the beginning of my career as an artist and photographer my work has been informed by the impossibility of ever achieving a definitive picture of one's self. By this I mean that our identity is fluid and constantly evolving." Originally,

Figure 1.3. Underwater Puerto Rican, ADÁL, 2016. Bold Destrou. From series *Puerto Ricans Underwater/Los ahogados*. Strange Cargo Press, San Juan, PR, 2017. Courtesy of the artist.

as ADÁL explains, he created "self-portraits in order to work through existential worries of being and not being and unhealthy feelings of displacement."[16]

Moved to document a "collective identity," he "began a series of portraits of prominent Puerto Rican figures who transcended their circumstances."[17] For the artist, Ricanness is shaped by a collective colonial condition, marred by debt, existential angst, displacement, and dispossession. A way out of such terror appears for the artist through aesthetic fortitude. In his own analysis of the series *Puerto Ricans Underwater/Los ahogados*, he explains the personal and political feelings of negation, or subject incompletion, lack, and loss under unsovereignty:

> I think mainly and most importantly, it's the sense of denial of self-determination by having the federal government sort of impose their agenda on you. That feeling that you get from not being in control of your own life. That will manifest differently depending on different people . . . but I would say that's pretty much it; not having a voice, feeling impotent inside of your own condition.[18]

ADÁL's images and analysis of his series critically capture the place of internal compression and negation: how does one rightfully release oneself of existential strife while holding one's breath under water? Even with the subject's breath lines floating to the top of each image, the droplets of air fail to negate the excess of silence and imminent death, all in the compact zone of a bathtub. Yet ADÁL finds that muted voice, not by creating conventional sound but by forcing us to listen to images. In these photographs, I see why idealist subjects are arguably the saddest, sometimes drowning in order to survive their own disparaging dejection. They are sad because they are tenaciously expectant of something better. They are unwaveringly hopeful because even a bathtub is big enough to hold, regard, and dispense life, even if one's breath is held under water.

Roland Barthes argues that "because each photograph always contains this imperious sign of my future death that each one, however attached it seems to be to the excited world of the living, challenges each of us, one by one, outside of any generality (but not outside of any transcendence)."[19] Akin to Barthes's testimony, these photographs brush up against mortality, insisting on a reframing of Rican historiography, and instigate a time lapse into both the past and future. In this case, a series made in 2016 extrapolates Ricans under water in the form of images, transporting the eternal with such force that it cycles into its own history and future, "not outside of any transcendence" but certainly beyond its frame. Aesthetic interventions such as this one speak against practices of oppression in historical time, whereby the always enduring Rican subject is left both unwanted and eminently needed, in which their servitude is the imperative mechanism sustaining all life on constant loop.

In colonialism's refusal to follow the light out of this world, then, ADÁL asks how temporality, and not history alone, unearths its eternal recurrences in sites of displeasure, negation, incompletion, deadness, in which the wretched point us in the direction of the most promising of Rican domains. Seeping into every photograph is the vigorous force of subjugation in the subject's call to existence, in the space of embodiment, always near to death. Time shows us how to differently breathe in and out within these painful confines; and these anticolonial photographs bring to light the power of aesthetic transmission in ADÁL's personal and provocative version of Ricanness.

Like ADÁL, I, too, am concerned with what happens when colonialism is not ancillary to Ricanness, but rather its frame, shot—the mechanism that sustains its duration. These renditions of Ricanness do not labor against an anticolonialist discourse in reference to the Puerto Rican condition.[20] Reading such an existence through the lens of colonialism is not a choice, it's historical realism, asking us to feel and sense the "impotence" ADÁL experiences. In an immediate account of the deadly enterprise of colonialism, and akin to Briggs's position of the island, Puerto Rican scholar Jorge Duany explains that "no country in recent history has undergone a more dramatic, prolonged, and massive displacement of its people."[21] In refiguring globalization and spatial politics, Duany conjoins cultural migration patterns and Rican existence itself under forms of unsovereignty, and adds, "Such dizzying nomadism—a constant dislocation and relocation of peoples, practices, imaginaries, and identities—has been posited as one of the defining moments of a global, transnational, or postmodern age."[22] Here, one is forced to look into the intricate and internal mechanisms of a tiny colony to understand and relocate the course and currency of the global. Similarly, Frances Negrón-Muntaner argues that Puerto Ricans are "imagined as 'territorial' citizens whose citizenship standing and national worth significantly shifts according to location."[23] In acknowledging how displacement, relocation, and dispossession shape Ricanness, she adds that endurance practices of Puerto Ricans stem from a "gradual exhaustion," an act of suffering that is a result of the long-standing struggle for economic and political self-sufficiency.[24] To be Rican, then, means to ride out the inexhaustible constraints of one's life under limited self-control in a nonstop state of economic and political impotence.

Like the work of these scholars of Ricanness, ADÁL's work illuminates how Rican subjectivity is recognizable beyond a geographical understanding of the United States and Puerto Rico, even in the transient, isolated, metaphorical space of the tub. He exposes what embodies Ricanness, that is, from the mainland to the transoceanic, to the edges of shorelines, to those local social spaces on and in between worlds. In doing so, he also depicts the temporal distance of Ricanness, and how Ricanness is animated by acts of political and aesthetic endurance, those moments of staying power in the face of cultural, personal, and national subjection.

Traveling through Puerto Rican subjectivity this way, as ADÁL also confirms, will not solve the colonial problem; alas, it will also not drive us past the inconclusive debate on the status of the island and its debt crisis. Yet political work does not always need to be set to the speed of emergency, or to historical time.[25] Believing in the potential of different political velocities may help us press pause on linearity, the horological event, consecutive narrative structures, historiography, and chronology. At times, political work looks like a hushed subject submerged under water in a cramped bathtub; still and patient, this human learns to wait or wade against the political current. At other times, this human rises from the bathtub, stands erect outside its depth—tall, firm, and clean—and then courageously goes under again. This is all to say that I am interested in what the aesthetic teaches us about bearable ways of "doing time" with our own bodies under subjugation. Throughout this book, I search for alternative ways of being and becoming in time: for the pause in tight spaces, in all those wretched domains that lend us something by way of Ricanness, death, and even humanity.

Even though postcolonialism contends that turning to historiography supplies both the answer and redress to all temporal problems, I argue that the only way to "authentically" access Ricanness is through various nonlinear and insurgent breaks in time—a disruption of history that accounts for time's looping nature against postcolonial promises. In *Ricanness*, I reshift our normative assumptions about linear time, and by consequence existence, through spaces of negation, incompletion, exhaustion, violence, and impending death, alongside those moments of pleasure, desire, redemption, and love. These moments exist in a series of sites, from theater and experimental video to activism and durational performance art, in which the social and psychic merge at the site of aesthetics, uncovering what's really at stake politically for the enduring body.

Enduring Durational Aesthetics within the Contours of Performance and Rican Life

My investment in Ricanness, guided by performance practice, is tied not only to conventional markers of revolution, protest, and resistance (as the following chapters will disclose), but also to the experimental as a powerful aesthetic force against the burden of liveness and racial/sexual transparency for minoritarian subjects, specifically those in colonial destitution. In engaging politics at varying velocities, at the site of colonial violence, I rely on endurance and durational art for direction. That is to say that I turn to how these particular aesthetic traditions, beginning in the 1970s (shortly after the insurgencies of the 1960s), develop and extend two important conceptual and performative turns: the body as an aesthetic site in corporeal suffering, pain, violence, debility, and anguish; and how to counter the demands of "capital time," or in my case, colonial time, through variations of time itself.[26] Durational art, while not always defined by bodily pain, is concerned with how "to disturb or suspend narrative resolutions and consolidated identities."[27] Particularly, durational art is attentive to "the notion of persistence, or remaining through time, and is inseparable but shadowed by the term endurance, which is often associated with sufferance" and body art.[28] In order to mobilize the temporal and bodily dimensions of Ricanness, I turn to how both these performance art practices might inform an understanding of the colonial body suffering through time. At times the connection to endurance and durational art is specific in these chapters and one notices the silent cameos of famous endurance artists like Chris Burden, Marina Abramović, Vito Acconci, Tehching Hsieh, Bruce Nauman, Zhang Huan, and Linda Montana,[29] but mostly I am interested in how these aesthetic concerns advance our assessment of temporality and the colonial subject, outside of and alongside these well-known artists. Or, who is let into this dominant archive of endurance art at the expense of those forced to endure outside of it?

While each chapter of this book illuminates a Rican event in historical time, the event itself is not the endurance act in the traditional sense of the term. For example, I am not investigating individual performances that extend over twelve hours, twenty days, or a year, other than the act of colonialism itself, which is indeed never-ending. Even though endurance is often seen as labor sustained over linear time, in these chapters, the intensity of the acts stretches the brief time of the event into a cyclical, looping eternity, which models the eternal recurrence of colonial practice. In all these moments of sufferance, performance transgresses the boundary between nonlinear time and affectation, as the spectator learns to assume the bodily effects of each artist and activist. The events of this book, whether a political assault against the state in under twenty minutes, a dramatic durational text of an hour, a one-minute avant-garde video, or a highly intensified performance art piece of ten minutes, capture the effects of Rican colonialism—a practice composed of both timelessness and too much time at the expense of the negated body. In doing so, I reorganize our recognition of endurance, and our automatic assumptions and responses to duration. In consequence, violence and the body are also brought into the spotlight under different determining factors, meaning that I ask readers to rethink their supposition of violence altogether. Might violence, if viewed outside its often debilitating optic, drive us to transcend our own repulsions, our abject relations with others? I place semi-short durational acts, not necessarily long-term actions, in direct confrontation with the everlasting effects of colonial time and history in very aggressive scenes.

Endurance, as I have translated it to fit Ricanness, is about laboring to eventually stare past the horizon with apprehension, longing, pain, and pleasure—no feeling invalidated by another in the long pursuit of liberation and continual existence. This is the crucial component guiding my figuration of Ricanness, for if one is to speak fairly in matters of ontological inquiry, endurance must sit at the center of such conversations. Another way of saying this is that to be delimited in the world, from the onset of birth, means to always already be running vigorously behind the hands of the clock, and when that colonial clock stops ticking, either for repair, disciplinary reform, or capitalistic gain, the unwanted continue laboring: above water or below ground, stumbling, falling, even in the event of no mechanical time at all.

This material exhaustion is indisputable in ADÁL's photographs: the subaquatic Rican body steadily controls itself against suffocation; spasmodic breath after breath, this subject works against the break point. The image, however, appropriates the abject feeling of drowning as an interminable sensation, one analogous to the draining awareness of subjection, regardless of one's short mechanical time submerged. ADÁL's images grant us an emergent performative practice in a space of duress: the choreographic glare of stillness, a perceived corporeal deadness at the hands of a snapshot. Holding one's breath here is about surrendering any and all grip to historiography and plunging in dynamic nonlinear time in order to declare something about the living while prefiguring the dying. Against all odds and between all currents, his "drowning" subjects are examples of the capacity of endurance within the aesthetic domain.

The endurance mode throughout the book extends from, into, and beyond the privileged domain of durational aesthetics reserved for certain visual and performance art canons. This trope is also a temporal intervention in how we may begin to imagine different forms of antioppressive, anticolonial performance. Taking a direct cue from my training in performance studies, I travel the course of aesthetics and politics enduringly. In this interdisciplinary exploration of the concept of Ricanness, I disclose an ontology of Rican anticolonial aesthetics. This ontology, this theory of being, is grounded in a sustained dislocation of a colonial hierarchy of the senses and bodily habitus within oftentimes brutal encounters. These violent encounters are not always as motionless as ADÁL's photographs; at times, they disintegrate the subject, forcing the colonial subject to disappear and then reappear as another being in the world.

That is to say that if colonialism remains a thriving enterprise, we cannot follow its execution linearly.[30] We must form new temporal alliances in spaces of the event to unearth the deadly effects of oppressive time. I am deeply invested, here, in how Ricanness expresses the duality between excess time and no time, between history and the past under restrictions of colonialism and coloniality, at the site of performance. If Ricanness is always already colonial, sexualized, racialized, native, debt-ridden, at its base dangerously queer, enduring, and in constant existential crisis, my archive reflects this ontological inquiry. I move through anticolonial and postcolonial theory, Continental philosophy, psychoanalysis, feminist and queer theory, Puerto Rican and Latinx studies, under the liberating guidance of performance studies.

Performance studies is the critical mechanism by which these fields distinctly come together throughout these pages. As a theoretical paradigm, mode of analysis, and heuristic to read aesthetics, culture, and sociality, performance studies works between multiple ways of meaning making, from the intellectual corpus to the materiality of the physical body. At the apogee of performance exists the manifestation of the subject/object, a subject's way of being, doing, and redoing that breathes new worlds, oftentimes untenable under the regulating conditions of heteronormativity. Performance is also "a restoration of behavior" in which human actions are the results of an aggregate of past behaviors that are reorganized and remade according to an infinite number of possibilities—a temporal condition that parallels but also reshifts masculinist, linear temporality.[31] Restored behavior, then, provides a framework by which to understand how we *do* culture and also learn to revitalize it against impending odds. I imagine this field as a para- or even meta-discipline, in which it is both alongside and beyond itself, extending the limits of its own chronology and linearity, while simultaneously being aware of performing such acts. As an almost meta-futural "discipline," performance studies has regularly gained its aesthetic and political force by critically traversing systems of knowing, being, and doing, repurposing objects alternatively appearing lifeless in the overhaul of liveness. Strictly speaking, performance is always outside itself, in the world; as such, it simultaneously replays the social constructions it hopes to both demystify and engage. And, it has always left the door wide open for this tension, revealing that at its core lies a fertile aberration against normative rules of conduct and composure.

Chasing Philosophy, Following Fanon: The Corporeal-Performative Politics of Colonial Endurance

The material life of Ricanness is best gleaned when the psychic and the social touch, and when endurance and its deliberate effects restage survivalist scenes in nonlinear time. In turning to performance sites as practices of philosophy, I read for sustaining bodies at the limits of humanity. Just as ADÁL's overtly still subjects provide an existential snapshot into the drowning life of Ricanness, Fanon, through his body, extends an alternative corporeal gesture in time—as both an act against unwantedness and a directive for life.

From 1952, with the birth of *Black Skin, White Masks*, until *The Wretched of the Earth* in 1961 (the same year of his sudden death at thirty-six years old), Fanon produced some of the most comprehensive and provocative scholarship on the psychic and social constructions of colonialism at the site of his own enduring body.[32] Influenced by psychoanalysis, political philosophy, existentialism, phenomenology, and Negritude theory, Fanon demonstrates his fullest contribution to those universal debates concerning existence, the human, freedom, and authenticity. Through the personal and political exploration of Blackness, he deploys a new humanism, a revised metaphysics—not by beginning with the universal subject, often depleted of race, sexuality, and gender, but by starting from the subject in descent. At the horizon of death and forced rebirth, Fanon specifically describes the close encounter between the social and psychic, as he returns to his own act of bodily endurance in "The Fact of Blackness."[33] Staging a conversation between Continental philosophy and his marked body, Fanon evolves into a phenomenologist consciously aware of his psychic life. Allowing for the aesthetic moment to enter the space of politics, he describes what the choreography of everyday life might look and feel like for a colonized subject of Blackness.

In demonstrating again how performance is cultivated from scenes of *redoing*, I want to reproduce Fanon's existential performance piece below as a performative, bodily, existential act. After being hailed into the world by a child, as either a "'Dirty nigger!' Or simply, 'Look, a Negro!,'" Fanon demonstrates the metaphysical link joining the conjunction above.[34] "Or" is used not simply to link alternatives, but to signal similarity. What, if any, does the world see as the difference between these two designations? It is Fanon's act of endurance that supplies a response to conventional, majoritarian understandings of Being. He states,

I came into the world imbued with the will to find a meaning in things, my spirit filled with the desire to attain to the source of the world, and then I found that I was an object in the midst of other objects. Sealed into this crushing objecthood, I turned beseechingly to others. Their attention was a liberation, running over my body suddenly abraded into nonbeing, endowing me once more with an agility that I had thought lost, and by taking me out of the world, restoring me to it. But just as I reached the other side, I stumbled, and the movements, the attitudes, the glances of the other fixed me there, in the sense in which a chemical solution is fixed by a dye. I was indignant; I demanded an explanation. Nothing happened. I burst apart. Now the fragments have been put together again by another self.[35]

Even if eventually bursting into pieces, Fanon's desire to exist in the world, to be allowed the space to be existential, lives beside his singular facticity. In comparing himself to "objects in the midst of other objects," he encounters his objecthood and, in the process, stumbles into "nonbeing," moving toward "an explanation" of another type of subjectivity. But the explanation is never attained because his being "bursts apart" and "the fragments" are put "together again by another self," another version of Fanon built from the Other. In this collapse and crumble of self, through both language and body, he elucidates how a standing and still body is ripped apart and decomposed, leaving little ontological alternative for colonized subjects. These fragments unveil a past self that can never be detached from his now-present composition, making one question his entry into the future. What can Fanon's bodily decomposition teach us about being human in the space of unwantedness?

Fanon's multiple disembodied selves are made possible through different choreographic movements: stumbling, breaking, fragmenting, and bursting work in relation to being an object, rather than a whole subject, or what Fanon calls a being in triple consciousness. They underscore the numerous choreographies of oppression and incompletion for the colonized other: one may stumble, fall, implode, explode, but one continues to sustain the act of human endurance, even if "by another self" within the narrow space of negation. Incompletion here works as the incentive to keep on keeping on, rather than the source that impairs the subject. Fanon's words above operate as a physical score of existential right, a recitation in bodily gesture propelled by the psychic life of an alienated subject. He illuminates what it viscerally feels like to wear colonialism on the body and within the spirit, revealing the boundaries of both existence and ontology, while summoning the desire to be wanted, valuable beyond (but with) one's facticity.

In that space Fanon calls "a zone of nonbeing," he is in deliberate conversation with philosophical narratives of subjectivity. Throughout his writing, he stages openings between his "zone of nonbeing" and Hei-degger's *Da-sein*,[36] Nietzsche's construction of human tragedy, Hegel's "being for others," Sartre's subject at the space of Nausea and nothing-ness, Lacan's barred subject laboring under the state, and Merleau-Ponty's charge against a being without bodily intellect.[37] In Fanon, like in Merleau-Ponty (whose lectures Fanon attended while in France),[38] the bodily schema is the main site to understand the subject's interiority. It is Fanon, however, who institutes the hard labor of interrogating race, both psychoanalytically and philosophically, even when the call to the human is situated universally. Consequently, I cannot turn away from his work, even when I feel most estranged by his homophobia.[39] His corporeal plea for being, and the desire to be wanted in a world that does not want him is a reminiscent sound, and this sound seeps into the pages of this book, guiding the interconnection of colonialism and Ricanness. In this take on Ricanness, the tight spaces of negation, dread, violence, despair, incompletion, combustion, and disintegration—informed by colonial practice and residue—help one find the time to breathe within the closed quarters of depletion and alienation. In following a Fanonian compass, this exploration of Ricanness turns to the philosophical, social, and psychic, as they meet at the site of the enduring body within the aesthetic domain.

I understand the risk I run of conflating identifications and construc-tions of Being throughout this book, but I deliberately turn to Blackness as a philosophical framework to read existence writ large, against and with other figurations of Being. In saying so, I want us to consider what Blackness unearths about life and death that other analytics might not ever understand about existence. Or, what can Fanon teach us about Ricanness? What can Ricanness teach us about Fanon, and all of these philosophical zones of being and nonbeing alike?

Fanon—like Heidegger, Bergson, and Merleau-Ponty (as I will show later)[40]—provides ample mileage to read for Ricanness within Being. When Continental philosophy refused the commitment to race, Fanon lent his spirit, allowing one to enter these metaphysical debates through the utility of one's own viscerality. I'd be hard-pressed as a scholar if I tossed his work, or any flawed text, into the dustbin. Fanon, like the fig-ures of these chapters, is productively complicated, incomplete, wanting in his unwantedness. I have learned, through performance studies, to recycle and co-opt dominant narratives that attempt to both define and erase me. How else might I see myself, the supposed problem within the human, in philosophy's performative contemplations of existence?

Similar to this philosophical preoccupation, the aesthetic is the other constant variable of this book. An investment in Puerto Rican subjectivity, through aesthetic interventions in time by artists and revolutionaries who essentially espouse their own philosophical truths in their work, directs these pages. This book concerns the openings and boundaries of philosophy, which the subjects of these chapters explicitly invite the reader to travel. ADÁL, Dolores "Lolita" Lebrón Sotomayor, Papo Colo, Pedro Pietri, and Ryan Rivera live at the horizon of existence; and it is through performance that their existential desires and phenomenological affinities are revealed.

Such affinity is also visible in the twenty years I've spent chasing philosophy, determined to see racialized, colonized, sexualized, queer, minoritarian beings at the center of conversations about existence, time, essence, selfhood, authenticity, and freedom. It is unsurprising, then, that I would take such flights into the philosophical alongside these concerns and these Rican cultural figures. Throughout this long run, Fanon has been both the compass and compact armor against this refusing world, guiding me through the white maze of philosophy and psychoanalysis at the performative spot of both social and psychic debates that have maintained Western metaphysical thought. This is all to say that I am interested in what an ontological excavation of Ricanness (what is this thing's essence?) reveals about existence and subjectivity in the very life of the aesthetic. Philosophy may not want *me*, but its perpetual obsession with death proves that the field cannot survive without *us* at the limit of existence. Even when we are not written into print, we are on the pages, silently waiting to be wanted alongside the unproblematic universal subject. This book turns to the Rican subject in anticolonial performance to tell life stories at the perimeter of mortality.

Importantly, I must also explain my connection to certain disconcerting philosophers: I pull from Heidegger's ideas about the transformation of the subject enduring through time, because by rethinking temporality and its linear authority, one reshifts the human condition. I am aware of the discomfort that will arise from my use of Heidegger in conversation with colonized subjects, considering his deplorable and inexcusable affiliations with the Nazi Party. Yet, my engagement with Heidegger is specific: I need to understand the ontological relationship between temporality, existence, intersubjectivity, and death in a way that both uses and departs from his rendition of Being within the philosophical tradition, but also provides an escape hatch for alternative continual becomings. He will never be able to offer an ontological corrective for Ricanness, but through his work on time, I can extend Ricanness into the domain of temporality. Heidegger, like the expanse of Western metaphysical thought, is not critically concerned with the racialized other, but I read Ricanness into philosophy. If Ricanness is always already dead, or near to death, I must turn to philosophy's obsession with death for a fuller understanding of existence writ large.

In Heidegger's understanding, the subject must always reckon with "the temporalization of temporality," since time equals not a final departure, but rather a subject enduring in time.[41] There is no way to separate being from temporality: they exist as counterparts in one's search for conscious awareness and freedom. *Da-sein* is interpreted in various ways as the meaning of existence, the essence of what it means to be human;[42] being-thereness;[43] and presence itself.[44] Heidegger himself explains the term as "the site of the understanding of being"[45] or "that entity which is characterized as *being-in-the-world . . . being-with-one-another*."[46] For Heidegger, *Da-sein* does not live within one isolated agency of time, such as the past, present, or future, but joins together these three states. He sees temporality as "ecstatic,"[47] as relating to the interconnected experience of these states of time—with the *futural* holding the most promise. In other words, "This ecstasy makes it possible for Da-sein to be able to take over resolutely the being that it already is" and what it might become.[48] But *Da-sein*, lest we forget, is not equivalent to a human being; even in its many layers and translations, it rather signals what it means to be a being within time.

Heidegger's construction of *Da-sein* is generally viewed as linear—the living subject confronts their inevitable death, while also never able to experience the individual death of another. In this situation, the finality of death marks the end of the subject. But this death-bound subjectivity, or the anticipation imbedded in one's future as "being-toward-death," merely offers the perception of linearity.[49] The reality of the subject's transformation, for Heidegger, is not a temporally collapsing one, but one in dimensioned time, which moves beyond a series of points and into the complex properties of the subject enduring through time instead.

In and of itself, Heidegger recognizes that the linear notion of time is "vulgar,"[50] limiting one's access to an "authentic" life through the prime example of the mechanistic clock. In an endeavor to expose us to the durational moments of a clock ticking us into existence, he shares, "If we approach an event with a clock, then the clock makes the event explicit, but more with respect to its unfolding in the now than with respect to the how-much of its duration."[51] In expanding this idea, he adds, "What primarily the clock does in each case is not to indicate the how-long or how-much of time in its present flowing, but to determine the specific fixing of the now."[52] Still unsatisfied with temporal linearity, he asks the following questions: "What is the now?"; "Am I myself the now and my existence time?"; and "Or is it ultimately time itself that procures for itself the clock in us?"[53] These questions mark the internal depths and arbitrariness located within time, and Heidegger's desire to change linear time—not defend it; knowing all too well that linearity will never be able to reveal the exquisite and complex qualities of the *futural* and authentic freedom of the subject.

Therefore, I understand Heidegger's idea of *Da-sein* to be not a linear one, even if the clock is the most linear of objects and *Da-sein* ceases to be when it "has reached the end."[54] Not knowing what this end is, or how one releases oneself from a constant state of endurance, I question whether one can actually end or die, or if all of meaning and existence is just one big run toward something else, maybe something already dead. In a poignant moment of temporal clarity, Heidegger defines the meaning of *Da-sein* in time and death, characterizing it as a "running ahead to its past."[55] He expresses this condition in several choreographic ways, wherein running clarifies the nonlinearity of human existence and time itself: "running ahead to the past is Dasein's running up against its most extreme possibility";[56] "this running ahead is nothing other than the authentic and singular future of one's own Dasein";[57] "maintaining myself alongside my past in running ahead I have time."[58] And importantly, "Running ahead seizes the past as the authentic possibility of every moment of insight, as what is now certain. Being futural . . . gives time, because it *is* time itself."[59] In the above descriptions of time, there are no sequential markers in these running scenes. In fact, in these activated scenarios, time is not a measuring system used to sequence events; it is also not locatable within a Newtonian theory of absolute reality, moving chronologically on a straight line. Although the linear presentation of a past, present, and future announces a type of protracted movement in time, time's ontological speed is faster than its duration.

In further clarifying his commitment to different movements in time, Heidegger shares the paradoxical, but looping nature of *Da-sein*. He states that it "is not itself historical. Dasein, however, is in itself historical in so far as it is its possibility. In being futural Dasein is its past . . . the past—experienced as authentic historicity—is anything but what is past. It is something to which I can return again and again."[60] In this looping rendition of time, Heidegger challenges historical presuppositions and linear presumptions—both used to "time" the subject into spaces of infinite stasis, in which death is the only thing that can define, start, and end a being.

If "Dasein is the whole of time,"[61] then time has no real end. Time is the future.[62] And since we haven't landed on that future just yet, time is but a beginning and a perception of an ending, not the ending itself. According to the philosopher, we never experience or know our own death; thus, we may never accurately experience finitude. He offers a promising rendition of finality, however: there is no real end in time, that is, when its "ecstasies" are on the horizon. The crucial matter, for Heidegger, as it is for me in this book, is that we recognize "time as the underlying structure of being";[63] without this idea of an enduring subject in time, there are no planes by which to understand a being in the full sense of *Da-sein*. If we *are* essentially how we *live*, I am interested in discovering the Rican subject's life course within colonial temporality; or the potential of the Rican subject's freedom, both fraught with no time and extra time, wherein their surplus, and lack thereof, produce and advance temporal looping. In saying so, I am also asking us to reconsider how Ricanness begins enduring in time, in this act of a looping subjectivity that reorients our linear understanding of the human.

In a similar political expenditure of my own, Chicana feminist philosopher Mariana Ortega spells out what's at stake for women of color doing and enacting philosophy, especially when engaging with Heidegger.[64] On writing with, for, and against the discipline, she says, "Feeling comfortable in the world of philosophy has not been easy for me";[65] she adds that this writing is her attempt "at finding a sense of belonging and ease within a discipline that forgets the contributions of those regarded as 'others.'"[66] Pulling from both the personal and the political, Ortega locates those lived experiences, delineated by race and gender, at the apex of metaphysical thought. Of her use of Heideggerian existential phenomenology in particular, she states, "My view of multiplicitous selfhood does not constitute an endorsement of his political or personal views but rather an engagement with valuable phenomenological insights from his description of the self as *Da-sein*."[67] She also declares her fantasy against him, too, which is similar to my own: "I wish to shatter Heidegger's account of *Da-sein*—to see all the different directions in which Heidegger's view can be taken rather than staying confined" by the parameters he sets up for existence.[68] In wishing to shatter his account of existence, she defies disciplinary borders, moving from Latinx feminist thought, existential phenomenology, and critical race theory to stage a conversation with Heidegger that challenges heteronormative constructions of being-in-the-world. Through a close exploration of social spaces like the borderlands, specific cultural localities, notions of home, the place of *mestizaje*, and world traveling, Ortega reforms identity, selfhood, and belonging. Social spaces afford her the capacity to read for those "othered" and still becoming subjectivities. In doing so, she translates Continental philosophy, and so I follow her lead in this book, but also provide another escape hatch. From start to finish, space and spatial politics conjoin her ideas; in this way, Ortega speaks to the cultural lexicon that tightly sustains Latinx studies. It's a cultural logic I have been struggling to find my way through, and in doing so, I have turned to how time reorients spatiality and Latinx studies, too.

Like Ortega, Fanon helps me translate the time of *Da-sein* as he explicates the following position: "[The] challenge to the colonial world is not a rational confrontation of points of view. It is not a treatise on the universal, but the untidy affirmation of an original idea propounded as an absolute"[69]—and, I would add, composed of different temporal states. In rethinking *Da-sein* against its universal agenda, I am reminded of the following beautifully aphoristic moments in Fanon's work, wherein he shifts our temporal understanding of Being altogether: "I am part of Being to the degree that I go beyond it";[70] "The body of history does not determine a single one of my actions"; and "And it is by going beyond the historical . . . that I will initiate the cycle of my freedom."[71] These moments sufficiently emphasize what's at stake for all colonized subjects: a reordering of time at the deliberate expense of linearity.

To explicitly expose the internal clock of colonized subjectivity, Fanon extends his own genealogical compass into a deeper analysis of W. E. B. Du Bois's double consciousness with his version of a third-person consciousness.[72] In Fanon's three psychic states one is always aware that one is being looked at; one is always having to see oneself as one is seen; and last, a legitimate idea of self and other is always mitigated by the invasion of the psyche. By differentiating between "the third person" and "the triple person," he shows how the latter consumes his own subjectivity.[73] To exist in "triple person" is a psychic and bodily laboring that is filled with exhaustion, unquantifiable in mechanical, linear time. Just as Fanon's consciousness (unconsciousness!) becomes a manifestation of endurance, the characters of this book express such sustainment, too.[74]

But how does this subject obtain ontological value under restrictive time? How does one "initiate the cycle of freedom" Fanon advances? One way to answer these questions is to directly address the concern of mortality, or death, which is the central preoccupation not only of philosophy, but of Ricanness (although Albert Camus would say philosophy's main concern is actually suicide).[75] Although many argue that being-toward-death overshadows life, specifically for those subjects still living on the margins, this critique falls into a dangerous dialectical trap, refusing to exit the paradox of existence. Being unable to read for existence outside the poles of *life* and *death* in the *here* and *now*, the idea is that if the living are condemned to perpetually *be* with death in everyday life, how do they actually start existing? Surrounded by the dominant discourse of death, how do the most vulnerable, still living, actually live? Death appears to erase pleasure and desire for life and to cement the transparency of the subject, for who are we really if we live only as fragmented versions of ourselves? The incomplete moments of being human remain bearable, however, if we rethink the boundaries of life and death simultaneously. In *Ricanness*, death and life are not antithetical to one another: there's a continuum of existence that abides between, before, and beyond them. Death is also not a hauntology or a symptom of racial melancholia; it's more than its perceived end. It's even more than the end. In fact, it might be where we all begin, even if slightly deadened from the start.

Ricans, as I argue throughout, begin their call to life on unsteady ground several steps behind in time, in a position of descent—similar to those positions explored by both ADÁL and Fanon. This unsteadiness, as a phenomenological read presumes, lingers in the present, but is also a wormhole for time travel into the future. Against a universalistic rendering of experience, I am not convinced that all subjects exist in the expansive realm of Being under oppressive time, or that all choreographic acts of existence feel the same. Colonial subjects experience a different form of alienation from beings who do not descend in life first, sometimes dead, or dying a little before living, in their enduring pursuits for liberation and freedom. Being-toward-death, in these cases, is not a daunting manifestation; it's an insurgent alternative to a limited existence.

Death has always been available, even "free," to colonized subjects, so disbanding from its logic will not free us from it; we have always already been somewhat dead in our labor, sheer physical appearance, or want for recognition. Discussing death not necessarily as an act of biopolitics and necropolitics but as something more futural and promising, might land us in search of ourselves, in our wanton liberations against our unwantedness. Exchanging glances with mortality is an event no one can escape, of course, but one I see as a different experience for Ricans, for all colonized subjects. This book is invested in how death, just like other exercises in movement and time—falling, collapsing, pausing, waiting, running, jumping, being still, physically and painfully enduring—becomes a bearable, auspicious, and insurgent act under restrictive temporalities. Or, how do the "dead" live?

Incomplete Subjects, Unwanted Beings: Deathly Methods in Puerto Rican and Latinx Studies

My version of Ricanness imagines past the horizon—not as a recapitulation of the nationalist debate, or a sentimental reading of what could be in independence, but how each artist/activist learns to endure through performance in order to create their own dimension of bearable existence, even if in the space of imbued violence and pain. In saying this I find myself again halted by the Puerto Rican studies Superego (of course, I have partially invented this figure). It perpetually advises me to push against the "nationalist/colonialist binary" that manages most debates about Ricanness. It compels me to work ethically against nostalgia, to think critically alongside lack and incompletion as viable pathways to subjectivity, and to remove myself from the romance of liberation, revolution, and communal longing. Earlier, however, ADÁL created the space to rehearse such deathly conversations; his work releases this very apprehension from Ricanness into the aesthetic domain. In this version of Ricanness, I am interested in how incompletion, negation, even at the level of oppressive perception and at the extent of death, foment bearable ways of being in the world, and invite not-so-pleasant, violent moments of being-together, being mutually transformed.

My argument is that Ricanness functions as a continual performance of bodily endurance against US colonialism, unfolding via aesthetic interventions in time. The Puerto Rican situation exists simultaneously under too much time and timelessness: on the one hand time has appeared to stand still for the island, basically unchanged in its quasi-national status since the annexation of Puerto Rico to the United States in 1898. The island's lack of a "liberatory moment" makes it difficult to read through traditional constructions of time and subject completion, so I turn to temporal acts of excess and redeploy them as resistance, inner strength, survival, transformation, and self-determination through scenes of endurance. Through performative interventions in the temporal, the cultural figures I highlight challenge the colonial legacy that has perceived such diasporic subjects as tragically incomplete, fractured, lacking, ahistorical, and/or delayed. There's a way to read with and through unwantedness, I suggest, that does not destroy the futural prospects of the subject under a looping colonialism. This book attempts to tell that story.

My understanding of Ricanness is highly indebted to Latinx studies scholar Antonio Viego's intellectual labor. Somewhat of an outlier in the field, Viego boldly explains how critical race and ethnicity scholars often fall prey to the dominant discourses they hope to work against. In examining the Latinx subject, he turns to how Lacanian psychoanalysis might help us resist and reimagine racist discourse. In doing so, he subverts this discourse, building on the very foundation of negation and incompletion to read for subjectivity, even in spaces of death. The racialized hysteric, for Viego, is viewed as a subject who is actively resisting the Other through reinvention, or the creation of new symptoms. This requires the master to constantly create new labels to continue to suppress the subject. For Viego, themes in social and ego psychology, framed by the desire of the whole and complete subject, actually strengthen violent discourse against racialized subjects. Incompletion, as a benchmark for subjectivity, is not a negation of a limited life, adversely encapsulating evaluations of the subject. A lack of wholeness, and racial and sexual transparency, does not delimit the prospects of being in the world. In fact, as Viego claims in a critique of critical race and ethnicity studies thinkers who rely so heavily on social and ego psychology schemas to read the Brown subject, the "repeated themes of wholeness, completeness, and transparency with respect to ethnic-racialized subjectivity are what provide racist discourse with precisely the notion of subjectivity that it needs in order to function most effectively."[76] In an attempt to get out of this trap, this book continues this line of thinking in hope that negation may lead us to the spaces where the unwanted are essentially desirable on their own terms, and outside of pellucidity.

Like Viego, Patricia Gherovici turns to Lacan for traction in *The Puerto Rican Syndrome*, in which she examines the origins of the titular disorder, created by US Army doctors in the 1950s. Doctors observed Puerto Rican Korean War veterans with afflictions such as "anxiety, rage, psychotic symptoms, and unpremeditated suicide attempts, followed by depression and often amnesia about the spectacular crises."[77] This syndrome, which is also known as *ataque de nervios* in the psychiatric community, is a hysteria in response to colonialism, as Gherovici argues. These symptoms actually reflect the Other's (in this case the United States') message of violence in order to demand liberation.[78] Working against the master/slave dialectic, here, the author exposes, too, the psychical residue of both war and racism, how it infiltrates Ricanness and becomes the impetus for its erasure.[79]

Frances R. Aparicio has similarly argued that Puerto Ricans in the United States "continue to be seen as Racial Others who need to be contained, supervised, and controlled by the state, and its institutions." The designation of Puerto Ricans as an "ethnic group" serves not only as an entry into the system of institutional multiculturalism, but as a method to subvert both racialized, subordinated views and radical, self-constructed views of Ricanness.[80] Viego, Gherovici, and Aparicio offer us a way to read for psychical time in Ricanness, even in spaces of Brown obscurity, and provide a way out of this trap through the very language of incompletion, otherness, and fragmentation that is often subsumed by the burden of liveness and transparency.

But how do subjects really come to know one another through their negation in life? Do these fragmented subjects link bodily forces and build a signifying chain of perceived completion? Are they always as still as ADÁL's subjects, or as combustible as Fanon's? For José Esteban Muñoz, the temporal valences of Brownness register as a "mode of affective particularity that a subject feels in herself or recognizes in others."[81] Subjects, in this sense, come to know one another through their negation. Muñoz argues that Brownness's real sense of political and social power is found in how such identifying subjects come to know, feel, love, and exist with one another. This occurs through theatricality, speech acts, quotidian occurrences, and performance more generally—a way of acting and feeling both on- and offstage, in the space of ephemerality and the documentation of any happening. Working from this tradition here, then, Brownness, like Ricanness, is about feeling, doing, emoting, and sensing—and also, as I contend, how we learn to wait with/for/on the other and the self in incompletion, even if one never fully exists. In this waiting, we learn to co-opt heteronormative velocity and use its tempo in our exchanges with one another. In particular, we access our own unrealized subjectivity through our intersubjective relationships on constant loop, rotating to the cadences of coalesced existences.

Muñoz, always Browning the queer archive and queering the Brown one, suggests that ontology itself is a process and product of the future, something still unrealized. In suggesting that "queerness is not yet here"—a claim that is equally spatial and temporal—he also provides a slight adjustment: utopia is not always a place; at times it is a temporal conviction, an instantaneous want, an ephemeral act that alleviates the horror, terror, and apprehension in the *now* for queers and people of color.[82] That is to say that Brownness is not only in this here and now, but always already oriented toward transformation—its essence is formed by the potential of utopia in a quite dystopic world. With and through Muñoz, I have come to search for moments that compose the nexus of queer, Brown, and

Rican temporality, whether in elongated or shortened temporal scenes. In a further theoretical leap, I want to suggest, then, that the Brown subject, always first by way of the Rican body, experiences an incompletion also by orienting itself to what lies beyond the beyond: a meta-futurity wherein the future always pushes up against its own future.

In Latinx studies, spatial concerns and historiography, not necessarily these temporal charges, have dominated postcolonial discourse, Latinx feminisms, and critical race theory. Queer studies, in contrast, remains transfixed by temporality, adjusting the present to fit into the future by challenging the horizon to best glean the subject's past. Queer theorists like Muñoz, Sara Ahmed, Jack Halberstam, Tavia Nyong'o, Roderick A. Ferguson, Dana Luciano, and Elizabeth Freeman, to name only a very few, have placed pressure on the heteronormativity of time by exploring new temporalities as crucial acts in the evolution of theory and practice.[83] This gesture is also a political exercise in creating new alternatives to reproduction—alternatives that are not always linked to baby making and marriage as ultimate signifiers of valuable life, living, being-with, intrasubjectivity, and the transparency and completion of the minoritarian subject. For example, Freeman's brilliant, Marxian-infused work stages aesthetic and political encounters in art, film, and literature through various temporal modes. Linking all of these phenomena is her concept of *chrononormativity*: time that pushes and manages the subject's body to its maximal potential in the name of capitalist productivity and gain.[84] Sara Ahmed, in a similar maneuver to that of Freeman, mobilizes phenomenology as a viable analytic for queer studies, an act I follow in Latinx and performance studies. In avant-garde articulation of corporeal endurance, Ahmed shows how human interactions unfurl under the graceful watch of space—not outside of time, but with space as the director of these exchanges. By turning to phenomenology's investment in the body, a deliberate charge against the Cartesian mandate (only the mind, mind before body, mind with no body), she exposes how subjects, objects, and the "thing" itself are all emotionally and sensorially "oriented" in space and time, and how queer ways of being-in-the-world disorganize and reorient heteronormative ways of existence.[85] Time and its anxious residue sit at the very interior of queerness.

Pulling from queer studies, phenomenology, political philosophy, and psychoanalysis, I turn to the ambivalences and negations found in aesthetic spaces to feel for the incomplete minoritarian subject moving toward the futural. In doing so, I continue to build on Muñoz's work, placing pressure on the field of Latinx studies to move from a typically spatial obsession with border violence to encompass expansive queer temporalities. This intervention, at times, has been read as a dismissal of the present state of emergency, a disregard for the dangerous state of politics for people of color, but a closer look might unlock what's really at stake, specifically for those of us committed to riding this train. Muñoz understands what's missing in this world, in this here and now, precisely because he theorizes from the glum reality of the present in a hopeful stance toward something better.

Similarly, *Ricanness* is not a rejection of the here and now, but a "running ahead to the past"[86] in order to land on something else we haven't yet dreamed up. Or as Fanon reminds us of colonial life, "The real leap consists in introducing invention into existence."[87] In demanding space within the future, I also ask Latinx studies to continue remarking its spots, even if such markers land us on X.[88] As a *via negativa* through the living death of colonialism, *Ricanness* is an intersubjective relational type of dreaming of an otherwise.

There's no denying that the present is both a terrorizer and a site of terror for queer, Brown, minoritarian, colonized, Rican subjects, always six feet underground, or submerged under water, or engulfed by heteronormative strategies run by colonization, racialization, and sexualization.[89] But since temporality is not prescriptive or linear, and is deciphered in our pleasures, displeasures, longings for one another at the site of death, negation, fragmentation, despair, and alienation, we might see these enactments as gestures toward the illuminations of the horizon. In my *futural*, the unwanted find refuge in their imposed and communal maladies in the compressed places of violence, pain, and suffering, alongside love, gratification, and resilient dreaming. In these spaces of negation and methexis, I work with—not against—fragmentation, ambivalence, and repulsion as vital sources of existence in both the psychic and social life of the unwanted being. Oftentimes these moments are internally transformative, wondrous, and exquisite—not necessarily pain-free, but certainly cathartic.

The Logic of Nonlinearity in Ricanness

Ricanness is organized somewhat chronologically, tracing the threads of post–World War II Rican cultural history; but it simultaneously disrupts that lineage, pressing against linear time in a looping nature. Each chapter focuses on a different measure of time as both an aesthetic and political medium: the artists and activists of this book either press pause on time, or wait with time, run us into exhaustion or drag us through dread and dying. They do so by staging scenes with death, running against time, and jumping into its confines, banging their heads against chronology to underscore the unique temporality of colonial residue. The following chapters spell out how each cultural figure of this text is actually ahead of their time, that is, if we reorganize our understanding of linearity. All of the cultural figures featured in this book stand against the heteronormative grain, either through a critique of übermasculinity in racialized subjectivity, fighting against normative constructions of femmeness, advancing erotic energies that signal new ways of belonging, and pushing past dominant stories that hold race, ethnicity, and the nation sacredly together in contempt of an impotent sexuality, and a transparent Rican and Brown subject.

Chapter 1 begins in 1954 on the US congressional floor: the day Dolores "Lolita" Lebrón Sotomayor and fellow members of the Puerto Rican Nationalist Party (formed in the 1920s as a response to US colonialism) staged an armed assault against the United States. I look to Lebrón's actions in the Capitol as a way to discuss how the subject offers death as a way to access subjectivity. In paying close attention to Lebrón's bodily endurance as evidence of her desire to offer death for the independence of Puerto Rico, I assert that the only thing that she, as a colonial subject, rightfully owns upon entry into the world is her own death. An understanding of her death drive is linked to Lebrón's presentation of self, challenging the traditional, androgynous view of a female revolutionary. The important aesthetic details of her performance are not, in my argument, antithetical to other markers that claim and seek to trivialize her: former beauty queen, mother of the nation, femme fatale, beautiful convoy, and hysterical, suicidal depressive. Lebrón symbolizes the relationship between aesthetics, death, and gender. She walked into the Capitol building wearing the struggle and desire of the prospect of dying as fervently and fearlessly as the glamorous attire, red lipstick, and gun that were her signature accessories. I suggest that Lebrón is more than a sacrificing mother, a pathological terrorist with red lips, or an accomplice to male leaders; she stages a site through which to dismantle Rican patriarchy and restage death, both imposed and re-created by colonialism.

While this was not the colony's only attack of its kind, it was the first time a Rican female revolutionary led the revolt against the United States on mainland territory. This is symbolic for several reasons, which force a return to the 1930s to understand the magnitude of Lebrón's actions in the 1950s. During the 1930s, sterilization policies were designed to control an ostensible overpopulation issue on the island. These procedures became widespread in Puerto Rico, and by 1965 it was reported that 35 percent of Puerto Rican women had been sterilized. Sterilization policies were officially in practice from the 1930s to the 1970s, and the resultant massive extermination of a population left a stench of impending death that saturated the very essence of Ricanness.[90] The female body, once a sight of life and reproduction, became a site of finitude. During the 1930s, Lebrón was in her teens, learning to survive her own extermination. And still she carries the stench of death onto the congressional floor in 1954 and stages a new political and philosophical conversation with death. In her, we see the resilience of the femme, female, feminist, mother of the nation who refuses the call to suicide, and instead offers us a recitation for Being.

Chapter 2 highlights multidisciplinary artist Papo Colo and his 1977 performance piece *Superman 51*. In *Superman 51*, Colo runs down the West Side Highway in New York City with fifty-one wooden planks attached to his back; he runs for ten minutes until he falls from exhaustion. In the performance *Jumping the Fences*, Colo leaps over fifty-one fences in Puerto Rico, New York City, and other locations around the world. The number fifty-one symbolizes the possible future of Puerto Rico as the fifty-first state. This chapter, then, explores the conceptual artist's mapping of temporality against an already imposed choreography of Being through acts of collapse and the movements of running and jumping with the number fifty-one. I argue that Colo's übermasculine public acts of endurance among the concrete, metal, and cement of the globe serve a revolutionary function for the Rican subject; he stages time on the building materials of space itself, illustrating the temporally futile components of masculinity.

Although Colo's acts can be considered revolutionary much in the same way we read the actions of Lebrón as a highly aestheticized performance, revolutionaries such as Lebrón and conceptual artists such as Colo work in different contextual domains, awaiting different consequences. Colo, while he runs at full speed down a highway, does not pull out a .38 Luger pistol and begin to fire in the actual place where policy is made legible. Yet, his performances of exhaustion highlight both the limits and potential of the Rican body bound by a geopolitical state of neither here nor there, now or then.

Chapter 3 transports us to a fancy French restaurant, or a Bronx hallway toilet, highlighting the work of Nuyorican icon Reverend Pedro Pietri with a particular focus on his experimental and existential one-act endurance play *The Masses Are Asses*. Pietri's crude play takes place "sometime last week" with two characters, Lady and Gentleman.[91] The play's events occur in timed sequences that repeat and loop back on themselves, and become clear indicators of the colonial time of dread. While the play tackles socioeconomic issues such as poverty and imperialism, and the bourgeoisie's control of mankind, it also highlights domestic violence and sexual abuse of women. As readers we travel a treacherous terrain: Gentleman beats, verbally abuses, and rapes Lady precisely when she desires to release herself from the quagmire of life's despair that he has helped to create and sustain. Through this hardship, the reader is forced into the cramped space of colonial violence in the site of a bathroom, with no way out.

I suggest that the social spaces of this play invite us to read the text through the measuring stick of temporal dread. The characters *descend in time* in order to finally exist again. And descent, in this chapter, demarcates how downward movement is a revolutionary action that ultimately serves to resist or ascend in the face of colonialism. In this piece, endurance is a hardening and precipitation of being—one animated by the ultimate intimacies of vulgarity.

In chapter 4, I share the archive of the late New York–based queer Rican avant-garde multimedia and performance artist Ryan Rivera by examining his experimental videos. In his 2002 videos, less than a minute each, Rivera remains abstracted, drawing the spectator's attention to the psychical states of self-injury and suffering. Through close-ups, a manipulation of real time, splicing, and overexposure (all techniques that make seconds feel like hours), Rivera pushes the spectator to endure a series of grotesque actions; he repeatedly bangs his head against plexiglass, places his fist down his throat, holds his breath, retches, and violently punches and slaps his face. If the senses are where being is constituted, how do we, as spectators, learn to *wait* with this disembodied artist? This chapter explicates the political and aesthetic consequences of waiting in the seat of sensation with and for a bodiless Rican subject. Rivera compels us to wait in dissonance through the exploitation of the senses as a way to redeem our own materiality and engender a type of queer calling. Rivera urges us to sit with him as he beats his head against the never-quite-postcolonial, creating new forms of Brown and Rican intimacy. I showcase the narrow space of a video screen as Rivera, on loop, reformulates the Cartesian split and illuminates the Rican thinking mind without a body that must bang its queer postcolonial head against the fast-paced heteronormative world.

All of this book's aesthetic sites are located on the East Coast, a geographical location that has been home to millions of Rican subjects (New York's Puerto Rican population is the largest of any city in the world) for more than a hundred twenty years.[92] While it seems, through my depictions of these places, that *Ricanness* is about the formation of subjectivity through social spaces, I am most concerned with how these tight locations unveil something about Ricanness that is profoundly temporal and on loop in an act of eternal recurrence.

All of these artists/activists teach us something about the racialized overtones found in gender, sex, and sexuality at the site of colonial practice. The reader will notice that I turn to concerns of gender and sexuality through the trope and trajectory of impotence: whether through an unrealized and exhausted hypermasculinity collapsing on the highway; the beaten-up and sweaty face without bodily organs; the constant execution of gender violence, rape, and abuse; or the death that is not taken in a final act of femme empowerment; the construction of "barrenness" situates the call to existence in this book. To "feel impotent inside of your own condition," as ADÁL himself explains, is one of the deepest concerns of both endurance and Ricanness. This impotence, however, does not minimize life, but rather is used to propel one forward through the mired maze of colonial existence.[93] The colonial enterprise is always already set to a certain sexualized tempo at the expense of the racialized subject bound to the nation.

Each chapter of *Ricanness* presents the artist or revolutionary as a harbinger of existential right; and I "reproduce" the existential work already explored and executed by all of these subjects of analysis. In each case, politics and philosophy merge to create a space for the aesthetic. But these cultural workers, too, do the hard labor of philosophy, expelling their own ontological reality on the breadth of Ricanness.[94] Or rather, the philosophical and political quests of these artists produce an aesthetic event whereby existential concerns meet performative ways of being-different-in-the-world.

1

Lipstick Revolutionaries

Dolores "Lolita" Lebrón Sotomayor and the Site of Rican Death

Yo no vine a matar. Yo vine a morir.
—Lebrón, during her arrest in 1954

Minutes after members of the House of Representatives began to trickle into the US congressional chamber and the Speaker of the House tallied its members, approximately thirty gunshots sailed over the proceedings.[1] The gunshots sprang from Puerto Rican Nationalist Party members Irving Flores Rodríguez, Andrés Figueroa Cordero, Rafael Cancel Miranda, and Dolores "Lolita" Lebrón Sotomayor,[2] who previously purchased four one-way tickets from New York City to Washington, DC, to execute a meticulous incursion on Congress in the name of Puerto Rican liberation.[3] Even on the heels of the attempt on President Truman's life, spearheaded by the party's own leader, Pedro Albizu Campos,[4] all four compatriots passed through security with their concealed weapons and were freely admitted into the Ladies' Gallery on the very floor above House members. They sat armed in the second row, peering down at an assembly of white men in lawmaking suits.

Lebrón, alongside comrades, fixed both hands on her .38 caliber pistol and fired several shots at the housetop, not with the intention to harm, but to free herself of colonial domination.[5] Unfurling the Puerto Rican flag after her hail of bullets, Lebrón, too, vehemently cried for the independence of the island.[6] And in a statement of unmistakably existential import, she screamed *"¡Viva Puerto Rico Libre!"*—thrusting the name of her island between the dual imperatives of life and freedom.

The year was 1954, and Lebrón was dressed to die, not to kill. In her version of a clever suit, she dressed in hyperfeminine combat gear: the thirty-four-year-old donned crimson-stained lips, manicured eyebrows, a black hat atop coiffed hair, a chic scarf over a double-breasted skirt suit, high heels, and dangling pearl earrings. Toting a black purse, which contained a "suicide" note, and, at one point, her loaded Luger, Lebrón staged a scene in anticipation of her own open-casket reveal on the afternoon of March 1.

But soon after Lebrón and her comrades opened fire, a representative, with the help of several spectators, climbed the stairs to the gallery and subdued Cancel Miranda and Figueroa Cordero, reblocking the Nationalists' deliberate political staging. Lebrón was apprehended at the scene without any bodily harm, and shortly afterward, Flores Rodríguez was apprehended by authorities, after his brief attempt to escape.[7] Five congressmen were injured and immediately rushed to hospitals, but no one was killed during the attack. However, the four subjects were instantly charged with sedition, assault with a deadly weapon, and intent to kill. Lebrón, however, was acquitted of assault with intent to kill and sentenced to sixteen to fifty-six years in prison. While her compatriots suffered larger sentences of twenty-five to eighty-one years each and were found guilty of assault with intent to kill, the defense argued that Lebrón aimed her gun at the ceiling rather than the House floor; as such, she received the most lenient of sentences.[8] Ironically, her offense carried less legal ramification, and while fortifying her political and personal premeditations, it also separated her from male peers.

Yet in a news conference directly after her arrest, Lebrón exalts herself as the insurgent act's authority. While she is recognized as less dangerous under the law, the newsreel highlights Lebrón's unwavering commitment to a life inextricably linked to the possibility of death, a disposition one sees during her trial as well. Latently foreshadowing the event's phenomenological and performative weight, the narrator depicts the event in the following way: "a wild hail of bullets" hits five congressmen after a "fantastic sudden shooting" by Lolita Lebrón, one of the "would-be assassins" who "boldly claims she is [the] instigator of the murder plot" and "brazenly sprayed bullets."[9] Hailing, here, becomes significant for both its physical fracturing of space and time and its ideological interpellation of the subjects involved. At first, her small stature is enveloped by Miranda's larger frame, but eventually the viewer of the newsreel is equally hailed, led directly to the face of Lebrón. The viewer notices Lebrón with perfect posture, just like a trained model groomed for the camera. When asked by a reporter if she shot to kill, she turns to the screen and slowly parries: "Not to kill," signaling once again her desire to offer death, not take life.[10]

"What was the purpose of this shooting?" a reporter asks. Lebrón pauses and responds calmly, "The purpose of this shooting was for the freedom of my country." She alone is further queried by another reporter: "Miss, can you tell us whose idea this was?" She confirms, "Sir, it's my idea . . . our idea." It is only after proclaiming that the event is her idea that Lebrón faces Miranda and declares, "our idea"—a subtle detail that reifies, but complicates the communal authority at once.

The interaction between Miranda and Lebrón further intensifies this tension: when called to respond to the reporter's questions, Miranda's responses are obscure—"I don't know" and "It is not necessary to answer that." Lebrón senses his displeasure, or desire to remain clandestine, and compels us to watch her further: she shifts the top portion of her body in Miranda's direction, and whispers something to him under her breath, simultaneously fingering the back of her left earring. With posture still intact, she pretends not to have uttered a word, although the viewer notices her moving lips as she places her finger against her ear. In less than two minutes of footage, the viewer is closely acquainted with Lebrón's complex and performative personage, alongside her steadfast commitment to national sovereignty. Demonstrating to the wider audience that she is the progenitor of this revolutionary happening, she exudes the command of a strategic agent more than the expected obsequiousness of a forlorn captive. Lebrón's responses, given at a time when dissenting subjects—especially women—were violently silenced, invert the threatening narrative of Otherness always already defined as pathological under imperial power, and especially during the height of the Red Scare.

In an extended campaign against communism, the United States moved strategically across continents to control the global stage;[11] at the same time, its tiny colony of Puerto Rico, led by this feminist revolutionary, moved cleverly as well, staging an attack on the very heart of the American Empire. This hair-raising performance by a pistol-carrying femme envoy for the party, alongside her resolute decree upon being arrested—"I didn't come here to kill, I came to die"—has made her one of the most celebrated revolutionary icons in Puerto Rican history. Lebrón's now-famous words, while signaling a form of autonomy under colonial life, also direct the porous boundaries between life and death; that is, if both might be seen as modes of becoming in Ricanness. Lebrón's existential mandate also redirects something altogether equally as important here: the fine line between madness, sexualization, and race at the site of death, which often reifies the dissenting woman of color as resolutely insane.

Although her 1954 scene of insurgency was "over in a matter of seconds,"[12] the spectacle of this "sensational act," as Lebrón calls it, begets an extensive reformulation of the event and the revolutionary herself in order to discern the social, aesthetic, political, and psychic figurations of Rican subjectivity. Though my analysis also traces the antecedents and aftermath of this action, this chapter accentuates a historical moment in time, in which Lebrón challenges the constriction of linear time via her enduring body. She is *that* site of Rican death, an image/representation of the resistant subject who reveals her intimate social and psychic contours in order to break through colonial time. As such, I read all of *her* as an aesthetic site, while willfully knowing what's at stake by attending to her act against the state as a highly aestheticized performance. While her act is certainly not the same type of performative exercise enacted by the other artists in this book, the aesthetic is always more than a heightened encounter with beauty for colonized subjects; it is politically larger than its performative stage within the limiting and violent script of existence for those unwanted beings in the world. That is to say that I restage, here, the spectacle Lebrón already orchestrated in the 1950s: a dramatic scene in which the United States is forced to take her death seriously. Lebrón walked into the Capitol building wearing the desire to die as fervently as the glamorous attire, lipstick, and gun that have since become her signature accessories. For Lebrón, politics and aesthetics are inseparable, all of her aesthetic choices are inherently political ones, and she alone retains the pleasure of performance, at the extremity of her own horizon.

Lebrón's performance on March 1 is both an aesthetic and a political intervention that deconstructs the teleology of American Expansionism and the incessant civic desire for world domination in the very portal of death. She is *that* prime example of those contingencies between death, colonial pathology, liberation politics, gender performance, and bodily endurance, as they sit at the center of Ricanness. If colonial subjectivity is structured around the management of life and death—not only at the level of political subjugation and revolt, but also in the psychic life of the gendered and racialized oppressed—then a major goal here is to establish a framework by which to speak of death as a bearable (maybe even productive) form of existence under colonialism. Lebrón directs this interarticulation between Ricanness and the onto-historical conditions of colonial life and death by consciously stopping time on March 1. In other words, I argue that she forces historical, colonial, masculinist temporality to pause in the very space of lawmaking. While she is ill fated in offering her life, she manages to display her only material property under colonialism: her death. For this reason, this chapter engages both the philosophical and psychoanalytic outlines of the Rican death drive as they surface through the life and activism of Lebrón alone. In attempting to undo a certain cliché of the femme, a cliché that often reduces Lebrón to a hysterical tool of masculine conspiratorial design, I expose how, at the pinnacle of the Cold War, she shakes the very leveling ground of democracy, gender, race, sexuality, and humanity. Lebrón offers her death not as a melancholic, mad subject, but as one compelled by a metaphysical conviction to transcend unsovereign oppression.

Enter the Queen of Terrors: Who Is "Lolita" Lebrón?

Even in this unshakable pledge to offer up her death, Lebrón is an enduring mystery. Her iconicity is affixed to her lack of transparency, sustaining the multidirectional narratives that frame her. Yet, the uncritical attention given to her femme aesthetic is so much of what superficially constitutes Lebrón. One such instance of this is found in the photograph in figure 1.1, which exposes the signifiers used to misread her. In 2004, Manuel Roig-Franzia, a journalist for the *Washington Post Magazine*, covered the fiftieth anniversary of "Lolita's" attack on Congress. The article, "A Terrorist in the House," also containing an interview with Lebrón, illustrates a cover photograph of Lebrón seized minutes after her arrest in 1954; directly under her close-up shot, the headline reads, "When terror wore lipstick." This headline perfectly encapsulates the paradoxical personage of Lebrón: how can a strikingly gorgeous woman also be a terrorist?[13] Or what happens when the language of terror accompanies a beautiful face?

This image disrupts our original understanding of a terrorist and also reframes our notions of a femme revolutionary. Like the headline, this Puerto Rican Nationalist is known by many other opposing names, too: teenage beauty queen, Catholic zealot, mystic visionary, martyr,

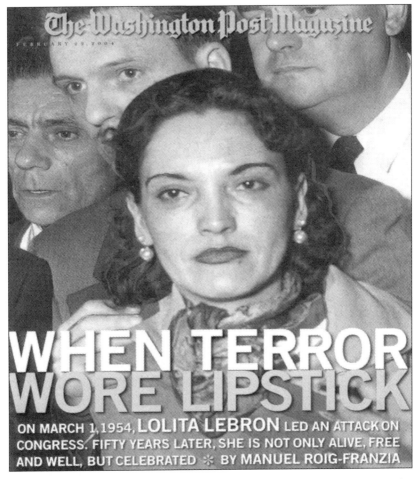

Figure 1.1. Cover of the *Washington Post Magazine*, February 22, 2004. Photo copyright Getty Images.

madwoman. While she is understood as the all-sacrificing mother of the Puerto Rican nation, her notoriety is also closely tied to the sexual fantasies surrounding her. For Puerto Rican scholar Ana Y. Ramos-Zayas, Lebrón's womanliness "is sexualized as the fantasy of the male revolutionaries: the beautifully manicured Lolita Lebrón wearing four-inch heels and a fitted dress during her anticolonial attack on the U.S. Congress."[14] Lebrón—"the revolutionary woman par excellence"[15]—is a product manufactured by colonial patriarchy, and while she may offer her death, for Ramos-Zayas, it is an action sustained under the limits of sexualization. But is "Lolita" just a Lolita, someone marked by the heteronormative standards of beauty—or an irrevocable terrorist dressed of her time? To push this even further, how does her name Lolita—"the tip of the tongue taking a trip of three steps down the palate to tap, at three, on the teeth. Lo. Lee. Ta.,"[16] as Nabokov's opening lines harmonize—a sultry utterance of the tongue, engender terror? The sexualized depiction of Lebrón places the female body, at once a femme fatale suddenly turned gun carrier, at the center of the terrified nation, making the body *humano* representative of social practices that mitigate and reimagine the racialized body politic.[17] Neither masculinist nor androgynous, Lebrón complicates our understanding of revolution itself, wearing both the fantasies and paradoxes that frame her, much like her male counterparts wore masculinity—often as excessive affectations doubling as subversive supplements under colonial life. The representation of Lebrón is as powerful as the revolutionary herself, and both work diligently to offer us a figure we may never intimately know outside of contradiction and incompletion.

While imagined as the mother of one nation, Lebrón is also understood as that mother who abandoned her own children for the revolution, shifting quickly from a sexual icon to an invalid maternal figure. She is, as Ramos-Zayas warns, always that Rican teenage pageant queen turned sexualized desire for the male party. For many others, however, her image is holy ground, and her sacredness muddies the clear waters between religion and communism: Lebrón is a devout Catholic first, who only secondly engages with socialism. For others, some very close to home, the fantasy of her rubs against a psychical nightmare and Lebrón is that suicidal subject led by a religious delusion. Or, she is that typical hysterical woman of color—"jabbering," "shrieking," and "crying about for 'freedom.'"[18] For those who've encountered her only as a footnote in US history, she is, as Roig-Franzia suggests, a terrorist who also wore lipstick—not an activist, thinker, political prisoner, and published poet. Lebrón is all these labels that "women with politics" are often branded as, none of them a small gesture in the larger scheme that is her long-standing celebrity. The task at hand, here, is to reconcile these incompatible ideologies, working alongside Lebrón herself as she negotiates the call to existence between the limits of race, gender, and sexualization, along with the nation, motherhood, anticolonialism, and religion. Convinced that one could never be a terrorist on stolen land, Lebrón endures the conflicting bedrock that informs subjectivity itself.

In her interview with Roig-Franzia, she firmly declares, "Who calls me a terrorist? The most terrorist country in the world! What other country dropped the atomic bomb? And they call me a terrorist. I went to the U.S. in a fight against terrorism."[19] At a time when subjects were forced to participate in performances of disavowal under McCarthyism, Lebrón utters a profound decree against the state, one precluded by the label of communist terrorist, dissenter with red lips—shifting the entire ontological terrain to the fecund ground of life and death. So how do we critically attend to these opposing entities—all of which are equally potent versions of Lebrón? How do they reinvigorate the rhetoric of terror, colonial servitude, and also withhold the subject's intricate interiority? And importantly, how is such vibrant terror even born?

Dolores "Lolita" Lebrón Sotomayor was born on November 19, 1919, in Lares, Puerto Rico, a town in the northwestern section of the island famous for El Grito de Lares.[20] Unlike those of the leader of the Nationalist Party, Lebrón's roots were not steeped in nationalist politics, the law, or rebellious aspirations, and yet she was born at the very site of revolution, within the most celebrated, rebellious territory of the island—Lares. This *jíbara* attended school through the eighth grade and trained as a seamstress. As a teenager, she was proclaimed the "Queen of the Flowers of May," a title she proudly wore; simultaneously, however, her political consciousness galvanized around the grips of colonialism with the Ponce Massacre of 1937.[21] By the time the United States entered World War II in 1941, Lebrón was already in New York City, leaving her daughter behind for her mother to raise as she searched for a better life as a seamstress.[22] In 1944, Lebrón married and had a son, but sent him to live with her mother and daughter, too.[23] Disillusioned with the fallacy of the American Dream, racism, and US belligerence, Lebrón confessed that she was hired by textile companies only after denying her Ricanness and claiming to be of Spanish descent.[24] To her employers' dismay, she soon spoke out against the mistreatment of garment workers.[25] And by 1947, completely discouraged by mainland racism and sexism, she officially became a prominent member of the Puerto Rican Nationalist Party, where she introduced feminist, socialist, and religious ideology to the political platform.[26] It was here that her life as a devout revolutionary began, culminating eight years later with her "cry for victory."

Lebrón has claimed that the Nationalist Party was a refuge in her everyday trials as a New Yorker. As she herself shared, she grew "tired of the daily humiliations she experienced and felt badly that she and her compatriots had had to leave their homeland in search of work, only to land in a place that did not want them."[27] Tormented by the "oppression of Puerto Rican women, who in addition to caring for their homes and families had to go out to work and then come home to put up with difficult husbands," Lebrón established the party as her new homeland and addressed these very feminist concerns. This oppression she experienced as a Puerto Rican woman had already been long established, encasing the contours of Ricanness at the site of the female body. Lebrón was keenly aware of the sterilization policies of the late 1930s, which provided the Puerto Rican government (under US authority) the right to manage what they perceived to be a problem of "overpopulation" on the island.[28] Rican reproduction, then, became viewed as an issue to seize, for if not, it would keep the island mired in poverty and "backwardness."[29] Cast as both a "demon mother" and a victim of *machismo*,[30] the Puerto Rican woman, via both angles, was also inherently pathological and in need of emendation.

The Nationalists began to protest these very policies, particularly after 1937, when the Puerto Rican legislature passed a bill to legalize birth control and create a Eugenics Board to review sterilization practices.[31] Under the Nationalist agenda, "women, children, and the poor would be able to thrive" under a just society.[32] This profoundly appealed to Lebrón, and she served several positions within the party as an expert on the topic. But in the very year of her action against Congress, Albizu Campos selected her as the general delegate to that Nationalist Party— the highest position within the party itself.[33] Though there have been claims that Albizu Campos ordered the attack, Lebrón was driven by the reported torture of the party leader in prison.[34] Lebrón reportedly planned every detail that occurred on March 1, telling Roig-Franzia, "I had all the secrets, all the plans. Me and me alone."[35]

I see March 1 not as a hysterical terrorist action, but as an action that in its purest philosophical pursuit expresses how the Rican female body is always a site that unwillingly seizes life and owns death. I understand

Figure 1.2. Lebrón after her arrest, March 1, 1954. Photo copyright Associated Press.

Lebrón to be working against this very history of sterilization and death of the Rican woman in contempt of sexual and gender violence. Resolutely aware that she never owned her life under the law—one needle always away from eradication—Lebrón chose to offer her death, a decision she deliberately makes, and repeatedly shares in her subsequent memories of 1954. Profoundly aware of the fading line between death and life, Lebrón endures against the scenery of her unwanted existence, showing us just how constructive the space of negation can be for certain subjects. The productive space of negation that I illustrate throughout this chapter, via Lebrón, works against the state's construction of the revolutionary as a maladaptive citizen-subject. The colonial state generates the rhetoric of terror that paints Lebrón as both a "terrorist" and an unhinged lunatic. In order to substantiate this story, revolution itself must be seen as lawlessness. To complicate matters further, when the revolutionary wears a femme aesthetic, the aesthetic is dismissible under the pretense of hysteria, and dissent is then read through the ongoing lens of pathology. But Lebrón is more than a radiant accessory; her femme aesthetic is an insurgent act, which recalibrates the very time of colonial politics.

A Recitation for Existence: The Suicide Note as Philosophical Disclosure

Like Lebrón herself, the "suicide" note found in her purse on the day of her attack is also more than an accessory: it is key to understanding how her radical performance encapsulates a tireless Ricanness on the global stage of American imperialism. Her handwritten note, retained after her arrest, mounts a critique of linear notions of life and death. Her note reiterates her declaration to die, not to kill:

> Before God and the world, my blood claims for the independence of Puerto Rico. My life I give for the freedom of my country. This is a cry for victory in our struggle for independence. Which for more than a half century has tried to conquer that land that belongs to Puerto Rico. I state that the United States of America are betraying the sacred principles of mankind in their continuous subjugation of my country, violating their rights to be a free nation and a free people in their barbarous torture of

our apostle of independence, Don Pedro Albizu Campos. . . . I take responsible [*sic*] for all.[36]

While the above note is often limited to the psychoanalytic language of
suicide,[37] or that suicidal subject desiring to rid herself of unbearable
despair, I read these words as a recitation for existence, a call for life
through the gift of death, in which this subject deliberately comprehends
her Rican ontology. That is to say, what if this suicide note is actually not
so suicidal? What if, instead, it is a public declaration of independence,
challenging the interarticulation of melancholia and race that continually frames the colonized other, the hysterical Rican woman?

"My life I give for the freedom of my country" extends an existential
trajectory: Lebrón *gives* her life and does not *take* it, and that ultimate
affirmation of struggle emerges as the ammunition of her political convictions for the nation. I propose that the important distinction between
the words *give* and *take* destabilizes the dialectical permanency of suicide. Just as an unwanted being in the world, a position Fanon expressed
earlier, is not the same as no longer wanting to live, giving necessitates
calculated agency; and unlike taking, it works outside the space of intended violence and assault.

Lebrón, here, confronts the image of the docile, uncommunicative,
disposable Rican woman and narrates her own interpretation of a discursive subject, one not limited to eulogy. In showing how the universal
"sacred principles" bypass her very existence, Lebrón endorses a new
kind of political humanism—one constituted by a desire to be seen and
regarded as human. Especially germane in this regard is her use of the
words "sacred" and "continuous subjugation": there is an obvious temporal inflection in the latter, and the former underlines an eternal summoning along a sacred-profane continuum, which profoundly informs
Lebrón's understanding of the meaning of life, in which both God and
the want for liberation guide her calling. Her cry for victory is a religious
one, yes, but it is also a phenomenological battle call to commemorate
those unwanted existences. As her writing suggests, this call is ambitious
in its attempt to offer one death to save many lives. Maldonado-Torres,
also following a Fanonian compass, explains this phenomenology of
the cry as the "first marker of an enslaved and suffering subjectivity" in
which "'crying' [that battle cry] is connected in the struggle for recogni-

tion."[38] This cry is a gift exceeding the parameters of colonialism, an existential recognition of self-giving that surpasses mechanical time. This twinned relevance, here, suggests that crying is a lamentation, but also an all-embracing moment when the subject embraces the limits of the materiality of their body, a reminder of their liveness at the site of both sound and flesh. This note, then, is a public admission of endurance, one fundamental to my theory of Ricanness, in which at its very center sits an entity crying against the colonizer's "barbarous torture," to remind us that terror's lips are often unpainted.

Lebrón's penciled note is an incantation for being—a song, chant, cry—a linguistic, sonic expression accompanying her already enduring body.[39] Within this cry for victory, however, how does Lebrón understand the conscious decision to want to die? To uncover what's eternally at stake in her incantation, I will further extend a performance studies lens here and return to the scene of the "crime," hoping to excavate what's really put to death on March 1.

Silent and still in the Ladies' Gallery, Lebrón first gives face—"a large, definitive, and demanding" gesture—while listening to congressional deliberations and anticipating her dramatic cue.[40] "Between embodied gestures of expression and iterative structures of power," the law and performative action confront one another.[41] I understand her moment of waiting to offer death, here, as a distinctly Rican type of suspension under colonial rule: in the very place where policy scripts determine and reimagine life with the inaudible flick of a pen, Lebrón releases her own call to arms. It's a moment of hailing with varying gestures, tones, battle cries, and lips; and in her hailstorm of bullets at the ceiling, there is an immediate enactment of the Althusserian interpellation. She crosses the law, the congressmen, and the armed guards, forcing them to hail her—a hailing so forceful that she consequently hails herself, an always-already subject looking straight into the eyes of death. Althusser explains ideology and the interpellation of subjects as similar phenomena: "Ideology has always-already interpellated individuals as subjects," which means "that individuals are always-already interpellated by ideology as subjects, which confirms that "individuals are always-already subjects."[42] In Lebrón's moment of political agency—an instantiation that magnifies erstwhile inscrutable ideological coordinates—lies an intersubjective performance in which an armed authority and this armed woman finally face off. It, too, is a Foucauldian type of relationality, which forces sovereign power and the docile body's revolt to disciplinary power to restage their "means of correct training."[43] Behind these multiple encounters, Lebrón demands recognition under the law, on the lay of its land, as a Rican woman. In this dynamic constellation of the always-already subject, Statehood, and the interpellation between them, Lebrón redirects the Hegelian dialectic, obliging the law to recognize and confront its self-consciousness through an immediate unconscious response to the other's mortality. To invoke both Althusser and Hegel once again, at the very moment of the congressional speech acts, she becomes the recognizable Other, importing her own set of dialogic and material terms.

But death becomes neither the revolutionary nor the congressional male on March 1, leaving a desire for continual iteration and bodily vindication through the failed attempt at both mortal sacrifice and revolution. I suggest that this misfire casts a spell on the existential life of the colonized subject and is the start of the performative act in which the law stands guard at the resistance of the subject; or that moment when, like Fanon shares, the lifeworld of the colonial object meets the lifeworld of the enslaving Other. Fanon, if we recall from the introduction, desires to be a being amid the larger call of Being, but realizes that the master (as in Hegel's master/slave dialectic) casts him (prior-to-being) as an object.[44] This determination as an object/slave compels Fanon to fight and engage the master through conflict in order to reach a state of shared recognition between opposing subjects. From Fanon we learn that Being is linked to combustible acts—objects like himself that also crumble, fall apart, burst into pieces, and are made anew into another formulation of self.[45] But this new self, as he shares, is always joined to conflict; one must confront the entity that made one an object. It's this very state of objecthood that sets the stage for revolution.[46] Fanon critically writes that "he who is reluctant to recognize me opposes me" and "in a savage struggle I am willing to accept the convulsion of death," making it apparent that the impulse to strike back when stricken releases in him a resistance to a persecutory life in favor of death.[47]

In the strict Hegelian sense, self-consciousness is never actually achieved: it is rather a social creation helping the master and slave to preserve one another; power and this constant "savage struggle" to retain recognition prevent any resolution. Like Fanon, Lebrón incurs a necessary struggle to attain recognition; neither Fanon nor Lebrón enters conflict with the Other to murder, but instead to defend themselves against the "sacred principles of mankind." This internal uprising offers us a complicated glimpse into death, which cannot be easily understood by conventional negations of life versus death, or dying versus not yet living. Both Fanon and Lebrón extend their own hail for existence under the precept of their unwanted lives.

These encounters necessarily induce a confrontation of both physical and immaterial elements. That is to say that the material body is always already connected to one's speech act, too. Lebrón's handwritten note and her incantation for life are Austinian promises, which in their very utterance and public circulation unfurl a scene—*do* something. Austin understands the performative utterance to be run by a temporal meter: the performance of the articulation (the locution) to its intended meaning (the illocutionary act) to the consequence of the speech act (the perlocutionary act).[48] In Lebrón's speech act, the illocutionary act is the declaration replete with meaning: Lebrón achieves "independence" in the audibility of her cry, in the very moment of that utterance, on March 1, 1954. In these illocutionary moments, she is the writing/speaking subject, forming insurgencies out of syllables. In this occurrence, both Lebrón's calculated recitation and her aesthetic gestures unfold within the event, the rehearsed action lingering within the taken-for-granted script against which performativity becomes legible. The unwelcomed and unwanted Lebrón orchestrates a relational affectation in her offering of death—a showdown that instantiates a Rican existentialism in a space that historically and legally mutes and erases her. The reddest of all scares, then, is the painted face of Lebrón in the very locus of Rican death.

This recitation for existence calls forth alternative ways of being in the world that must overcome insurmountable odds. Lebrón's words outline the figurative framing of her revolutionary life, but also provide exegetical insight into the existential, phenomenological, and psychoanalytic parameters of a Rican colonial subject. While Fanon is a major analytic of this book, I also turn to his multiple guiding compasses to discuss the transformation of the subject. So here I anticipate Heidegger and Lacan—who also follow a Hegelian compass to unearth the conscious and unconscious properties of the subject. These philosophical and psychoanalytic conversations concerning existence, while excluding the Rican other, help me to rehearse the conditions of Ricanness: it is expansive in its historical call to life of more than five hundred years of colonial servitude, and also exclusive in its act of colonial endurance. That universal desire Lebrón calls forth in her recitation for being, much like Fanon's, is made of broken and alienated parts, letting in the most valuable and pushing out the most severed.

A Brush with Death: Surviving Conscious Portals into the Future

The puncturing act by which Lebrón inserts herself into the historical and temporal ledger on the congressional floor delineates her sense of being in the world, her (pre)life, and her eventual death. Rican death, whether given, planned, imagined, or taken, is a condition of the colonization of time itself—one of the central preoccupations of this book. In my reading of her premeditated performance, I suggest that Lebrón hails humanity through death, that ephemeral grace she summons to answer the most savage of colonial practices under the very precept of Being. As such, Ricanness is a theorization that provides an opening for imagining the psychical reality of the socially limited colonial subject, and the potential of the subject to resist its ontological fate and move past disillusion.

This maternal idol of the Rican nation leaves her fingerprints on those totalizing renditions of social death and civic materiality, offering her version of Ricanness as a complement to both biopolitics and necropolitics.[49] Lebrón creates a blueprint for Rican death—both ontologically and in its everyday, prosaic occurrences—in her narrative for an always-already endangered entity struggling to achieve independence. Such death derives its force from the spaces of incompletion, negation, and unwantedness as viable metaphors for a bearable life within colonialism. Lebrón exposes how life's ability to intimate death is an ontological evasion: death is often speechless. So if death is the only thing proper to itself, as Heidegger will explain below, then what does the arrangement of a Rican coup de grâce offer Being more generally? And what does the potential death of a colonial, Rican femme constitute in its own desire to stop time?

This dramatic figure, as I see her, represents Rican death: a category that envelops Ricans of all walks of life, the (in)famous and the anonymous, the deliberately political and the quotidian apolitical, those underwater, those across the sea. In this way, Lebrón symbolizes a reproduction of life that stands outside the physical limits of mortality. In taking on this universal quality of mortality in order to complicate our understanding of death, Heidegger differentiates between two crucial components of existence: death and dying—the latter is the only thing the subject can experience in itself. But subjects, for Heidegger, can never experience finitude, although they discursively understand that they, too, will eventually fall off their perch. This difference is expressed through the pursuit of the meaning of existence (*Da-sein*) itself: "In dying it becomes evident that death is ontologically constituted by . . . existence. Dying is not an event, but a phenomenon. . . . But if 'ending,' as dying, constitutes the totality of Da-sein, the being of the totality itself must be conceived as an existential phenomenon of my own Da-sein."[50] There is never a complete representation of death in existence. Even when we witness the "ending" of someone else, we never attain the full experience of death proper. This *Da-sein*, as Heidegger explains, is an existential process universal in its kicking of the calendar, but particular to one's experience. Death is like an out-of-body experience that one never feels, and even if one sees someone else die, one is still too far removed from the immediate entity of death to actually engage it. Can one really die, then? The important matter for Heidegger, as for me with Lebrón, is the idea of coming to terms with one's mortality as a way to understand time, and one's ultimate nonlinear freedom. In Lebrón's case she offers her death, willing to die, acting out her "ending," and yet she remains further away from death.[51]

Death refuses her, even when she is not fully outside its range. Offering death, as she does, is a confirmation of her unique possession of existence, a self-gift that cannot be taken from her, and which becomes the intimate locus of her freedom, will, authenticity, and path along *Da-sein*. Heidegger shows us above that one's death cannot be imitated, borrowed, or passed on in time: each subject retains the admission of life through her understanding of mortality and path toward conscious freedom. But what of the colonial subject, at once conjoined to and disjoined from that larger narrative of existence? What becomes of one death in the name of those many colonized lives? Unwilling to see the colonized other in his demand for a universal understanding of mortality, Heidegger fails to see how *Da-sein* in its purest philosophical sense is first and foremost always already a category of enslavement: one knows death and can offer it, because one does not fully exist under the full possession of one's facticity.[52]

While Lebrón may not die on March 1, the congressional floor is forced to take the island, and her death, seriously. Lebrón answers the emotional and bodily incarceration of death and calls out the docility of the necropolitical subject under colonial time, transmitting instead a vital bearability under subjugation. I see her recitation for being as a performative act that redirects eternal despair and dread under mortal premises. As she yields "a cry for victory," I do not hear a melancholic subject, for Lebrón's offering is a question; with calculated prose she indicates her gift of death for the future of the communal good in a world stricken by the presentness of colonial disorder.

Hailing the Unconscious: The Madness in the Rican Death Drive

Gripping death produces an immediacy that most colonial subjects must work with and against in a world where linear time is used to restrict freedom and determine sanity. I would be remiss if I did not mention that Fanon departs from psychiatric practice to join a revolution against another type of disorder: the diseased nation itself, pathologically diagnosing colonial subjects in order to disguise, preserve, and advance imperial practice. As Fanon warns, the colonial subject is not mad, but rather becomes so through the very "sickness, and the inhumanity" that colonization has historically produced.[53] In the case of Puerto Rico, the historical is simultaneously contemporary, exposing the myth of the progress narrative in linear time. Development is never chronological when the racialized, sexualized, colonized subject sits at the center of its building blocks.

To explain this scripted relation of alterity, madness, and Rican colonialism, Lacanian psychoanalyst Patricia Gherovici turns to Puerto Rican Syndrome, a disorder created in the 1950s to identify "inducted Puerto Rican soldiers" during the Korean War.[54] According to Gherovici, army psychiatrists developed a foreign diagnostic system to fit a set of local, male, subaltern symptoms at a time when the Nationalist Party expressed dissenting viewpoints against the mainland.[55] This national label, most commonly recognized as *ataque de nervios*, actually reinforced the threshold of colonialism:[56] if the United States hailed its subject as the abnormal other, then Puerto Rico was not only economically, politically, socially and culturally determined, but also psychologically constrained. Ricanness, that syndrome now akin to hysteria, manifests astride a set of symptoms that are indeed politically motivated. In these connections between war, race, and hysteria, Gherovici stages a conversation between the psychoanalytic and social, pulling from the Freudian female hysteric and pushing into the new docile and diseased racialized male Rican. That is to say that symptomology and hysteria are never outside the parameters of national violence, protest, and racialization when the Rican subject is implicated. Gherovici explains the important connection below:

> While it would be rash or misleading to collapse the hysterical symptoms manifested by Puerto Rican soldiers during the Korean War and the violent political actions led by various groups of nationalists because they somehow took place at the same time, I wish to stress the similar pathologization of these disruptive manifestations. While violent demonstrations, shootings, and rioting in the name of nationalist resistance cannot be called hysteria but political struggle, when this is perceived from the point of view of the Other—that is, in this case, from the American doxa of law and order—then the subversion of order can only be made sense of by being reduced to a madness seen as stubbornly opposing civilization.[57]

While warning us against historical conflation, she does not dismiss the reality of imperial essentialism. In fact, her psychoanalytic and social turn, here, exposes the convergence of colonialism and mental disorder. The stubborn colonial savage is incapable and undeserving of sovereignty—not only in 1950 but in the eternal recurrence of colonial domination, in which the master's discourse is at the apex of any figuration of Ricanness. To understand how Gherovici arrives at Ricanness as a dialogue between the Rican subject and Lacan's Other, insofar as the Puerto Rican subject creates an unconscious connection to the Other, we must again return to the recurring Hegelian face-off between the master/slave that appears throughout this chapter in varying performative ways.

Influenced by Hegel's notion of subjectivity, Lacan reconceptualizes the master/slave dialectic in psychoanalytic terms: he extends Hegel's notion of being by transforming this very binary tension into discourse through the position and language of the Other. Let us recall again that in Hegel's dialectic, the aspiration for self-recognition hinges on the desire of the other; that is to say that the subject who is recognized (master) hinges on the one who recognizes (slave). In this struggle for domination and desire, self-recognition is actualized by the negation of the other, a confrontation that will eventually, as Hegel hopes, offer mutual recognition. But since there is often room for only one master, when does this mutual recognition occur? Interested in the connection between the social, political, and psychological implications of the subject through different forms of communication, Lacan explains that "what dominates society is the practice of language." Lacan sees discourse living in all of our social interactions, while also organizing and framing every speech act. In seeing discourse this way, Lacan attempts to reshift the tension between the master and slave through a reevaluation of self-recognition itself, or what he calls misrecognition. He argues that the master speaks to the slave as the slave labors to produce for the former;[58] however, the slave never attains the benefits of this production. Instead, what is produced is consumed and appropriated by the master—this includes the slave's language as never being independent from the master's discourse. In this sense, the master reaps not only the benefits of the subordinate's disposability, but also any "surplus" that exceeds what is needed to exist, including the slave's language.[59] While this surplus exists, the master, in all of his desire, never actually attains it; he, too, is left endeavoring to contain the desire in language itself. Lacan wonders, however, what is this desire? Might it be actually misrecognized through the misperception of the Other's wants? Might it actually be something more than freedom from domination for the oppressed Other?

At stake for Lacan is how the master creates a language that is used to estrange his subordinate. While language brings the subject into being, it is not without recourse, for language is an alienating force that contributes to the subject's split. In rethinking the master's discourse, here, Lacan imagines this barred subject as the split between the ego (never fully actualized) and the unconscious (the signifying chain), with the ego composed of "internalized ideal images," which are used to make sense of the world.[60] Just like our desires, however, these images and our attempts to translate them can often be false, thus rendering malformed and incomplete the resultant subjectivity. On the other hand, "The unconscious is the Other's discourse in a very straightforward fashion: the unconscious is full of other people's conversations, goals, aspirations, and fantasies (in so far as they are expressed in words)."[61] The distinction between these two psychic states shows how subjectivity is never stable, for in Lacan's barred subject, the influence of the Other's language still infiltrates both states: in the first, one is cognizant of language and its consequences, and in the other, a full realization of thought remains out of reach.[62]

If we follow Lacan's idea of the barred subject, as translated by Gherovici, the Puerto Rican colonial subject is recognizable in US culture only through the Other, an enduring unconscious infiltration from the start of existence. The state, the master's discourse, is always already inside the colonized mind, making it impossible to attain freedom outside some sort of showdown, dialectical recognition. If we extend this even further into the realm of the Rican revolutionary, as Gherovici sees in the Nationalists, then the desire to offer one's death becomes an embodiment of madness; the madness of the revolutionary is made legible only through the lens of melancholia and suicide, a further perpetuation of the Other's oppressive discourse. Even Lacan notes that the one who protests and revolts against the law is seen as an abiding hysteric. In this case, the gendered and sexualized gestures of hysteria fail to surpass Lebrón. They, in fact, symptomize her revolutionary act, for how else might we arrive at a concrete understanding of subject self-recognition and ideological fortitude? How else might an act against the Law of the Father be legible to the general public—that is, outside a system of pathology?

Lebrón is described by mainstream culture as a "convicted thief and forger who spent much of her adult life in prison," and a "fiery divorcée," a "shrieking" subject "jabbering in Spanish."[63] This discourse, here, suggests that both a deviant criminal and a hysterical woman were unleashed on March 1. Even the governor of Puerto Rico at the time, Luis Muñoz Marín, labeled the event as one of madness, and conveyed to President Eisenhower that the act was a "savage and unbelievable lunacy," fervently suggesting that the Nationalists, including Lebrón, were a "virulent germ of infection."[64] In analyzing the political significance of "the *ataque* as the Puerto Rican syndrome," Gherovici explores the Nationalists' actions as a "defensive attack" against the United States, and explains that this cannot be viewed outside the purview of hysteria's historicity itself: "The 1950s, the time of the invention" of this disorder, was "also a period of intense unrest that turned out to be the real breeding ground for this hysteria."[65] But when political action is advanced against the state during perilous times, how might violence be reframed as a defense against both oppression and pathology? Gherovici points out that Lebrón was acutely aware of the wider pathologization of insurgency and identifies Lebrón's essential clarity of thought during her trial. Gherovici, in her defense against defense, shares that "during the trial of Lolita Lebrón and her three co-defendants, [Lebrón] interrupted the proceedings, crying 'no!' three times when lawyer Ehrich tried to claim that the defendants were insane."[66]

Lebrón deliberately "aimed her fire directly at the Great Seal of the United States, injuring no one, and could not be convicted of assault with intent to kill."[67] Her companions, too, shared that "they did not take aim, or shoot to kill; and indeed the five injuries were the ricochets rather than direct hits."[68] In particular, Lebrón firmly declared "that if they planned to kill anyone, it would have been simpler to hurl a single grenade."[69] Lebrón, with great conviction, confirms that she "deliberately committed a sensational act calculated to shock the U.S. Government into awareness of the cause of Puerto Rican Independence."[70] This discrete, punctuated attack against the US government (less than two years after the establishment of the Commonwealth status) was chosen for several reasons, including to coincide with the Tenth Inter-American Conference. Held in Caracas, Venezuela, this US initiative intended to solidify anticommunist sentiment and support from across the Americas.[71] But this date inspired the Nationalists more fundamentally because it marked the anniversary of the passing of the Jones-Shafroth Act of 1917, a law that replaced the Foraker Act and granted citizenship to Puerto Ricans.[72] This act also called for the creation of a legislative and executive branch similar to those of the United States, with the exceptions that the president appoint the governor and that the US Congress approve all cabinet members and still hold the power to veto any legislation.[73] For Lebrón, the revolutionary act was planned to strike against such pro-American affiliation and to resist the political and economic imperial ambitions of the United States.[74]

Alongside this clear pronouncement of her sanity and premeditated plan, Lebrón expressed another clear conviction during the entire trial: Lebrón read the pages of her Bible as if a transcendental force were also endorsing her actions. She did so even as "her brother Gonzalo, a first-rank militant," testified "against her as a witness for the people."[75] Just as the judge, Lawrence Walsh, was about to hand down her sentence, Lebrón asked "to speak from the bench of the accused."[76] In a distinctively forthright speech before the jury, Lebrón confirmed a set of unruffled principles. Emphatically positioning herself as a savvy independent vis-à-vis the tentacular reach of US imperialism, she shared "how she preferred to look for coins in fountains rather than accept public assistance from the oppressor nation."[77] According to Conrad Lynn, Lebrón's lawyer during her trial, her speech was so moving that "even members of the jury wept . . . even Judge Walsh himself had to interrupt [her speech] momentarily in order to go to his chambers and dry his eyes."[78] More than just the personal charisma of an individual, the emotive, theatrical, and sensational power of these scenes conveys a cognizant Rican woman, enlivening the metaphysical dimension of subjectivity.

Lebrón's disidentification with colonial epistemes enables her to independently reconstitute existence, on both conscious and unconscious planes—neither of which unveils a conventional hysteric. Similarly to Gherovici, Latinx studies and Lacanian psychoanalytic scholar Antonio Viego reconstitutes the hysterical subject by revealing how the racialized hysteric ceaselessly creates new symptoms to satiate the desire for new forms of knowledge.[79] This desire, as Viego explicates, strengthens her unconscious relationship with the Other in order to best understand her sense of being in the world. This perpetual reinvention undermines "the master," since he consistently produces symptomatic labels to index phenomena observed from/in the hysteric. For Viego, the racialized hysteric works diligently for complete knowledge, and through her very actions, labors to expose any "hole[s] in discourse."[80] The master, on the other hand, attempts to undermine this move and prevent any challenge by the hysteric. Viego argues that this marginalized subject is "often instantiated as lacking in the social" and "must learn to imagine alternative ways of making life pleasurable, tolerable."[81] He adds that this subject must labor to find "new ways of accessing the dialectical movement of desire, without being convinced that building the ego's defense is the answer."[82] These alternative forms of being in the world, as Viego notes, are actualized through archetypal reinvention; as such, I see Lebrón reinvesting in an alternative and bearable existence by stopping the master's clock, pressing pause on outdated citational pathways that lead one into the space of pathology. While she may embody those symptoms placed upon her as a Rican femme colonial subject, she also extends these symptoms, producing new knowledge, in her endeavor to offer death; importantly, she leaves a blueprint for a Rican future in her plea for existence through the space of death.

In this case of Ricanness via Lebrón, Lacan's barred subject, racially reformulated by Gherovici and Viego, supplies us with a valuable way to imagine the ontology of a subject who lives in constant incompletion, negation, abjection, hysteria, and unwantedness. If colonialism is always predicated on pathology, as Fanon, Gherovici, Viego, and even Althusser—working from Lacan—confirm, then its unconscious structures are equally relevant to its social demands. If existence is always constituted by the language of master versus servant, and this dialectical recognition is both a conscious and an unconscious affair we experience at all times, then death is not finitude, death is not the end of time; it surpasses mechanical time, uniquely, for some exquisite futural gain. Thinking of death along these lines rejects the suicidal, melancholic racialized subject unable to move past her despairing and disparaging symptoms. In this understanding of death, new symptoms produce emergent life worlds, especially when certain subjects might already be dead.

Perhaps a consideration of Freud's construction of "mourning and melancholia" may help us uncover how melancholic Lebrón never actually was. In mourning, as Freud explicates, a nontoxic reaction to a lost object forms, in which the object is eventually renounced and supplanted. Melancholia, however, works as a pathological relationship to loss and the lost object itself.[83] Freud contends that suicide is always an aggressive act against the love-object that was once toxically internalized. Lebrón's note and her revolutionary actions during 1954, however, never indicate a subject struggling with unbearable angst; instead she yearns to die, in the now, for the independence of Puerto Rico, and thus she extricates her impulses of all traces of existential nausea, for the future. One certainly mourns while being oppressed, but internalizing the lost object, as it occurs in melancholia, suspends the transformation of the subject. Such introjection is enduringly toxic, engendering a subject that cannot release herself of the grips of—in this case—colonial life. Instead of replacing the lost object, the subject internalizes its identity into a new way of being in the world. This harmful relationship to loss foments the subject into one of perpetual suffering; unaware of any time here, she then carries the lost object into the present toward a toxic future. We must move past this interconnection between melancholia and race, gender, and sexuality, in which colonized subjects are always the saddest, most vulnerable, and unwanted of the world. So how can thinking beyond this introjected loss allow us to see death as an alternative pathway to another type of living? How might "suicide notes" be poetic recitations for existence from femme, feminist Ricans?

While Freud argues, in his death drive, that the subject wishes to return to an organic state through death itself, Lacan sees death as a citational pathway to the renewal of the subject. In his reading of the myth of Antigone—a subject entombed (and who subsequently commits suicide) for providing a proper burial for her brother against the state's demand—Lacan considers the anticipation of death, or the death that comes into life. In an act of ethical conviction, Antigone takes her life, defiantly grabbing death and placing it around her neck. What fascinates Lacan, here, is the idea of living between the first death (one's bodily death) and the second death (where regeneration is impossible). Lacan's death drive does not allow for a return to an original preexistent state, however. Instead, he wonders how restoring the beautiful (found in the limit of the second death) helps one understand one's own relationship to mortality and existence.

In returning to the story of Antigone as a parallel for Lebrón, let us recall the details of her demise. In order to bury her brother, Antigone chooses to die, with a conviction demonstrated by her verbal declaration of always having been a dead subject. Marc De Kesel shares of this already dead subject: "The idea that a human being, as a real being, is always already 'dead' lies at the heart of the Lacanian theory of the subject. Being the subject/bearer of signifiers, human beings have left behind their real being and only live by grace of the signifiers that represent them."[84] This "already" dead subject, an ongoing deadness, is fundamental to human existence inasmuch as it is circumscribed by the semiotics that sustain it. Both Antigone and Lebrón answer to the call of owning death, of being already enmeshed in death under the state. Unlike Antigone, Lebrón is that colonial subject born dead, who must offer her already dead death again so that others, too, may exist in the future. Both women, however, answer the emotional and bodily incarceration of death, even if already dead. Lebrón, in particular, lends us an antidote to the necropolitical subject under colonial time—transmitting instead an essential bearability under oppression by stopping historical time.

Her recitation for being is so profound that it redirects despair, longing, dread, and death itself. Her powerful performance yields "a cry for victory," not a call for a life destined to perpetual melancholia and suffering.

Freud claims that the melancholic subject "represents its ego to us as worthless, incapable of any achievement and morally despicable; he reproaches himself, vilifies himself, and expects to be cast out and punished."[85] Nothing in Lebrón's words or actions would suggest a subject wishing to be disciplined or castigated. To read beyond unbearable loss, here, is to assess the beauty and productivity of death. Offering death is a constructive means of existence, a realization for Lebrón that death was always already hers to own. What she owns—death—is not what she aims for in life; it is what she already had to offer. That is to say that her performance in 1954, as her letter indicates, is the uncompromising manifestation and unity of both unconscious and conscious desires.

If the only thing Lebrón owns in this struggle for liberation is her death, then such an offering must face off with the potentialities of the body. Judith Butler describes the material body as a canvas for both politics and aesthetics, showing how subjects consent and disidentify with dominant social constructions of gender and sex, while also refashioning the very ontology of corporeality.[86] For Butler, gender is both a performance and performative, and never outside history, constituted firmly by laws and doctrines. Working from an Althusserian construction of ideology, Butler explicates that the subject is always already discursively formed, hailed even, before entering the world. In showing how the material body actually speaks, Butler unveils the power of performativity in acts of repetition, reiteration, at times even exceeding the boundaries of language itself by translating latent drives into their physical incarnations. As a corrective to a more purely linguistic model of performativity, Butler *feels* for the materiality of the body and, in doing so, reanimates the indispensable quality of the psychical, those unconscious parts of subjectivity that reveal their own performative force. The body's movements come, as Butler discovers, from those deeply rooted feelings of being, belonging, and existing within one's body, with other bodies, which often surpass the body's very intentionality. That is to say that signification is always already deeper than the conscious intention can bear. Most specific to this point, Lebrón willingly punctures an all-male congressional floor with four-inch heels, consequently halting and

activating the law, policy, gender binarisms, and chronoheteronormativ-
ity. In reordering the ordinary script of the law, Lebrón, in her "excitable
speech," does more than appropriate heteronormativity;[87] she restages
that Althusserian call through her recitation, a type of vulnerability that
Butler claims carries a legacy of history that the subject is born from and
into, and from which she can never escape.

There is also a certain material, phenomenological, and self-
transformative gift that unfurls in this process, particularly for the
woman-of-color feminist intending to exist in the world. To draw out
these transformative moments in both aesthetics and politics, I suggest
that Lebrón refashions the numerous incantations of the body. Ricanness, in this chapter, demands multiple existential and psychic turns,
as I have shown throughout: Lebrón's radical act against Congress is an
integrated engagement with the linguistic, material, affective, and genealogical body, creating both the theatricality and reality of the historical event. Untenable without Lebrón's material body, this femme Rican's
sacrificial offering, while seductive, is the enactment of the resistance of
the object. It is also the bedrock of the fantasy of Lebrón as Ramos-Zayas
has revealed. Within this dynamic projection, Lebrón, the beautiful,
mysterious femme fatale and mother of the nation, fulfills the fantasy of
the body politic, enabling a new metaphysical corporeality through her
mortality. These intertwined bodies are choreographed by her *recitation
for existence*—a way of being-in-the-world that translates the call for
death as an antidote to pathology and suicide. Likewise, her performative gestures allow her speech act to transform the linguistic body of
history, the law, gender performance. In Ricanness, then, what does it
mean to relisten with and for Lebrón in her bodily gestures and speech
as a femme, feminist revolutionary?

María Josefina Saldaña-Portillo explores this relationship between
the revolutionary icon and the progress narrative. Placing in conversation twentieth-century development theory and revolutionary ideology deployed across the Americas, Saldaña-Portillo contends that such
a relationship is mired by the exacting indexicality assigned to race
and gender—those categories that sustain post–World War II capitalist
rhetoric. She states, "The convergence between late-twentieth-century
discourses of development and revolution cannot be explained by
a mechanistic derivation of one from the other, for developmentalist

and revolutionary speech acts are constitutive of each other."[88] This assertion places seemingly antithetical theories of progress on conciliatory ground: developmental and revolutionary speech acts arise from similar calls for social and political change, stemming from the colonial doctrine of "human perfectibility," which is marred by racialized and gendered exclusion. Echoing Marx's dictum that capitalism contains the "seeds of its own destruction," she argues that "we cannot simply read revolutionary movements of the period as against colonial and neocolonial capitalism. We must also read them as *within* a racialized and gendered developmentalism."[89] Subsequently, the revolutionary subject must shed the "feminized ethnos" of race and gender and be that androgynous figure that unites the nation in order to catalyze social, political, and cultural change. However, once the revolutionary begins to circulate globally, as Portillo shows through iconic figures such as Che and Malcolm X, gendered subjects remain lifeless while the "masculine" subject is lionized within the trajectory of a linearly understood history. She writes, "This revolutionary androgyny appears to have synthesized, dialectically, the thesis of a fully masculine, developed subject moving forward universally through historical time and the antithesis of a feminized, underdeveloped subject who gets left behind in the particularity of domesticity once the choice for progress is made."[90] Here one notices that the animus between chronology—"historical time"—and phenomenological renderings of experience—"the particularity of domesticity"—is reconciled as *History*, the gold standard of existence. Racialized masculinity is the measure and crest of all revolutionary life, and this masculinist narrative advances in time, while the femme subject descends into the space of the endnote.[91] So much of what makes Lebrón experimental and vanguard, I suggest, is her ability to retain the femme aesthetic as an insurgent act—part and parcel of the event, the revolution, her time, offering up a flight plan to Rican subjectivity. Lebrón is futuristic, especially in a time and place where to be deliberately *other* meant death by the hands of the sovereign power. Lebrón is an armed authority against masculinist chronology, leaving her fingerprints on the fissures of those totalizing renditions of social life, political death, and civic materiality.

In the striking photograph in figure 1.3, taken after her arrest, Lebrón smiles haughtily into the camera, her body stretching closest to the lens

Figure 1.3. Lebrón smiling with Cancel Miranda, Figueroa Cordero, and Flores Rodríguez, 1954. Photographer unknown.

as her male comrades shift behind her petite shoulders and glare at her admiringly. She is the only one directly gazing into the camera, ostensibly contented after her failed attempt to offer death. Lebrón is the pulse of the image: she is both the frame of the cultural milieu and that pricking detail that reminds one how satisfaction and deliberate dignity visually meet. But there is a meta-punctum here, to invoke Barthes's *Camera Lucida* again: if the camera captures life in the flash of a "shot," then the presumably successful death here stands as in the photo, the photograph as the prosperous hailing bullet. As Barthes warns, the image as a symbol of death is illusory, for even the copy learns how to demand privilege and concession. As one's eyes remain transfixed by erotic curiosity, or ocular intrusiveness, Lolita "gives us life" and re-rationalizes the revolution, moves the viewer from a masculinist time frame to a femme aesthetic in the face of death.[92]

The Lady's Galleries: Prison, Poetry, Religion, and the Endurance of Death

Lebrón is that armed authority who stopped colonial time on March 1, but how do we reconcile her inability to actually give up her death?[93] How do we come to terms with a subject who, in offering her death, no longer owns her life? Lebrón offered her death in 1954, but death did not seize her until almost sixty years later. Naturally and without political conflict, on August 1, 2010, at ninety years old, the iconic revolutionary died of cardiorespiratory complications in San Juan, Puerto Rico. After devoting more than sixty years to the nationalist cause, twenty-five years spent in prison, postincarceration public demonstrations, and politically charged writings, she passed of old age—an elliptic moment of transition rather than a terminal period sealing an end of an existence. If this is how she conventionally ends time, how does she reimagine finitude throughout the remaining years of her long life? How might Lebrón's twenty-five-year term in prison help reorganize our understanding of endurance, as both her mind and body sustained and suspended the daily pangs of serving time under an intense desire to die? In its most literal sense, Lebrón, unable to offer death, *did* time—or, some might say, time finally *did* her. If we consider how she spent such time as a political prisoner, as a profound writer, we might see the enduring effects of political endurance itself—that matter at the very heart of Ricanness.

During her time in prison, Lebrón became a fervent believer that God had chosen her as a disciple for freedom, a religious-political determination making colonial life bearable, and rightfully evinced in her book of poetry.[94] In several of her poems, Lebrón addresses Albizu Campos and God nearly simultaneously—the former often as *Maestro*, a term frequently used in biblical texts—in a language that reveals her religious faith and adherence to a traditionally masculinist, even patriarchal platform. Both entities often become one in her poetry, a theme working alongside her feminist political convictions that also seep through the verses. One such poem begins, *"Respirame, Albizu! / En la infinita esencia en que arrulla tu vuelo."*[95] Imploring Albizu Campos to "breathe" life into her with the "infinite essence" of his "lulling flight" from this world, in this poem Lebrón refers to Albizu Campos as the *Maestro*, as the pedagogue sustaining her existence, pleading again, but differently: *"Respirame en tu llama, hoy, Maestro / en que arrullan campanas / y en Jayuya / Blanca Canales canta!"*[96] Here she also invokes the name of Blanca Canales and unites Rican freedom fighters in the name of feminism, God, and the platform. Lebrón reaffirms the "call" and "song" of both Albizu Campos and Canales, uniting this feminist and the masculine archetype in a single stanza. This gesture is a deliberate political move: four years prior to Lebrón's insurgent act, Blanca Canales, a member of Nationalist Party, organized the Jayuya Uprising—a three-day rebellion in which she literally supplanted the symbol of North American dominance, the US flag that conspicuously omits from its fifty stars a representation of its colonial island, with that of Puerto Rico. Distinct in her demeanor, Lebrón still belongs to a legion of women who have led resistance movements, a sororal connection she eloquently magnifies in the poem's lines above. But this poem also signifies the arduous task of being a complicated woman of color who refuses the transparent view of race, sexualization, religion at the forefront of disidentifying ideologies.

This is not to overshadow that women of the revolution have been historically sideswept by their male counterparts, having to painfully negotiate between strict national, sexual, maternal, psychic, and racial allegiances while also upholding radical feminist beliefs. These gendered images, as Saldaña-Portillo notes, are fraught with paradoxes, that is, in fact more true to human form than the myth of cultural unmistakability. There's a long-standing maladaptive trajectory of the revolution in general: a masculinist construct in which the "ladies" of any movement exist in the margins of the narrative, cut off from the female revolutionaries laboring before them. Contrary to this myopic construct, history is replete with women who have led the vanguard of ideological and political revolution, especially in Puerto Rico. Noting the eminently gendered role Lebrón has played in the consciousness of the island, it has been argued that far more than her male comrades, the femme revolutionary became a cause célèbre: "In a culture that reveres strong women, her mythic status lies somewhere between La Pasionaria and Joan of Arc." This comparison to two of the most legendary female revolutionaries of Western civilization—the former a Republican heroine of the Spanish Civil War and the latter the French canonized saint who was the heroine of the Hundred Years' War with England—positions Lebrón as a figure of biblical and European proportions. Under the long-standing colonial predicament in which she stands, Lebrón's story fails to fall neatly under the rubric of the typical revolutionary subject. Rather than an easily dismissed side note, Lebrón's poetry seizes authorship for her unrivalled role in the insurgent attack against Congress. And in her poetic verses we witness a version of Lebrón even more impassioned by national vindication, justice, violence, and want for a liberated life.[97]

Her writing while in prison demonstrates the inseparability of her political and religious convictions—ideological poles often considered antithetical. In one poem, she states, *"'La República está cerca,' Dios lo dijo"*—The Republic is near, God said.[98] In another, reproduced below, we see the motif of political sacrifice playing a paramount ideological and spiritual role. Lebrón undertakes this idea of "colossal sacrifice" in her 1975 poem "*Vamos*," written four years before her release from prison:

¡Vamos!	Let's go!
¡A romper las cadenas	To break the chains
del tirano!	of the tyrant!
¡Surjan los batallones!	Rise up the battalions!
¡Abra paso	Make way
todo libertador de nuestra raza!	all liberators of our race!
¡Aquí estan,	Here they are
AZADAS Y FUSILES,	HOES AND RIFLES,
FLECHAS Y BALAS,	ARROWS AND BULLETS,
LANZAS,	SPEARS,
MACHETES,	MACHETES,
ESPADAS!	SWORDS!
¡Raza de héroes!	Race of heroes!
¡Nuestra SANGRE *reclama*	Our BLOOD demands
valor y sacrificio	courage and sacrifice
por la Patria!	for the homeland!
¡!Ya sube la marea	The tide is rising now
en nuestra plaza!	in our square!
¡Se levantan las ROCAS	ROCKS rise
en la rosa y el alma	in the rose and soul
de Mariana!	of Mariana!
¡Adelante Boricuas!	Onward Boricuas!
¡Surge el ASTRO	The STAR arises
iracundo y triunfal	angry and triumphal
de la jornada!	of the day![99]

The poem is bold, opening with a declarative call for all "*Boricuas*"—the name of the indigenous, precolonial inhabitants of the island, used to resist the discursive violence of imperialism—to take arms against "the chains of the oppressor." She asks her fellow Puerto Ricans to "rise up

Figure 1.4. Lebrón speaks at a news conference on September 11, 1979, at the United Nations upon her release from prison. She, Flores Rodríguez, Cancel Miranda, and Oscar Collazo (who was incarcerated for his assassination attempt on President Truman in 1950) were released in early September 1979 when President Carter commuted their sentences (Figueroa Cordero died of cancer six months prior). At the podium, she said, "I hate bombs, but we might have to use them. Until my last breath I will fight for the liberation and freedom of Puerto Rico" (Schwartz 1979). Photo by Máximo Colón.

the battalions" and to move forward with force and weaponry in hand. Unlike her calm and collected nature back in 1954, her language here is one of guerrilla warfare—a call to fight against the United States by any violent means necessary.[100] In one pressing line, she claims, "Our blood demands courage and sacrifice for the motherland." These terms "courage" and "sacrifice" are ingrained in the philosophy of the Nationalist Party and highlight how Ricanness is a constant act of bodily endurance, spurring the subject into immediate action within a state of emergency. Lebrón "considers her time in prison a sacrifice, but not a waste," an extension of the death she could not offer on March 1, or an enduring act of dying in the name of Ricanness.[101] In comparing her short time on the congressional floor to a life behind bars, one might incur a new understanding of death itself. That is to say that Lebrón may not have died in 1954, but her stint in prison is a life continually in tension: she learns to amalgamate her opposing ideologies, and remain cognizant of the specter of death.

But according to Lebrón's granddaughter, Irene Vilar, Lebrón must confront a larger tension perpetually encircling her—the one of a hysterical mother at the hands of religious fundamentalism. In doing so, she travels through an analysis of the religious and maternal into the material figure of Lebrón in her memoir, *The Ladies' Gallery*. In this book, Vilar stages her own attack against the state, religion, the father, and the Law of the absent Mother,[102] intertwining her own life with the lives of her mother and Lebrón. Vilar's life melds into her grandmother's persona and the tumult of her mother, who committed suicide when Vilar was just eight years old. The memoir juxtaposes three historical occurrences: Vilar's first psychiatric hospitalization, the death of her mother, and Lebrón's actions in 1954. These life-altering events presage her detailed recollection of the two most important women in her life— subjects whom she does not fully understand, agree with, or forgive. Pointing out that her mother never fully recovered from the loss of Lebrón, she suffered from years of untreated depression. As Vilar explicates, she wore the same eyes as her grandmother, sensorially deadened, almost mute in her presentation of a nonpersonalized life. Her mother, as she frames her, was led by images and representations, searching for herself through the reflection of iconic figures. She donned wigs, artificial eyelashes, flamboyant makeup, and outfits to cover herself up as much as she tried to escape those carapaces. Lebrón always lingered in these images; an image herself, she became just another figure desired and recognized from afar, by none other than her daughter.

Both "motherly" replicas became one in Vilar's memoir, combining these two simultaneously absent and present maternal figures. Lebrón, seldom spoken of in her home, was a ghost-like figure looming in the interstices of desire and lack. In Vilar's account, one reads a memoir redolent of pain and hope within the image of the Mother. Vilar's interrogation of normative gender structures is apparent from the name of the memoir alone, the titular metonym providing a pithy summary of the prescribed place in the civic sphere for women during the 1950s—a moment of high modernity and rigidly gendered binarism.[103] Reflecting on the complex and remarkably religious manner in which Lebrón subverted and repurposed orthodox belief systems, she states,

In the case of Lolita, her destiny unfolded in her country's name, and, despite a leftist ideology, in God's name: the prismatic view which carries all the birth-pangs of Latin America's political consciousness. Lolita was to become the legendary woman who stripped herself of all "womanhood." A sense of offering, of sacrifice in all that she said and did, was always there. And her religiosity still amazes and disturbs many. My grandmother obviously saw herself as a martyr for the liberation of Puerto Rico. At some level, a woman firing a gun at congressmen of the United States of America must have been rather shocking. Yet, when I listen to people of my grandmother's generation speak, not only in Puerto Rico or in Latin America but also in the United States, I realize how much they see themselves, many of them, in Lolita's "act." With apprehension, certainly, but also with some gratitude. For she "did it for them." My grandmother must have seen it in the same terms.[104]

Yet Vilar writes cautiously when she asserts, "She did it for them," a tone that undermines the provenance of Lebrón's actions. While Lebrón offered her life for Puerto Rico—the infantilized nation—she did not raise her own children; in fact, the two children she bore "accidentally" died. In Vilar's view, Lebrón was not a martyr, but someone caught between religious fanaticism—especially during her twenty-five-year term in prison—and leftist ideologies that created a certain type of mother who was unattainable for the child proper. She provides this decisive detail in her narrative of Lebrón, sharing that her grandmother spent six months of her prison sentence at St. Elizabeth's Hospital in Washington, DC, after writing President Dwight Eisenhower the "*Mensaje de Dios en la Era Atómica*," or "Message from God in the Atomic Age," which was given to her by "a voice [that] came unto her from a blue silky flower."[105] Again, the mad Lebrón rears her head against the decree of ideological and philosophical conviction. While Vilar's loss of this icon is an absence we will never feel in the same way, the above description of Lebrón further magnifies the hysterical representation of Lolita. This figuration of her always factors into the subject none of us ever really know outside of her image. As such, we must labor to read her outside of pathology, with and against familial conviction.

Under this pathological lens led by religious conviction, Lebrón stripped herself of "womanhood" in order to be the sacrificing, unhinged mother for the nation. This concept of "womanhood" seems to be synonymous with ideal motherhood. Vilar proposes a perplexing relationship between "womanhood," motherhood, madness, and the revolution, in which it is difficult to disconnect one from the other. If colonialism always already stifles the proliferation of life—whether through debt, sterilization, illusory reparations, or disease—we must contend with how Lebrón refigures the Law of the Father and the Rican death drive in her conflicting, but powerful, ideological poses as a Rican feminist. How does this image of a figure filled with the desire to die for the lives of so many reposition the figuration of the mother proper under Ricanness? When Rican men abandon their homes for the revolution, are they also deficient father figures? Oftentimes, they carry the position of hero, the pulse of the revolution leading the revolt against colonial temporality. The religious conviction spearheading their politics, as in the case of Albizu Campos, is not generally used against them. In other words, this subject is read outside of opacity when he, too, sees, and convinces us of the relevant connections between God and man himself.

Feminist revolutionary Assata Shakur sheds light on the sacrificial role of revolution on the colonial stage in her description of the contentious relationships Lebrón experienced with visiting activists while in prison:

> After the resurgence of the Puerto Rican independence movement, Lolita was visited by all kinds of people. Some were pseudo-revolutionary robots who attacked her for her religious beliefs, telling her that to be a revolutionary she had to give up her belief in God. It apparently had never occurred to those fools that Lolita was more revolutionary than they could ever be, and that her religion had helped her to remain strong and committed all those years.[106]

Once again, we see the complex nature of Lebrón as a historical figure, in this case leaving her "pseudo-revolutionary robot" peers befuddled. Despite their dismissal of her religious beliefs, her resistance to colonial time is immune to oppression precisely because it admits no clean, easy-fitting categorization along religious and political lines. Echoing a long-standing animus between religion and Marxist thought, Lebrón's critics ironically reinforce her power by allowing her to circumvent simple classification. Obliterating the binary oppositions between religion and politics, death and life, beauty and terror is a way of being in the world for her. The potency of her contradictions is matched only by her principled convictions. In other words, Lebrón's supposedly paradoxical disposition does not render her a directionless subject. Led by ethical and political exigency, she is very clear about the ground on which she stands: "It would be a purer thing, a more beautiful thing for me to die in prison. And if I do, it will be for my people, without one regret."[107] Pregnant with contradictions and dialectical promise, her mélange of ideologies disrupts myopic ideas of Ricanness, femme, feminist, and revolutionary—none of which hang on pathology's thread.

I would be equally remiss, here, if I did not suggest that we look deeper into the political impetus of religious life. That is to say, listening to the cry of God is often a cultural exercise, undertaken by someone who is a harbinger of freedom, not necessarily psychotic. Religious incantations are more than just fantastical iterations for minoritarian, enslaved subjects; they are often one life force that untangles the colonized from the colonizer. It is easy to use her religious convictions as fodder for a justifiable diagnosis of madness; but God, whether symbolic, fantastical, or ethereal, provides a currency of momentary freedom when one is lost and searching for existential truth and human worth. In such an act, colonialism faces off with faith—that oftentimes bearable existence under uncontrollable angst. That is to say that the onto-theological plane of existence—that simultaneously physical and metaphysical essence of Being that Heidegger united—imbues Lebrón's calling for God with a bodily yet transcendent armor against US onto-political aggression and the forms of imperial knowledge that have historically erased unsovereign subjects. Lebrón's recitation for existence, her note, actions, revolutionary poetry, signal the melodic call for "freedom" in the temporal register of finitude.

Death-in-Life: Exit the Queen of Terror

Lebrón is a discrete site of authorial life, death, grand pleasure, and catharsis. In my attempt to understand the complicated Lebrón, I locate her subjectivity in a lifeworld always already predetermined by two kinds of mortality: the low-frequency hum of stifling incompletion, negation, and unwantedness; and the syncopated beat of death-in-life. That is to say that Lebrón's *gift of death* is one afforded by her prelife:

before entering the world she harbors the internal depths of her death. But this is an ironic twist of fate that reveals the uncompromising essence of death. In 1954, Lebrón offers death to an ideological cause, yet what she experiences is not the state of death itself, an impossibility already positioned by Heidegger. She experiences, as Fanon explains, too, the willingness to undergo the convulsive spasm of death. Put yet another way, Lebrón reinvents herself in her own death—her conscious and reflective aspirations grappling with the subterranean unconscious of which every invocation of death is at least a part, to invoke Lacan, Gherovici, and Viego again. Such desires are circumscribed by what she essentially owns—her femme Rican death at the reopening of Ricanness.

The dominant theoretical and philosophical thinkers in this chapter—Althusser, Fanon, Hegel, Lacan, Gherovici, and Viego, alongside Lebrón herself—take us through the social and psychical contours of death and a version and translation of Hegel's master/slave dialectic. As such, I have traveled through this dialectic via the very site of the anticolonial enduring body. That is to say that I have located the ways in which various forms of conflict—recognition, misrecognition, self-recognition, and nonrecognition—bear witness to emergent ways of being in the world. These dialectical engagements enable the unwanted to breathe out new pathways for existence, especially when the unwanted are viewed as nonessential/essential to life itself.

As Lebrón's note reveals, then, a recitation for being is an invitation for response, recognition, a coveted opening for those chants across colonial time. It is also a chordal pulsation, demanding the harmonic within the revolutionary solo: her siren song is a summons, transmitting vibrations within the dull and tragic life of US colonialism. And this revolutionary frequency is an exercise in multiple confrontations and corporealities, those limbs of bodily endurance that carry out Ricanness. Her "cry for victory" is an aesthetic and political one where the place of oppression meets the want for the "sacred principles of mankind" through acts of material endurance. "And so before God and the world," Lebrón's blood, her gift of death, is an offering of something greater, not a shedding of life always already slightly deadened. In fact, as she readily reminded us throughout her life, she came to die, not to kill, and the distinction is both the crust and the center of Ricanness. Lebrón's radical act reimagines how we get through the maze of colonial death.

2

Running Out of Time

Rican Exhaustion, or Superman 51

If origins are the identification of your past then the future is
the victim of your origins, making you a target of accumulated history and a colonizer of your own aesthetic discourse.
—Papo Colo, "The Hybrid State"

As the flight of the butterfly defines precise movements in-
comprehensible to us but in continuous transformation, the
logic of multiple layers of cultures woven across a pattern of
demographic dislocation seems chaotic but is precise.
—Papo Colo, "The Hybrid State"

In the summer of 1977, Papo Colo deliberately sprinted down the West
Side Highway scantily clad with a bare chest, short shorts, tube socks, and
tennis shoes, with fifty-one pieces of rope and wooden planks attached
to his back. He ran toward the Twin Towers on the cement's unforgiving
texture; heat and resistant pressure seeped through his sneakers as the
planks rubbed against the freeway (see figures 2.1–2.4). His cape was
heavy, bedraggled—it pulled him back as much as he pushed forward.
Even as the tangled thread and trailing sticks worked against his endurance project, with brute force he dashed across space—no stumble or
pause to catch the spectator's reaction, or his own feeling of inevitable
mortality. Yet after ten minutes of intention and exuberant masculinity,
he collapsed from exhaustion, making *his* superman unable to surpass
the regulating forces of time, space, imperialism, and tomorrow.

Superman 51 is Colo's most referenced and reproduced art object,
none more noteworthy for its Nietzschean implications. It's this very
aesthetic object that ignites and transforms the boundaries of Rican subjectivity in the public domain of politics. Or as Fred Moten confirms in

his evaluation of racial servitude and Blackness, "Objects can and do resist."[1] This chapter follows the resisting subject/object as he falls against
his own flight plan in a state of Rican exhaustion. I ask us to consider
how this object's currency and choreographic movement—both sym-
bolically and physically—determine its durational gravity. What is it, exactly, about this piece that reveals something about Ricanness, colonial
subjugation, bodily movement, superheroes, desire, and Rican time? In
its material composition and metaphorical implications, *Superman 51* is
an object that carries both aesthetic and political weight, and is also an
act of cultural resistance.

Colo—the Rican performance artist, curator, painter, writer, co-
founder and cultural producer of Exit Art, and founder of Trickster
Theatre—has created a tremendous body of work over the past forty-
five years, appearing in group and solo exhibitions at El Museo del Barrio, MoMA PS1, Museo de Arte de Ponce, and the Grey Art Gallery,
to name a recent few.[2] Similar to performance artists such as Marina

Figure 2.2. Still image from performance of
Superman 51. Photo courtesy of the artist.

Figure 2.1. Papo Colo, *Superman 51*, West
Side Highway, New York, 1977. Still image
(from video documentation of performance). Photo courtesy of the artist.

Abramović, Vito Acconci, Chris Burden, Stuart Brisley, Carolee Schnee-
mann, and Adrian Piper, Colo's very body is often the eminent domain
of the aesthetic process, confronting the precarious relationship between
the object, subject, and spectator. His provocative art, like that of his
contemporaries, produces a full somatic experience in which "the performers themselves become the text to be read."[3] But these texts sum-
mon a different kind of reading practice: the relationship between the
artist and viewer engenders a visceral intimacy compelled by the flesh of
the object. The artist's body, as Colo reveals, is enmeshed in the historical verity that colors its very visceral contours. Or, as the artist reveals in
the above epigraph, the body's "aesthetic discourse" is also a colonizing
practice, wrapped up in the accumulation of historical time. In Colo's
case, the colonized and racialized body is constructed from oppressive and violent epistemologies instantiated by the carnal desires of the
colonizer.[4] This process positions the other as a representational object
for erotic consumption, establishing a sense of existence mitigated by

Figure 2.3. Still image from performance of
Superman 51. Photo courtesy of the artist.

Figure 2.4. Still image from performance of
Superman 51. Photo courtesy of the artist.

longing, power, and concurrent sentience. Through acts of endurance, combining heightened physical force, athleticism, and seduction, Colo's work unfastens the tight grip of colonialism by envisioning the transformational power of aesthetics under a racialized masculinity.

Fifty-One Sticks and Strings May Break His Bones but Colonial Names Will Never Free Him

In an interview with artist and art critic Stefano Pasquini about *Superman 51*, Colo asserts, "The fifty-one sticks represent the fifty states of the USA and the one that wants to be. You can interpret this in [*sic*] three levels—the three ideologies of Puerto Rico: pro statehood, pro commonwealth and pro independence."[5] Colo's fifty-first piece of timber literally inhabits the other meaning of the word plank: a basic point of a political agenda. Its materiality parallels the ideological choices he runs for, against, into—even if such sprinting results in breakdown. As Colo demonstrates, these three ideologies constitute what it means to perform within Ricanness, in which the flick of a pen turns a political position into a fervent policy. Carrying the colonizer, colony, and future on his back, Colo runs within multiple time frames, demonstrating the speedy deliverance of national policy and the slow rise of changing politics.

This fifty-first plank also symbolizes the long-standing and contentious relationship between the United States and Puerto Rico since the late 1800s. As one of the oldest colonies to date, Puerto Rico is still granted minimal legal rights, even under the island's constitution and the Commonwealth status of 1952. While the Commonwealth status provides Puerto Rico some legal standing, the island's lacking "liberatory moment" and ensuing debt crisis make it difficult to read this site through a traditional progress narrative, although neocolonial, decolonial, and postcolonial injunctions share linear and defining evaluations of temporality. The Rican colonial subject is always already in a state of both absolute emergency and stillness, or as Elizabeth Freeman reminds us, time is never outside the markers of difference that instantiate and propel the subject forward; in fact, modes of difference and acts in time are conjoined.[6]

Colo's *übermenschean* project illustrates perfectly what it means to knock one's body against the postcolonial imperative—a discipline that repeatedly fails to live up to its own discursive demands, for what often follows decolonization is another form of global expansionism. Postcolonial scholar Homi K. Bhabha teases out this temporal disjuncture through his exploration of hybridity:

> Hybridity is the sign of the productivity of colonial power, its shifting forces and fixities; it is the name for the strategic reversal of the process of domination through disavowal. . . . It unsettles the mimetic or narcissistic demands of colonial power but reimplicates its identifications in strategies of subversion that turn the gaze of the discriminated back upon the eye of power. For the colonial hybrid is the articulation of the ambivalent space where the rite of power is enacted on the site of desire, making its objects at once disciplinary and disseminatory—or . . . a negative transparency.[7]

The colonial hybrid, then, becomes more than a category of opposing entities; it becomes the full excess of its contradictions. These contradictory positions allow the subject to look back "upon the eye of power," undermining this system that caused its subjugation. The colonial hybrid is brought into being via this "ambivalent space," and this space of varying valences is the only place where Bhabha's "mixed metaphor" can exist: "a negative transparency," then, is an expression of both negative affect and a negative exposure—almost like the photograph and its negative double. Yet, a negative double is not the opposite of the actual image or object; it is an "articulation," a representation of a perceived fixed category's ability to exist in differentiation. The mimetic impulses of hybridity are rooted in colonial time—a temporal composition that forms, frames, and enacts existence, even when one wishes to escape this historical enclosure.

Postcolonial scholar Gayatri Chakravorty Spivak might call this the difference between Time proper and "timing." She claims that "one common way of grasping life and ground-level history as events happening to and around many lives is by fleshing out 'time' as a sequential process."[8] She writes: "This I have called 'timing' . . . this feeling for life and history is often disqualified, for the sake of a dominant interest, in the name of the real laws of motion of 'time.'" And this demarcation of time, Spivak dubs Time proper, and goes on to state, "Time often emerges as an implicit Graph only miscaught by those immersed in the process of timing."[9] Spivak visually represents the spatial-temporal continuum, accounting for those social sites oftentimes discounted in the account of one's everyday life. She differentiates between a type of affective time and mechanical time, charting the consecutive and quotidian movements of the subject. For Spivak, "timing" pushes against History proper, helping the subaltern "time" or "graph" their way onto the larger, heteronormative map of existence.

But in his essay "The Hybrid State," Colo himself brilliantly theorizes this construction of "too much time and timelessness" for the Rican subject. Colo explains, "It is a matter of mutual occupation, the colonized paying back the colonizer. This is a fusion that is clearly a hybrid, an artificially forced union, a marriage for convention. This union becomes a conviction, a penetration of entities that explodes in our habitual coexistence."[10] In this doomed-for-divorce marriage, Colo captures just how colonialism is never ancillary to Ricanness, but rather its frame, structure; it's the mechanism and substance that sustains its duration. For Colo, they come together in the tight, fast, slow, and open spaces of his *Superman 51*, always hitting against the pavement. Colo's superman attempts to transcend both human and national boundaries under imperial domination for less than ten minutes. In such little time, he demonstrates the speed required of the minoritarian subject, who must labor to carry not only himself, but the legacy of colonialism as his ripped-to-pieces cape, lurching in double time. And as I argue throughout this book, this temporal positioning is not a strict opposition.[11] Too much or too little time is never the same as the concept of Time itself for those of us entering the world several steps behind. Ricanness, as Colo shows, is also an act of both acceleration and deceleration. The interplay between changing velocities reveals how falling from exhaustion captures both the dearth and excess of colonial time and the fragility of masculine fortitude.

One of the many ways Colo has consistently responded to history's colonial gaze is through the complexity of the aesthetic. In "The Hybrid State," he takes on the theoretical construction of hybridity via aesthetic terrain, merging performance and politics. He boldly writes that "art is the invisible opinion that manipulates by persuasion and perception and makes you see options of understanding and interpretation. When you experience art . . . you are conditioned to be convinced and to be touched inside your emotions."[12] Searching for that feeling within the political, Colo explains the emotional residue and aesthetic fortitude of his own experience of/as a superman. Of *Superman 51* itself, he writes,

> I want to use my body energy as an aesthetic and political metaphor. 51 represents Puerto Rico as the potential 51st State. Born in a colony, this is about exorcising my memories, political agenda, and being a Puerto Rican in North America. *Superman 51* represents the immigration of the individual and the integration of Puerto Rico as a State. Poetically it was a way to triumph defeat; the falling was premeditated and despite the knowledge of defeat (the eventual collapse) I will persevere. *Superman 51* is about the aesthetics of the body, brute strength, machismo, super-hero, cultural hero, power, and challenge.[13]

But what kind of superhero defeats the self, even if this self is a presentation of an alter ego laboring against the colonial mandate? In the above, Colo merges aesthetics and politics through the corporeal, demonstrating how they are imbricated with defeat for the colonial subject, but also the will to triumph over such lack. In this study of perseverance, the body manages the exchange between performance and politics, and Colo's bodily act becomes the site of and for Ricanness—a way of being in the world always on historical loop. It is also, as he expresses, an exaggeration of the *real* in which the symbolic implications of machismo maintain the privilege of inverted power and imagination, as his expression of masculinity ultimately fails him, and lasts for six hundred seconds only. Here we see the connection between colonial and macho temporalities, whereby the latter is always already conditioned by the parameters of racialized existence. Another way of thinking through this is to entertain how Colo uses the fallacy of masculinity, via a supernatural figure—as a man of color—to comment on the misogyny of colonialism. In this way, Colo's Ricanness reframes the masculinist other, asking us to reset the time of racialized masculinity, even in its incompletion and exhaustion.

Despite the manifest exhaustion that Colo projects in *Superman 51*, the elapsed time of ten minutes doesn't appear, at first glance, to be a typical endurance project compared to performance and body artists who have remained motionless for days or placed a knife repeatedly between their fingers (Marina Abramović), dangled from meat hooks (Stelarc), bled until enervation (Ron Athey).[14] Upon a keener look, though, this performance—and its continual circulation since 1977—offers us a snapshot into the apparent duality of no time and an excess of time that affirms Ricanness. Or what Colo calls the temporal consequence of decolonization: "The result is an elastic labyrinth of going back and forth, revolving into yourself, repeating the differences into a tornado of chaos."[15] This combination assembles the apogee of the subject in *Superman 51*, a prime entry point into Ricanness.

Of Will, Power, and Desire: Bodies at the Eternal Limit

In conversation with art critic Martha Wilson about his performance pieces completed between 1976 and 1986 for the exhibition "Will, Power, and Desire," Colo says of *Superman 51* that his act is compelled by "pushing" his "body to the limit" as an "extreme way to achieve ecstasy" through the endurance of both the body and mind.[16] But even the title of this piece and Colo's volitional collapse underscore the paradoxical nature of this artwork: supermen do not fall, nor do they carry the potential of their absolute failure with them into the future. They fight against immoral, opposing forces and triumph in grandiose style and elegance. Perhaps the performance's abbreviated but accelerated duration is the real measure of the extent to which he endures the call to Ricanness. Here, too, he expresses how a willful subject's desires against the state can provide social spaces of ecstasy—in the sense of both personal pleasure and collective futurity.

Colo's performative descent, or "premeditated collapse," underwrites the perception of the Puerto Rican subject as an incomplete being, so that what he descends from is the opposite and equal force of his negation. That is to say that he descends from the promising and yet ever-elusive status of the subject as a perceived complete being. Maybe this is also a way of asking: is this the metaphysical marker of time for the incomplete being, already ten steps behind? Achille Mbembé in *On the Postcolony* sheds further light on the temporal confines of coloniality and its perception of the colonial other as incomplete.[17] Referencing specifically the West's perception of Africa, he claims that the entire continent is envisioned as "incomplete, mutilated," just "close to" being, being human. Its invented lack taints its very process of becoming. He goes on to state that "Africa . . . is portrayed as a vast dark cave where every benchmark and distinction come together in total confusion, and the rifts of a tragic and unhappy human history stand revealed: a mixture of half-created and the incomplete . . . a bottomless pit where everything is . . . [a] yawning gap."[18] This dark cave he references is not Plato's cave. In Mbembé's cave, the colonial subject, unlike "the enlightened philosopher king," sees only the reality of his perceived incompletion. In this "yawning gap," what happens to time, then? What happens to the whole subject? How does the incomplete subject get out of this "bottomless pit"? What happens to the life of the colonial?[19]

Ricanness is "constructed, institutionalized, and communicated" in a manner that is as non-neutral as history;[20] Colo's failing superhero exposes this non-neutral and nonlinear construction, too. *Superman 51* leads me to consider a series of different feelings, orientations, and their political and cultural wear on colonial bodies. The status of Puerto Rico is an ambivalent way of being—not ambiguous—for the island neither belongs entirely to itself, nor reaps the benefits of full US citizenship. And yet, such a status exists within a specific dialectical continuum: on one end resides Statehood for Puerto Rico, and on the other end, Independence. If this argument holds, then Ricans—whether here or over there—are inherently barred, always already at some limit of their own bodily expanse. This important obscurity—an opacity often translated into strictly spatial metaphors of "island" versus "mainland"—has everything to do, I argue to the contrary, with the sensation of time standing immobile or merely moving across the possibility of these dialectical poles, which Colo's piece boldly personifies.

In contradistinction, the majoritarian subject does not descend in time and space first in order to move upward; he enters the world already perceived as complete; in effect, then, he understands himself within a predetermined prescription of perception—in a different state than Colo's hybrid one or Mbembé's half-created human. This realization is a projection not just of a metaphysical conjecture, but how certain subjects actually live within the domain of spatial and temporal incompleteness—a symptom of colonialism made explicit in Colo's performance. I want to be very clear that when I use the term "negation" in reference to Ricanness and incompletion, I do not mean this in the strict oppositional way of a static self-identity. Hegel's negation (or contradiction) represents a gamut of differences, oppositions, and relations.[21] It can signify the lack of—or incoherence of—a category. I am not saying that the incomplete being is merely its opposite, but that it exists like its many contradictions and moves into something more capable within the same category. If we turn back to Lebrón here, we will recall that death's opposite is also not life, especially when colonialism's essence and practice are on loop. Hegel's idea of negation, throughout this book, provides a way to reimagine the dialectical continuum of ideological states and valences, as Ricanness is not merely a packaged lack distributable upon sight. It is an internal bodily schema, as Fanon notes, which relies on the paradoxical as much as the surplus of these very contradictions. In such thinking, the concepts of incompletion and negation allow for a run toward the futural, one Colo advances in his *Superman 51*.

Colo's performance depicts Ricanness as a consequence of still time within colonial temporality, while he also runs vigorously forward to triumph against this very stillness. His collapse from depletion delivers a poignant point: subjects (citizens and noncitizens, complete or incomplete) always choreograph their bodies within time, regardless of social value. Heidegger attempts to understand this movement through space and time via his construction of subject authenticity, the want to actualize one's true freedom even in the face of modulated existence— bodily exercises that are ongoing, visceral, and laborious. But it is Viego's genius in *Dead Subjects* that might actually supply the choreographic antidote to an unrealized freedom for Brown and barred subjects.[22] Incompletion, for him, as for me, functions as an operable analytic and metaphor for subjectivity in real time, and not a signal of a restricted life. In his charge *contra* critical race and ethnicity studies scholars who rely heavily on completion to understand the Brown subject, he affirms that the trope of wholeness actually enables "racist discourse with precisely the notion of subjectivity that it needs in order to function most effectively."[23] In forcing the Brown subject to fall under this fallacy of completion, we've learned to contribute to and mount a hefty critique against incompletion, as if "unfinishedness" marks unintelligibility. This compromises the moments of potential for so many of us living outside normative grids, and who can't quite fulfill the illusion of subject wholeness because the state mandates our perpetual fragmentation. Viego's work shows us how to redress the conditions of an "authentic" life, especially one already marred by colonial protocols.

Superman 51, I argue, exposes how Ricanness and incompletion bear witness to one another in productive ways. This trope of completion has actually forced us to see the effects of colonialism within a narrative of resolution and finality. But Colo, entwined by the rawness of wood and tenuous string, highlights both the limits and potential of the body bound by a geopolitical state of a body neither here nor there and a time zone with ever-shifting parameters. In his version of flight, Ricanness is incomplete and fragmented. If at the very base of colonialism is the annexation of land, Colo pulls together decades of subjection in the course of six hundred seconds and reclaims territory himself on the West Side Highway. This is an act of temporal insurgency in the space of Empire.

In the title of Colo's performance we confront the meeting point of potential, incompletion, and failure—although with his face to asphalt, he will rise against his shattered impotence. It is no coincidence that the physical and psychical weight of the object forces this figure to tragically fail at being a superhero, falling from supernatural grace. This choreographic gesture is one we've seen before for colonial and racialized subjects in which the heaviness of life forces one to continually stumble. While the iconic Superman prevails in the face of immortality, fighting vigorously against opposing forces through space and time, Colo's superman is unsuccessful in retaining the rights to an assured futurity under unsovereignty. Even as he's caught between mortality and immortal want, Colo asks: what's the premeditated distance of Ricanness under colonial life? Or what's the temporal distance of the Rican subject, and how have the imprisoning conditions of this "here and now" actually mapped him out of the future?

In his painstakingly deliberate feat, Colo emulates a heroic archetype that is culturally ubiquitous, not only in the United States, but all over the world. The comic book Superman—the "Man of Tomorrow" who traveled "faster than a speeding bullet"—operated under a dual subjectivity, stemming from two opposing places: Krypton and Earth.[24] Born on Krypton, but the moral and ethical defender of Earth, Superman is left homeless and battles the duality of being inherently Kryptonian, but with the fundamental and formidable task of creating an alternate ego as an Earthling. Ironically, it is the green Kryptonite from his native "land" that destroys him. His tragic flaw, then, stems from the very space that gave him life. But even in 2011, the state of hybridity was too much to bear for the real hero: Superman renounced his US citizenship, stating that he was exhausted by the perceptions of other nations that he was merely an agent for the US government. This binary subjectivity is akin to the one Colo faces; however, Colo is not afforded the luxury of separation. Colo carries a different foreign weight, similar issues of displacement burden his cape, but unlike the original Superman, Colo cannot travel "faster than a speeding bullet"—although his intrepid display of persistence and resistance speaks to the trials and tribulations of his tomorrow.

Flying on the Ground, Walking Past the Site, Crawling in the Crevices: Insurgent Aesthetic Movements

I situate Colo's 1977 object as the precursor to other men of color in Superman outfits trying, through the heroic, to exist in the everyday beyond their symptoms. Although Colo's parallels to the fictional Superman illuminate the Nietzschean underpinnings of his performance, his staging occupies an aesthetic sphere populated by various artists and symbols. Colo endures the magnitude of a superhero across and in time, much like Jean-Michel Basquiat's painted superheroes endure in his artwork. José Esteban Muñoz provides a critical analysis of this piece, *Television and Cruelty to Animals* (1983), in which we see Basquiat's distorted depiction of the symbols of Batman and Superman painted alongside Nazi swastikas, a "magic" eight-ball, and Bullwinkle the Moose.[25] William Pope.L, a performance artist with similar thematic pursuits as Colo, crawled the entire length of Broadway, a New York street that is twenty-two miles in length, in a piece called *The Great White Way: 22 Miles, 9 Years, 1 Street* (2001–2009).[26] This artistic endurance act, originally intended to last five years, took nine years to complete; in it, Pope.L dressed himself in a Superman costume and tied a skateboard to his back.[27] Since the late 1970s, Pope.L has produced endurance acts across the streets of New York City and around the globe, exposing how his exercises in duration respond to the stifling scenes of urban verticality. Pope.L himself has said of *The Great White Way*, "Superman cannot fly anymore, just like the rest of us trying to make it through the day. Here, the heroic act is to give up his verticality, to submit to life as it is."[28]

Performance studies scholar André Lepecki argues that "crawling cracks open the kinetic assumptions related to ideological, racial, and gendered mechanisms of urban belonging, circulation, and abjection."[29] Being on the ground by choice is a revolutionary act—forcing people to disperse in order to have a clear angle of sight to see the oncoming traffic of oppression. Here, too, we notice the enduring/endearing connection between Ricanness and Blackness, in which hypermasculinity and sexualization confront race and the colonial in the expanse of bodily exhaustion.

Through urban space, Colo also enacts revolution through art; this time, however, his act is vertical—running through and against the space where traffic normally exists. The dimensions of the social and cultural field within which all of these artists create and perform suggest a certain ideological function of a minoritarian male subject wearing a superhero costume. Arguably, an incomplete being's possible options are twofold: on the one hand, perform such incompletion through the markers of recognizable minoritarian movements; or, on the other hand, cover those markers and by default wear the being of self, superego, and hero, even in the face/fate of collapse.

Movement(s) by minoritarian bodies implore a deliberate return, here, to the work done by Fanon. Let us recall that in conversation with the expanse of Western philosophy, Fanon stages the question of Being on murky ground—land already predicated on the experience of (an) other, and the facets of the world that exist prior to any experience of it. On unsteady land, Fanon shows us exactly through his enduring body what it feels like to be always at the thin line between objecthood and subjectivity; between a walk, stumble, and run; against death in life. Through movement, Fanon molds into a different understanding of self—one so shattering that he is left to pick himself up from the ground as another being.

For Fanon, as for the Puerto Rican colonial subject and Colo's flawed Superman, these multiple selves establish a real disjuncture between "[their bodies] and the world."[30] Unable to actualize the desire to be a (super)man amid men—not the last man, but a human of individual will—he instead unearths his vulnerable stumble and fall into life. It is Fanon who warns us that "every ontology is made unattainable in a colonized and civilized society" for the man of color.[31] Like the original *Übermensch*, the quest to find the meaning in life—even if going under to come up, falling to rise—remains at the core of subject transformation, the claim for which (Heidegger might say) is the frame for every death.

In large part because of this deathly frame, Heidegger developed his interest in the question of *how* "Being" means, a deceptively difficult question that involves three crucial steps. How does one understand to understand, first? And, second, how does one understand to think of how "Being" means? Last, how does one investigate how "Being" means when there are limits to ontology, when we cannot articulate the very entity we are but also hope to understand how (and who) we are as "beings"? For Heidegger, we are always "living away" from ourselves by not realizing the full extent of our existential freedom. That is to say, we exist without the full capacity of understanding ourselves.[32] And, "the common theme in all of these formulas is that we do not embrace the sort of entity we are, namely *Da-sein*, and live as if we did not have the possibility to gather ourselves out of our lostness in the Anyone and resolutely choose an owned life."[33] Retrieving oneself from this "lostness," then, involves both a falling and an authenticity—states of Being that Heidegger references as the beginning of the beginning.

In my translation of Being, the perceived incomplete being descends in time in order to move upward and begins his "owned" life on shaky and shaking ground—*terra (in)firma* that begins below the perception of completion and subject transparency. But, "What is the contrary of an owned life?"[34] The answer, for Heidegger as much as for artists like Basquiat, Pope.L, and Colo, is bound to flight. But this question, and its conditions of flight, must be answered differently for a subject in a position of abject difference, fixed within the temporal confines of the Other. To reframe this concern in other terms, we might investigate the properties and trajectory of this flight-to-being, or what Colo imagines as the flight of the transformative butterfly, expressed in one of the epigraphs above.

In a similarly aerial consideration, Lepecki juxtaposes two differing views on the philosophical question of "being" and the ontology of presence: Heidegger's and Fanon's.[35] Seeking to understand not only "the essent" in being for both of these philosophers but also the "choreo-political field of resistance in performance," Lepecki returns to Heidegger for obvious epistemological reasons.[36] As a scholar who politicizes movement, he recuperates phenomenology in order to engage in Fanon's idea of an incomplete ontology for the racialized-colonized subject. Fanon does not think that the man of color moves into incompletion; instead, he argues that locomotion must continue unabated. That is to say, as Lepecki argues, that the colonized subject must walk, stumble, or crawl—or mobilize some combination of all three—in order to adroitly move into some stable negotiation with "completion" or an amicable truce with ontology. In arguing so, Lepecki resurrects two important metaphysical questions: What is a body? What moves a body?[37] I locate these questions at the center of his intervention, for by *what is a body?* he adduces the Heideggerian body that exists in particular temporalities but that nevertheless oscillates; that is, the essent. And by *what moves a body?*, Lepecki also asks, what motivates the movement of a colonial body? What makes the ground—below Fanon, in particular—create an ontology of presence predicated upon shaking movements in being and becoming, such as falling, stumbling, at the very edge of death? Being, for Fanon—much like it operates for Heidegger—is a process always occurring in passage. The difference, however, is that Fanon's being starts moving from a different point, further removed from the horizon, making the journey a "longer" one. This journey exists by simultaneously accommodating the self and its dominant opposition, one Heidegger does not fully engage. Moreover, Fanon's ontological work is based not only on the phenomenological, but also on the psychoanalytic, and rather than view these as alternative methods, he embraces and develops the interrelatedness of these heuristic tools. In doing so, he shows us how conscious awareness is best gleaned by unconscious recognition.

The result of such a melding is a renewed focus on how colonized, racialized, and sexualized bodies relate to themselves and to other bodies in their immediate and distant surroundings, both consciously and unconsciously. I have tried with Lebrón to express how acts of endurance entwine the psychoanalytic and phenomenological, making it impossible for me to read for Ricanness outside this entanglement. That space between objecthood and subjecthood, or the unconscious and conscious, is an all too strong reminder of the durational gravity that propels the racialized, sexualized, and colonized body—a performing body that Colo situates at the perimeter of tragedy and redemption.

I'm reminded here, too, of Latinx performance studies scholar Ramón Rivera-Servera's own Rican phenomenological undertaking in which walking—like running for Colo, stumbling for Fanon, and crawling for Pope.L—serves as an aesthetic intervention into the constraints of heteronormative life, a quotidian insurgent act. The author provides us with a choreographic score, reminiscent of Fanon's plea for existence through the body, led by his very own body through the gentrified/ungentrified streets of Brooklyn before landing us in the dance club.[38] From walking in the hood, the Southside, into his jaunt through the Northside of Williamsburg, Rivera-Servera lends us his somatic experience of being hailed and renamed as a queer man of color, from both his "people" and his *gente*. As he explains of the Southside, "I often accelerate my walk and avoid eye contact when addressed with an effeminizing greeting or when I am simply called a faggot or *maricón* in the middle of the street. I know at times these scare tactics are performed upon me based on a perception of me as white and thus out of place in the neighborhood. 'Gringo!' often accompanies the homophobic slur when that is the case."[39] These interpolative moments help reframe Rivera-Servera's "lived time" or "human temporality" and psychical time—seen in both his choreographic strategies of acceleration and his own politics of slowing down. He states, "Once I cross the boundaries between my Latina/o neighborhood and the borders of gentrification, I change my attitude. My walk is less directed. I meander down the street at a slow, relaxed pace. Queerness abounds here. Not just in terms of visible same-sex couples walking about hand in hand, but also the overall attitude toward masculinity. A hipster aesthetic becomes the primary visual and performance code of this part of the street."[40] In his "deliberate improvisatory act," Rivera-Servera activates and extends the disidentificatory subject Muñoz provides as one way to live in a world that doesn't want you—that similar world that propelled Lebrón into an alternative kind of revolutionary act. Aside from reminding us that walking, too, elicits an act of politics, he lends us an answer to the temporal distance of Ricanness—one with less momentum, but with equal imploration. Walking, too, is an act of political force trekking into the fortitude of aesthetic determination.

Through the act of walking, and at the age of seventy, Colo offers his greatest feat of endurance against imperialism in his piece *Procesión-Migración* (2017). In this performance, he descends into El Yunque tropical rainforest to live off the land for four hundred days in complete silence.[41] *Procesión-Migración* is inspired by the 1953 play *La Carreta*, written by one of the most celebrated Puerto Rican authors, René Marqués, during the first large wave of Puerto Rican migration to the United States.[42] The play documents the migratory process of a family from Puerto Rico to the mainland in search of the American Dream. Unable to realize this vision, Marqués's family is forced to return to Puerto Rico, defeated by economic despair, but ultimately enlivened by a new cultural appreciation for the island.

Colo's *Procesión-Migración* mirrors the second largest wave of Puerto Rican migration. From 2000 to 2015, approximately 334,000 Ricans migrated to the mainland United States due to the financial crisis on the island.[43] In Colo's own rendition of migration here, about five hundred people—along with animals such as oxen and horses—joined him for a two-and-a-half-hour procession through El Yunque. Along the way, the procession made five stops to watch performers who were described by Klaus Biesenbach—director of MoMA PS1, chief curator at large at the Museum of Modern Art, and curator of the performance—as "beautiful tableaux vivant."[44] What followed this procession was the second and longer part of Colo's performance, in which he lived on his foundation grounds alone creating art.[45]

This piece, like *Against the Current* (1983), where he attempted to row a boat (as the title suggests) against the current of the Bronx River, and *Jumping the Fences* (2006–2007), in which Colo jumps fifty-one fences in locations throughout New York and abroad, functions to call attention to the protective and isolative function of borders.[46] More recently, in 2016, Colo spent every Saturday from May 21 through July 4 performing *The Cleaner*.[47] In this piece, he took to the streets of the Chelsea section of Manhattan, cleaning the sidewalks before arranging fifty one-dollar coins on each block, cleaning each coin individually. The piece is both a commentary on money laundering in Latin America and an aesthetic subversion of the Latinx as a janitor or cleaning lady. According to Colo, "'The Cleaner (or how to launder money and disappear)' is a show without the business. It's almost occult, an insane gesticulator of objects and symbols, a metaphor or an homage to the clandestine, a parody of the ability to beat the system and not pay taxes. The CLEANER is the pirate disguised as cleaner—he looks more like a señorito—that denounces by stealing."[48] All of these performances resemble the philosophical specter implicit in *Superman 51*, in which the trope of endurance facilitates the political intent.

Colo's Zarathustra: To Go Under and to Return Again

Colo's work considers the human features of superheroes, and how such features acquire eternal time in physically bounded bodies. While I've touched upon the iconic comic book hero before, I'd like to pause here with Nietzsche, for whom the act of heroism is best elucidated. In an effort to untangle the individual will of the human from the herd, Nietzsche, in *Thus Spoke Zarathustra*, posits an existential pursuit in which one's ascendancy in life is predicated on respective desires and values rather than ideals prescribed by institutional creed.[49] Fundamental to this concept is the dramatization of performance itself as a medium by which humans fulfill and exhibit potentials typically left unrealized. Nietzsche presents the concept of the *Übermensch*—or Superman—as the subject who aims for a superior ethical status over the masses. The *Übermensch* eventually overcomes himself and moves past sublimation. The flip side to this corollary, however, is that the last man—the one who follows protocol and is governed by religious, ideological, and political systems—remains mired in the traps and angst of everyday existence.

Arguably, Nietzsche makes his debut as a performance studies scholar in the opening pages of *Thus Spoke Zarathustra* via his exposition of Zarathustra's encounter with a tightrope walker suspended over the crowd of a small mountain town. Zarathustra ascends the mountain after ten years underground only to encounter the performer in the middle of his act, halfway across his tightrope. Beginnings and endings are a recurrent theme for Nietzsche's hero Zarathustra, who reenters civilization after living in the mountains, in an isolated cave. Describing his desire to integrate again into the world, Zarathustra states, "For this I must descend into the depths . . . I must go down as the human beings say, to whom I want to descend."[50] Zarathustra's movement "into the depths" transpires immediately in his prologue; it is a downward

journey that occurs in his physical act as well as in the psychic and emotional pangs he endures upon entering "the nearest town lying on the
edge of the forest."[51] The townspeople do not receive his prophesies with
open arms; in fact, laughter welcomes Zarathustra and his ideas of the
overman, a superman who places all of his hope not in a transcendental
force, but in himself. This overman must "go under" to overcome moral,
ethical, and absolute truths—much like the performance sites I underscore in this book, and nowhere more prominently as in the subject of
this chapter, Papo Colo.

There is a particular scene in Zarathustra's prologue that evinces the
difficulty of persuading the townspeople of the *Übermensch*: the performance of the tightrope walker, whose project in bodily endurance
ends in death. Attempting to move from one tower to the next, the artist slowly walks the dangerous line. He is methodical, valiant, and the
only one who believes in the idea of the overman. Yet, he never finishes
walking the tightrope; a motley jester taunts him into moving faster,
and abruptly jumps in front of the steadily walking artist. He falls. He
fails. Zarathustra, as if he were assuaging the tightrope walker's fear that
the devil caused his death, proclaims, "You made your vocation out of
danger, and there is nothing contemptible about that. Now you perish of
your vocation, and for that I will bury you with my own hands."[52] Zarathustra is forced to leave town, carrying a corpse on his back. Ironically,
he "walks" the man who walked a line for a living, failing to complete his
jaunt into superhuman status.

These acts of attenuated walking and superhero feats of endurance
are made most perplexing when further inquiring into the connection
between the tightrope walker and the jester, and subsequently their in-
trinsic relation to Zarathustra. For Paul S. Miklowitz, in *Metaphysics to
Metafictions*, Zarathustra is the "motley mask of Nietzsche's own face,"[53]
but Zarathustra is also both the "tightrope walker and the motley jester,"
or he is "'the mean between a fool . . . and a corpse' . . . he is both and
he is neither."[54] This means, as Miklowitz affirms, that Zarathustra-as-
Nietzsche is "*not* simply the jester: he is also the tightrope walker, and
he has not yet overcome the corpse of his own dead self when he meets
the jester."[55] The particular consequences of the intricate and altering
layers of subjectivity parallel the dynamic identificatory negotiations
Colo must endure in the face of national, racial, sexual, and ethical sub-

jugation. How is Colo all of these entities and also the hero with his wretched life to the ground?

I share the parable of Zarathustra for several reasons that accentuate Colo's work: first, to highlight the choreography of a prophet who must descend in life to reach some level of enlightened completion after many years in solitude; second, to expose the intricate ways in which this performance artist, like all performance artists, is always already near to death in search of subject completion; third, to expose the motley jester (or colonialism, or maybe Colo as the colonial project's desire?) as the fast-moving personification of mechanical time; fourth, to elucidate the infinite and paradoxical complexity of a hero, that simultaneously human and superhuman figure eminently encapsulated in the form of the Rican artist Papo Colo. Nietzsche's parable teaches us that being human is always an endeavor in performative heroism, and that sometimes, such heroes are already dead subjects, rewalking tight lines and carrying braided ropes and their own bodies for futural ascendency.

In *Coronation* (1976), a precursor to *Superman 51*, Colo extends a large cord between two buildings in New York City, reminiscent of Nietzsche's tightrope walker.[56] Along the cord lies a series of wooden planks tied to the rope so that they appear to be standing straight. The weight of the wooden sticks, however, pulls Colo's "tightrope" down, creating a dragged-down semicircle. Right behind this, unseen in the still image included here, are the Twin Towers again. This time Colo is not in the image, but I would be remiss here if I didn't admit that Colo's body of art—like all the figures of this book—returns me to philosophy in intimately racialized and sexualized ways. In searching through Colo's archive, my own existential wandering was activated, and Nietzsche *thus spoke* through all of these objects and themes—from the tightrope walker to the thick strands of rope, from the subject going under to arrive above, from walking the line to running for one's life; in all, the philosophical undercurrents demanded breath and space.

Inasmuch as artists like Colo establish a figurative drawing of such contours, their performance of walking, running the line inevitably involves a navigation of laborious and heavy boundaries. Such boundaries are, too, elastic and shape shifting: that is to say that Colo, in all his perspiring splendor, negotiates land and territory along fissures that are personal, social, cultural, and often already determined before he steps

Figure 2.5. Still image from video documentation of *Coronation*, 1976. Photo courtesy of the artist.

into the world. In his attempts to exceed even his own expectations, Colo's hypermasculinity—revealed in his running on concrete, his bare expression—cements his body into a time of being that is characterized by a labor both under constraint and thoroughly *overman*. Colo participates in Nietzsche's idea of the "eternal recurrence" of human circumstance by exposing the potential and prospect of looping in time, and subject incompletion particular to Ricanness. While he is not the *Übermensch* per se, he is also not precisely the last man, but rather a representation of how the broken-down subject learns to disidentify and survive in the face of political and national despondency. If the *Übermensch* is to move past sublimation (for Colo, colonial sublimation) and overcome himself, the performance he stages must also overcome an ambiguously defined social hurdle. Via this process of overcoming, then, whose hero does Colo actually become?

To render such sensations more vividly, Colo's *Superman 51* represents the symptomatic incarnation of failure—this despite the fact that Colo's collapse is an intended one marked and embellished by an endured and enduring body in time as a superhero. But, as stated previously, superheroes suffer different affective symptoms—such as bravery, moral indignation, intense strength, justice, *übermenschian* bodily endurance, and an acute and deliberate aversion to failure. Ironically, Colo's superman is a premeditated failing hero, running with a shorn cape, perhaps with less resistance to gravity—but lacking, nonetheless, the ability to fly. Perhaps, one might conjecture, it is the weight of the history of symptomatic traits attributed to the composition of a Puerto Rican subject—a burden Colo shoulders silently if also conspicuously—that grounds his takeoff before it can even initiate. It appears, then, that his presentation and transubstantiation of Puerto Rican subjectivity is one fraught with both symptoms of Rican colonial obduracy and the potential for complete national inclusion or independence.

Using a Lacanian lens, I suggest that Colo is embodying the prodromes that have been imputed to the Puerto Rican subject in an attempt to account for the existence of the subject. In this case, the Puerto Rican concretizes the "question of being" by justifying his or her place in the eyes of the Other. Colo is not only incarnating the traits but also extending them, bending them through his attempts to physically endure an ultimately unfulfilled endeavor to run to the end of the West Side Highway. Here we notice the brutal embrace between fantasy, reality, colonial introjection, and impotence—Colo must somehow wear both his projected cape and symptomatic wounds.

There's something inherently Rican in this object that refuses disappearance. *Superman 51* is an aesthetic object of the future, one that embroils Rican subjectivity in its very circulation and citationality across institutional sites and time. Most recently, in 2016, MoMA PS1 presented a small selection of Colo's early works, *Papo Colo*, which revolved around photographic stills from *Superman 51*, but also displayed *La Diferencia* (1986), a video that contained a montage of *Superman 51*, *Against the Current* (1983), and *Coronation* (1976).[57] After the MoMA PS1 exhibition on Colo's work closed, it traveled to a collaborating institution, Museo de Arte de Ponce, for three months.[58] In 2014, Colo's piece participated in another exhibition at El Museo del Barrio, this one titled *Playing with Fire: Political Interventions, Dissident Acts, and Mischievous Actions*.[59] This piece was included alongside those of other Rican avant-garde artists such as ADÁL and Pedro Pietri.

But it was at El Museo del Barrio's provocative 2008 exhibition *Arte ≠ Vida* that *Superman 51* commanded particular attention as the video of the performance on loop greeted the museumgoer at the door of the entrance to the museum, and a photo still graced the cover of the exhibition catalogue.[60] The decision to showcase Colo's work in this way was a politically strategic one by the museum, considering that this was the first exhibition to showcase diverse Latinx and Latin American avant-garde performance and visual artists from the 1960s to the end of the twentieth century in a historically Puerto Rican museum.

In 1969, Puerto Rican artist Raphael Montañez Ortiz founded El Museo del Barrio with funds given by the New York City Community Education Commission.[61] He formed a community advisory board consisting of parents and activists who had fought the New York City Board of Education over public school curriculum content.[62] After decades of ensuing debate with community leaders and the museum board members because of the institution's turn to a more Latin American emphasis, Colo's piece operated as a loyal gesture to Rican patrons.[63] This exhibition marked a large shift from a predominantly Puerto Rican museum indebted to the late 1960s and 1970s, to a larger comprehension of Latinidad that might have reshifted political and cultural understandings of Ricanness. This object's display invites a series of questions: How valuable is Puerto Rican art, Puerto Rican avant-garde art, art that makes non–Puerto Ricans uncomfortable? And how valuable is a museum that came into fruition under ethnic and racial premises, carrying—even if not with desire—the residue of past, present, and future conceptions of Puerto Rican subjectivity and colonial debris?

Tony Bennett, in *The Birth of the Museum: History, Theory, Politics*, investigates "the cultural function of the museum" by doing a "politically focused genealogy for the modern public museum."[64] His insightful investigation of this institutional site traces its advent not only as a space for disciplinary measures, but also as a depository for cultural codes of comportment. Bennett argues that the museum operates under a dual function: to be both an educational and behavioral site.[65] Subjects learn not only how to learn, but how to behave in a space of learning. Yet, in all of its universalistic intention, what and whom it informally and formally shuts out and lets in demonstrates the museum's exclusionary impact. I allude to Bennett to expose how the museum has the innate ability to control not only the subjects it deems reasonable for representation but how the viewer internalizes the interior life of the representational objects on display. Representation, presentation, and perception operate under slippery conditions already; it is no easy feat to adequately perform as a space of intended inclusion when the residue of colonial violence forms the museum's base. The problems that plague the museum at large also afflict this community-based museum wishing to expand its "exhibitionary complex."[66] Colo's *Superman* is not outside these parameters or institutional disorders.

This hang-up of expansion, for El Museo del Barrio, is bound to psychic mechanisms that actually create an "institutional complex" for a community of people. How does El Museo del Barrio negotiate Ricanness? The complex of/for Ricanness, a diagnosis formed from the onset of colonialism, even extends into a space for cultural expression and recognition. The museum, in this case, must expand its complex or compound in order to reconcile its internal neurosis. But what occurs is far less simple than an identity crisis; El Museo del Barrio must do without to gain; let up and let in; take down and reposition; return to the source to retrieve a new end. Ironically, Ricanness becomes an appendage to itself in a space designated for cultural, political, historical, and educational sovereignty in a larger nation of colonial subjugation.

There is no doubt that Colo's performance of bodily endurance highlights the never-ending question of Puerto Rico, but that is precisely it: Puerto Rico still operates as a question. There is nothing directly declarative in its status, and the ambivalence at the center of this signifier remains tied to conditions of stamina, endurance, perseverance, willpower, concession, and ongoing death. Colo's work cleverly calls to action a reading of Ricanness in two distinct sites here: the museum and the United States. I ask, then, how much longer can this object stand the test of time? How much longer will the question of the status of Puerto Rico condition the properties and currency of Ricanness?

Perhaps returning to the comic book character Superman, at this point, is a far stretch to reach some form of perceived completion. He is a fictive character, after all, and one who dies by the hand of his native home. But he is resurrected. The glue that binds him destroys him, but essentially returns him to us. I want to believe that Colo created a rendition of Superman throughout his work—and not another superhero—because of how this mythical character and popular culture icon played with time and space. He traveled through time, beyond space and back again, exposing the doltish belief of a monolithic and linear conception of time; and this he did by being both alien to Earth and the defender of a space that was never rightfully his own. Colo runs for six hundred seconds within over a hundred twenty years of colonialism, in many iterations of the "same" performance, decades apart from one another, in his own act of human temporality. But Colo's superman is not really the "Man of Tomorrow" traveling "faster than a speeding bullet." Rather, he represents the temporal valences of Ricanness, where standing still, falling from Brown exhaustion also move one into the performativity of tomorrow.

3

Countdown to the Future

The Dread in the Masses That Are Always Already Asses

Life is a toilet and all we ever do is go from one toilet to the
next. We can only pretend to be somewhere else!
—Pedro Pietri, *The Masses Are Asses*

Reverend Pedro Juan Pietri's absurdist, lewd, and intensely disturbing
1974 play, *The Masses Are Asses*, is a definite and soiled journey down
the toilet. Or, as the Nuyorican poet, performer, and dramatist himself
confers, the toilet is material sustenance; everything else is fantasy and
play under the precepts of existence. Written during the height of the
Brown and Black Power movements, and first performed at Miriam
Colón's Puerto Rican Traveling Theater in New York City, this "Sun Ra
of Puerto Rican letters" and "Poet Laureate of the Young Lords Party"
tests our social graces in this one-act piece by boldly moving between
abject aesthetics and futuristic Rican politics.[1] In this farce riddled
with obscenity, off-color humor, gender violence, domestic abuse, poverty, and impending doom, Pietri—aesthete and revolutionary—runs
past theatrical etiquette in favor of political satire, staging a boisterous
encounter between the disenfranchised and elite classes. *The Masses Are
Asses* is a play within a play, a Beckettian drama in which the poor use a
precarious fantasy of wealth as a weapon against social disparity. In his
own rendition of the theater of the absurd, Pietri, like the great Fornés,
turns to indecency and parody to sustain human tragedy, forcing dark
and fetid humor itself to be accountable to historical materialism, all in
one long act.[2]

Given the play's crude and emotionally triggering content, it is unsurprising that it has been out of print for over fifteen years, receiving
scant attention in comparison to his other play *The Livingroom* and his
famous political poem "Puerto Rican Obituary." More than a critique

of the vulgarities of capitalism, however, Pietri's play stages a dangerous and insurgent act against American imperialism that highlights
the fatal ramifications of the colonial project upon the lifeworlds of
poverty-stricken people of color. Transpiring in only one act that lasts
longer than one hour, *The Masses Are Asses* affords us a close-up of the
bodily endurance practices used to sustain colonial time in the narrow
spaces of domesticity. These tight spaces, such as the toilet, reveal all too
common narratives of assault often left unspoken. But in spite of such
silence, Pietri demands that we witness what comes to pass when the
colonized take on the essence and presence of the colonizer.

The Masses Are Asses, published ten years after it was first written
and performed, is led by two destitute characters feigning wealth, and
takes place in either a South Bronx hallway bathroom or a fancy Parisian
restaurant.[3] With intricate and intrusive stage directions, Pietri drives
the audience into this stark doubling of domain by frustrating the very
place of space:

> There is a small round table covered with a white tablecloth and 2 chairs.
> At the center of the table there is a lit blue candle in a candle holder.
> There's a bottle of champagne, a rose in a jar, two drinking glasses, silver-
> ware, napkins and two menus on the table. To the far right of the table
> against the back grayish wall there is a toilet with water tank overhead
> and a chain hanging down from the tank to flush the toilet. A roll of toilet
> paper is on the floor close by. To the far left of the table inbetween [*sic*]
> table and wall there is a bath tub. There is a telephone on the floor in front
> of the bath tub. The door is against the back wall in-between the toilet
> and table. There are no windows. A square shaped mirror hangs on the
> wall above facing the bath tub.[4]

This rigidly framed area marks the spot between culinary illusion and
fecal certainty. Both stuck in a place of no exit, the only two characters in this piece, a married couple—Lady and Gentleman—are pushed
to climb the walls. A cemented claustrophobia forces their fantasies of
affluence to rub forcibly against their gross and penniless materiality.
Could it be that the fantastical air in this room is also a pleasant breeze
instead of only an abhorrent accumulation of life, as Pietri contends?
Toilets, too, exist in all restaurants, even French ones; and even if filthy,

their use is universal. Still, what is the political calibration between a toilet and a fancy restaurant—even if the latter is imagined, and the former is never flushed throughout this play? What does Pietri demand that we remember by situating us in this crowded and foul-smelling domain in the South Bronx, that in imagination is also a plush restaurant?

Pietri's two characters are as ambiguous and unstable as the play's setting. Lady, either "30 or 93," and Gentleman, either "93 or 30," are a prototypical couple either living it up in their thirties or hanging on in their nineties, or in a mismatched pair of youth and old age.[5] In this circuit of another existential either/or, the cycle of life features already outdated gender performances in which Lady and Gentleman, not a/the Lady and Gentleman, remain affixed by obscurity, fake nobility, and obscenity. Without proper names and only a few physical descriptors assigned, the two protagonists stand in for everyone, someone, and no one simultaneously, two subjects moving from one toilet to the next, as Pietri affirms is the movement of human existence. It is only through their twists and turns in meandering dialogue, loquacious banter, and grueling physicality that the characters reveal their individual capacities for a *self* under colonial life.

Dialogue-heavy, the play creates garrulous characters who turn to repetitive, ironic, and comically rhythmic banter to sustain their fantasy (nightmare) of a harmonious and wealthy coupledom. Take, for instance, when Lady shares her most tragic fear with Gentleman: "Imagine having to work for a living instead of having others work for your living? Oh, how absolutely degrading! Just the mere thought of it sends chills up and down my upper class spine."[6] Feeling a similar sense of disgust, Gentleman refills their "champagne" glasses and offers a toast: "Give me prosperity or give me death!" And Lady, moved by his sentiment, lifts her glass: "Give me a mink, expensive jewelry and another mink!" But even Lady's actual costume—a blonde wig and old fur coat—cannot help her erase her glum imperial reality: she's a South Bronx native living in a culture of poverty.[7] Their very personages become tragic and plastic as they wait to matter in a world that doesn't want them. This South Bronx lovers' discourse is far from affectionate: their social and intimate vulnerabilities expose the binding of class struggle, race, and gender violence and how these very modes of difference both form and shatter already breakable subjects, wanting more than colonial life will extend.

Such descriptions warrant further inquiry into this existential either/ or that rears its dualistic head throughout this play as a political strategy against absolute determinism and unsought fate. Through either the doubling of space or the characters' ages, the dramatist forces his reader/ audience to form crucial affinities at the onset of the play and to be held accountable to both their fantasies and social horrors. These alternative angles present us with choices, choices that will ultimately guide and define us through the piece's narrative structure of impropriety and dread. For example, what would it mean if we aged these materialistic characters in their nineties—a poor, senile couple trying to beat the odds of their mortality? Might we be more accepting of the consequential pangs of domestic violence at this age, that is, rather than if these characters were both in their thirties? Here, I am suggesting that we all invent and purchase certain narratives for ourselves about the human condition in order to both witness and normalize violence. But why does Pietri deliberately redetermine our longings through these inescapable dualisms? These two characters, with Pietri closely managing every stage direction, expose the deadly scenes of colonialism, tapping into our own sense of humanity through violence and negation—in any which way we choose to restage the primal scene.

Through a combination of existential, surrealist, somewhat Marxian, and phenomenological sentiment, led by a heightened state of despair and violence, Pietri directs the speed of the script with accelerated dialogue and extreme physical endurance—both political strategies used as weapons against linear and colonial precedent. The characters are forced to bear witness to their own wretched lives in order to either die, or succumb to those unpleasurable yearnings under oppressive life. Even in its esoteric and absurdist sentiment, the play is framed by this looping narrative of linguistic and bodily endurance, preventing any Lady or Gentleman (or actor) from holding their tongue over the span of several tongue twisters such as this one uttered by Gentleman: "Because the masses are really asses exploited by the ruling classes with their military brasses and expensive champagne glasses because the gasses that passes from the asses of the masses not only smell like molasses it also stinks like perkasses!"[8]

Dadaistic and rhythmic lines like these structure the play's lingering momentum, forcing Lady and Gentleman to contend with a considerable amount of absurd dialogue and to deliver their lines in a rapid-fire manner, sometimes without definitive line breaks. Of aesthetic arrangements such as these, Puerto Rican scholar and performance poet Urayoán Noel in *In Visible Movement*—the first comprehensive history of Nuyorican poetry—proposes that we read Pietri's work from "a 'Dada-surreal' poetics that attempts a politically charged representation of a heretofore invisible reality without surrendering the 'solitary flamboyant' point of view of the poet."[9] From Noel's point of view, Pietri's writing must be read from within an aesthetic tradition that has invigorated Nuyorican poetic performances, informed greatly by the body of Dada-surrealist work produced by Pietri, the performing poet himself. Noel further notes, "Pietri developed a poetics of radical inversions and Dada-surreal images that veered off the page, toward performance and conceptual art, buttressed by a tragicomic self-mythology." As Noel shares, Pietri's writing eclipses the written word, "veer[s] off the page," extending into the realm of performance, whereby political sentiments inform aesthetic, cultural, and embodied practices.

It is in this context that Noel asks us to read this poet as a performance artist, too, one fully aware of the embodied techniques necessary to sustain both the closing curtain in live performance and the incessant page turning of print culture. These aesthetic affinities and enactments intimately match Pietri's political aspirations, or what Noel calls "Pietri's eccentric brand of decolonial anarchism" when he shares, "Although Pietri shared the Young Lords Party's focus on decolonial direct action as well as its commitment to Puerto Rican independence, he ultimately rejected its Marxist hard-line approach and characterized his own views as 'strictly anarchistic,'" never denying his full "poetic autonomy."[10] Noel's important analysis extends an essential genealogy of uncharted poetry and showcases Pietri the poetic genius. In this chapter, however, I am interested in rediscovering the playwright, not by dissolving his poetic voice, but by further attuning to his performative representations within a play-for-performance that measures the length of human endurance.

With regard to the previous assertions, it is crucial to note that the tempo of the entire play is perpetually a gallop at full speed: the two characters expend a tremendous amount of their energy talking quickly, but also in fight scenes, in which their sustaining bodies match their verbal acrobatics. This hungry and disgruntled couple spends one act moving between social refusal and affirmation, by playing out all too familiar scenes of domestic abuse: Gentleman beats and rapes Lady, and Lady attempts to leave him, but eventually remains; Gentleman verbally assaults Lady, and she responds by internalizing the abuse into her own sense of gendered anguish.

At one point, however, Lady manages to break the fourth wall, no longer desiring to stay in his torrid nightmare/fantasy, by declaring, "Cut my vacation short. I've had enough of this pretending to be rich nonsense";[11] but as she attempts to exit the bathroom, she finds herself beholden to his delusions, perhaps as a way to sustain her own desire for wealth, or is it his own colonizing glare? Within the sixty-five to seventy-five minutes it takes to stage this fast-paced play, Pietri vigorously compresses the unwanted of the world in the smallest of spaces. That is to say that this tiny bathroom reveals the tangled and tortuous tendency of imperial life, attachment, and marriage, to such an extent that not even love can escape what Paul Virilio calls the "post-modern world" as one framed by a "crisis of speed";[12] velocity, via the tightness of space, exposes the detrimental site of human life in this play.

To enter Pietri's mise-en-scène, one must be willing to be mocked, shamed, uplifted, temporally redeemed, raped, and then simulated back to an ass en masse. Throughout these vacillations of spirit, the play affirms the vitality of the Rican subject: the characters, despite their circumstances, offer all they have to the absurdity of life, even in the space and time of deep-seated and soiled negation. This sense of angst is viscerally experienced through the temporal ontology of the play: the "space" of the play happens "sometime last week."[13] Setting this story of social aspiration and poverty in the past creates a temporal disjuncture that is felt profoundly throughout the piece, particularly because of the doubling of space. Following Pietri's lead, here, I argue that even without a specific calendar, this tragicomedy is managed carefully by temporality. In saying so, I turn to philosophical constructions of time to expose how the strategic compression of time often converts it into social space. Pietri offers the audience a way to read these social spaces through distinct meters of time. That is to say that the South Bronx, a toilet, a hallway closet, a make-believe French restaurant, fantasy, and violent domesticity frame the text's velocity, such that a play with only two stock characters invites Time proper to be the third actor. Pietri rewinds time while also manipulating it: he is the record keeper who forces the characters to *descend in time* in order to continue existing into the future. I use the term "descend" here to illustrate how the characters' downward movements in time actually function as revolutionary exercises that ultimately resist or ascend in the face of the American Empire.

The future of the characters and the play hinges on the elasticity of numbers, or what Henri Bergson argues against—mechanical time. In other words, Pietri micromanages our sentiments of dread by forcing us to feel angst second after second through the execution of excessive and prying stage directions. The dramatist uses repetitive, everyday actions as stage directions, from clearing one's throat snobbishly for fifteen seconds to reading fake menus for eighteen seconds.[14] These extended quotidian acts are coupled with outside noises, such as blaring sirens, ringing telephones, knocking at the door, and screaming neighbors. For example, Pietri sets the dramatic dinner scene between Lady and Gentleman by breaking up their ironic banter with stage directions like these: "Gun shots are heard again. They rise and hide under the table. Police sirens are heard. Firing continues for 90 seconds";[15] "They slap each other five, rise, take a drink from the bottle and start cat walking";[16] and "They rise and waltz to the sound of the telephone ringing."[17] These measured intervals abruptly interrupt the linearity of the play, and while moments in this play often happen in succession, first in ascending order and then in descending order, the play eventually pauses us all *at* zero seconds.

The play mostly moves nonlinearly, with events occurring in timed sequences alongside interruptions serving as sonic intervals, such as a persistent ringing telephone. Pietri uses this form of counting down like a musical score to eventually land (end) the characters in silence *on* zero seconds. For instance, as the characters read their fake French menus, "*Loud knocking is heard. The LADY and her GENTLEMAN remain silent until the knocking stops 19 seconds later.*"[18] As they return to reading and bantering and bickering, the "*phone rings*," and "*they remain silent*" until it "*stops after the 10th ring.*"[19] This numerical countdown is best elucidated in the last moments of the play, which are revealed in stage directions: "*They make a 10 seconds* [sic] *toast. Finish drinking in 9 seconds. Rise in 8 seconds. He blows out the candle in 7 seconds. She picks up her wig in 6 seconds. Puts it on in 5 seconds. He takes her hand in 4 seconds.*"

They walk to the bathtub in 3 seconds. They climb in in 2 seconds and disappear in 1 second. They snobbishly clear their throats in zero seconds." And then: *"Silence is heard"* after fifty-five seconds of movement. But since the play begins in the past, one is left wondering if these failing subjects even still exist; or if these sonic interruptions are more like repeated death knells? Might they already be dead? Might Pietri be (re)counting down their days, the way he recounts the lives/deaths of Juan, Miguel, Milagros, Olga, and Manuel in "Puerto Rican Obituary," when he claims, "All died yesterday today, and will die again tomorrow?"[20]

Within the first five pages of dialogue in this seventy-three-page play, Pietri further distorts our sense of dimension and distance by replaying a tape recording of Gentleman and Lady in full banter. As the characters pretend to eat upscale French cuisine, the recording situates their voices: "You look terrific. You look fantastic. You look gorgeous. You look marvelous,"[21] providing us with a sense of live Dadaistic poetics, but leaving it unclear if these characters might have already existed in another time and place. Are we just left listening (perhaps?) to a prerecording of their once-lived past lives? Gentleman shares, "I have been secretly taping all the compliments we have exchanged." But for how long? How do we know that this play isn't just one big tape recording, and that these two characters are none other than the ghosts of Lady and Gentleman? Or every other poor couple of color living and watching daily death scenes?

This seemingly small detail—the tape recording—actually governs the temporal proclivities and ontological depth of this theatrical farce. And, as I will show throughout this chapter, the tension between an already-lived life and potential death, or the life that is already dead, requires the audience to also carefully stare into the brink of existence every step on their way down to zero. To offer the clearest understanding of what's at stake in such temporal shifts, my writing in this chapter also reflects the nonlinear construction of Pietri's form and content, moving the reader between past, present, and future without conventional narratological regard. In essence, this chapter is a close reading of a nonlinear play that exposes the pertinent and realistic doldrums of colonial precedent at the expense of the always already enduring colonial subject.

It is in this context that I should also note that Pietri is a poetic genius at keeping time. Each measured action of *The Masses Are Asses* is part of a larger durational plan occurring through his rhythmic control.

These exercises of duration are performed through strategic meters of time, essentially informed by the manipulation of our sensory perceptions. These intermittent seconds braided into the endurance of the play mount a theatricality that gives us life through everyday vibrations, even if such experience is actually the sound of dread. The elongated sequences break space, presenting the actor and audience with the means by which to be silent in the time of both sound and noise, blaring sirens and repeated knocks at the door. Both characters labor to somatically respond to one another as they move in the interstices of silence, laughter, and quotidian despair in the tight space of the toilet. Time, here, reminds us how to feel something *real* through the quandary of hunger and pain, and in the face of endless colonial life. As such, this chapter mobilizes temporality as a mode of critical attention that illuminates gendered and sexuality-based interventions in Rican subjectivity. In particular, I turn to different measures and readings of time—mechanical, durational, perceived, psychic—to underscore the condensation of dread within Ricanness. That is to say, what is the time of dread, and how does it access, break down, and remold the transformation of the subject? Or, how does dread activate the endurance of the subject, even if already dead?

Ears of a Vindicated Poet: The Reverend's Beat in the Rican Dramatist's Time

While Pietri's play does not reference terms such as Ricanness and Brownness, or race more generally, many textual signifiers point to these modes of difference.[22] There's an affective and cultural particularity within *The Masses Are Asses* that cautions one not to overlook racial and ethnic undercurrents, specifically in the space of the South Bronx, or the wretched-life-as-toilet for people of color. Many scenes within the play resemble the powerful stanzas in "Puerto Rican Obituary," wherein Pietri situates the dead Rican amid a barrage of labor and want:

> They worked
> They were always on time
> They were never late
> They never spoke back
> when they were insulted

They worked
They never took days off
that were not on the calendar
They never went on strike
without permission
They worked
ten days a week
and were only paid for five
They worked
They worked
They worked
and they died
They died broke
They died owing
They died never knowing
what the front entrance
of the first national city bank looks like[23]

In this piece, as in *The Masses Are Asses*, Pietri pushes against aesthetic tradition in favor of a performative and frontal attack against imperial rule—both in the world and in the space of conventional drama and poetry for people of color. But it is in *The Masses Are Asses*, unlike in his other work, that he forces us into the ghastly residue of imperial life and demands that we replace the façade of cultural capital (a fancy restaurant) with the horrors of racialized capitalism (a filthy toilet). Singular to this work, Pietri compresses all social ills and evils into the smallest of windowless squares, making us think we choose our own exit path, when in fact, for some us, that path is set with our colonial noses to the ground.

As a central organizer of the Nuyorican movement, alongside Nuyorican Poets Café founders Miguel Piñero and Miguel Algarín, Pietri demonstrates the inherent and inextricable connection between poetry, drama, performance, and protest, shifting from art to politics in the face of social grief and want for Puerto Rican liberation.[24] Such anti-imperial dreams were an integral part of Pietri's formative years. Born in Ponce, Puerto Rico, Pietri and his family joined their father in New York when he was just three years old. He began writing poems as a teenager, in-

Figure 3.1. Pedro Pietri performing at the Poetry Project in New York, 1991. Photo by Jacob Burckhardt.

spired by an aunt who read poetry and directed theatrical productions at the family's church in East Harlem. He graduated high school in 1960 and obtained a job restacking books at a library at Columbia University; it was at Columbia that he became familiar with poets such as Neruda, Yeats, and Hughes and began to write his own work.[25] After a tour with a light infantry brigade in Vietnam, he returned to New York and devoted himself to writing and performance.[26]

Pietri established his voice by navigating the borders of drama, performance, politics, poetry, and language itself. When asked if he felt more like a poet or playwright by author Carmen Dolores Hernández, he replied, "I'm a poet who writes plays through the eye of the poet and the ear of the poet."[27] Unsurprisingly, his expertise in poetry and drama brought him to the center of performance art. As a staunch advocate for safe sex in the late 1970s, Pietri often sold poems attached to condoms.[28] He distributed condoms on New York City streets, wearing a cross and signs reading "Safe Sex Not Jesus Saves." Pietri described himself as extremely religious, renaming himself Reverend and stating that he was ordained at the Ministry of Improvised Salvation in 1990 and the head of the Iglesia de la Madre de los Tomates Inc.[29]

Without leaving his political convictions behind, beginning in the mid-1970s, Pietri turned to theater as an aesthetic and political outlet and staged many plays with New York–based theater groups such as H.B. Playwrights, Public Theatre, and the Puerto Rican Traveling Theater as well as groundbreaking New York City institutions such as the Henry Street Settlement, La MaMa, New Rican Village, and the Nuyorican Poets Café.[30] During this time, Pietri was also collaborating with Miguel Algarín and other poets and performers who first met in Algarín's apartment, like Jesús Papoleto Meléndez, Lucky Cienfuegos, and Miguel Piñero. The Nuyorican Poets Café was founded in 1973 as a creative space for these Nuyoricans. With the help of poet Jesús Papoleto Meléndez and Pietri's brother Dr. Willie Pietri, *Seven Roosters* and *Three Drunken Poets* debuted in 1975. The next year, the trio staged *To Get Drunk You Have to Drink*, and Pietri himself staged *Lewlulu*. In 1977, the Nuyorican Poets Café staged Pietri's *Jesus Is Leaving*, and in 1978 Pietri staged *Appearing in Person Tonight: Your Mother*.[31] One of Pietri's plays produced during the mid-1970s, *What Goes Down Must Come Up*, which required a performance space to workshop and rehearse, led to the creation of the New Rican Village,[32] a forum for artists that opened its doors in 1976 under director Eddie Figueroa.[33] Familiarity with the corpus of his work and the extensions to which it led, then, provides the important context within which *The Masses Are Asses* becomes culturally and socially legible.

Whereas Pietri's early work established him within critical social networks, it was during the 1980s that Pietri became a member of New Dramatists (1982–1990), an organization that provided playwrights with space and resources to create new work. Revealing his prolific output, Pietri also wrote *The Kid with the Big Head* (1981), *No More Bingo at the Wake* (1981), and *Eat Rocks!* (1985). He also participated in the New York Shakespeare Festival's Festival Latino, a yearly theater and film event established by Joseph Papp (founder of the Public Theater) that ran from 1976 to 1990 and featured many Nuyorican writers; Pietri staged *Rent-A-Coffin* in 1985 and *Mondo Mambo/A Mambo Rap Sodi* in 1990 at the festival.[34] In 1998, Paul Simon enlisted Pietri as a dialect consultant for his ill-fated musical *The Capeman*.[35] Pietri stated that he was the "Spanglish Metaphor consultant" for the musical, which was about the life of Salvador Agrón, a Puerto Rican sentenced to death row as a sixteen-year-old in 1959 who began writing poetry in prison.[36] After winning several grants from the Creative Artists Public Service Program (CAPS) and the National Endowment for the Arts (NEA), Pietri demurred that they "amounted to chump Change."[37] The paltry financial awards notwithstanding, Pietri's impressive oeuvre of published works includes not only *The Masses Are Asses* (1984), the topic of this chapter, but also *Illusions of a Revolving Door* (1992) and the narrative *Lost in the Museum of Natural History* (1981).[38] What emerges from this bibliographic portrait is a clear picture of a poet who was also a prolific dramatist, and a body of work that takes as its motivating force a tender concern for the existentially tragic in the move toward a futuristic Ricanness.[39]

As Pietri shares, he began to involve himself in theater in 1971, when he saw the Young Lords and Black Panther movements tragically declining; he became disillusioned with these platforms and other political organizations that enforced singular views of race, ethnicity, gender, sexuality, and politics. Pietri states, "It was people in the theater that got back my trust in human nature."[40] These biographical details position Pietri the person, I hope, in such a way as to understand his full contribution in *The Masses Are Asses* in a time of international war, domestic conflict, and racial and sexual colonization, both internal and external to people of color and gender-nonconforming others.

Indeed, Pietri seals his own temporal fate, with both his past and the future, in the space of intense drama. In affirming his own tragic sense of self, he claims to have been "born in 1898, during the climax of the Spanish/American War." He adds, "I say 1898 because that was the year that the U.S. invaded Puerto Rico, the year when they colonized us."[41] However, for Pietri, his birth fails to account for his multiple beginnings, or temporal conditions, under colonialism. In what appears to be his own monologue on colonial life, Pietri restages his birth and death as a Rican subject in the theatrical space of a funeral home. He continues,

> Now, I was born again in '44 to my mother in Ponce, Puerto Rico and again in '47, at the age of three, when my folks migrated to New York City through the epic of Operation Boot Strap. We're all part of the casualties of the Inquisition, the American Inquisition. I also say I was born in 1949, because that's the day I went to the first theatre with my grandfather, who felt deceived by Operation Boot Strap and committed hara-kiri, but I don't think it was suicide. He was killed by the system that deceived him, the system that made him sell his land in Borinquen. What happened was

Figure 3.2. Pedro Pietri reads at a party at Taller Boricua, 104th and Madison *en el Barrio*, March 10, 1973. Photo by Máximo Colón, who describes the evening as "a wild party" with many poets in attendance, including Tato Laviera, Americo Casiano, and José Angel Figueroa.

the disillusion. The voices in his head were of the Central Intelligence, compelling him to sever his jugular vein. Think about his friends. There's nobody to talk to, nobody to communicate with, and there's nothing to go back to, but the industrialization of the island that had deceived so many people. So, that was the first theatre I went to, at Monje's Funeral Parlor, in a brown suit. Actually, that was my first teaching, or my first awareness of Puerto Rican history. Puerto Ricans die and go to a Puerto Rican funeral parlor.[42]

Above, we see the playwright locating the theatrical in everyday places; quotidian life becomes the most viable site for the exploration of the subject, or as he explains, Puerto Rican history itself. In a Goffman-like turn of events, Pietri locates Rican existence in the presentation of death in everyday life, in which a funeral parlor becomes a theater, and all stages contain deep and intense histories.[43] This funeral parlor, like his fetid bathroom in *The Masses Are Asses*, is a site of profound learning, living, and mourning wherein Pietri modifies the mundane into the extraordinary, exposing the genuine nature of absurdity in a world ensnared with death and violence.

Residual Desires: Duration, Perception, and Its Discontents

This biographical information about Pietri and the description of the play fall short of entirely capturing the psychic interiorities of this *obra de teatro* that functions as a microcosmic snapshot of the vaults sustaining oppressive life. Pretending to be affluent, while in reality welfare recipients, the two characters quickly come undone. As they dine over talk of wealth by dismissing the lower classes, they also suggest that there is no way out of imperialism's quagmire, even though Lady reminds the audience that "the rich don't shit any better than the poor. More maybe, [but] the sounds and odors are identical."[44] The characters remain enmeshed in their own war on poverty. Surely, all classes—upper and lower—must expunge to exist, exuding a scent both so odious and universal, as she explains, that it drifts across the border of us and them, across a pretend Europe and a South Bronx America. Yet Lady and Gentleman "don't even know what Staten Island looks like," let alone Europe;[45] cannot afford to purchase a "third-hand stereo" and thus "wait for the phone to ring" to dance;[46] and, as Gentleman explains, must learn to "move [their] bowels like an aristocrat, not like a welfare recipient."[47] For theater historian David Crespy, this play "manages to dramatize . . . the absurdity of everyday painful reality that is not only part of the Nuyorican and Latino experience, but the experience of all oppressed peoples."[48] Pietri's setting, here, discloses how Lady and Gentleman desire to be bourgeois, but in fact, they are pedestrian de facto; they drink cheap wine instead of champagne, dream of eating like the *beau monde*, but remain tasteless. They mimic aristocratic speech, but always enunciate like the depleted lower classes.

While the play sells the audience a story of a poor married couple with all too expensive dreams, it also announces how fantasizing is always already colonized, sexualized, and racialized, how the fantastical always hits against imperialism's pestilence. Alongside Lady's and

Gentleman's sorrowful delusions, the play's repetitive vulgarity helps depict the repugnancy of human existence, both debasing the audience and unveiling the limits of human vulnerability, second after second. The audience travels quickly from two characters dancing and coyishly laughing in a fancy restaurant to salacious banter and sexual and physical violence in a New York bathroom with an unflushed toilet reeking of a few weeks' worth of feces. Time, here, unsettles our feelings, both producing the conditions for excrement and consumption, and crossing the line between reality and desire. As readers, we proceed cautiously, unaware of when Pietri will turn a joyous moment between Lady and Gentleman into a frightful event, all in the course of several seconds, a tremendous amount of feeling, and an exuberance of sounds and smells.

Such a position warrants another assertion, too, that is drafted directly from the mind of Pietri. In this play, shitting is the great equalizer, the actual and symbolic residue of the human in the shape of abjection. Locked in a windowless room, these characters encounter the body with laid waste; and the toilet becomes a site within a site, or a relational object that forces Lady and Gentleman to break through their farce or eternally commit to it. Any comprehension of fantasy in this play is predicated on a reality mediated, staged, and recalibrated by our foul perceptions. In consequence, any understanding of perception is always already bound to parameters of colonial and imperial time, purposefully remanaged by Pietri within the space of stench.

In thinking through Pietri's deliberate disturbance of time, I turn again to Bergson's interarticulation of perception and duration. For Bergson, temporal linearity, much like this play, is a binding farce. Time is not a straight line, or an enclosed circle; its directions are limitless. The politics of our logic, as Bergson sees them, are conditioned by chronological, mechanical time and Western philosophy's fascination with space, leaving little room to account for the temporal interiorities of the subject. By placing one's lived experiences at the center of subjectivity, including our senses and affect, Bergson challenges the horizontal inflexibility of the future by working against normative constructions of time, perception, and reality.[49] Uninterested in mechanical and fixed time, Bergson distinguishes between "lived time" and chronographic time, marking off this distinction in the following way: "Pure duration is the form which the succession of our conscious states assumes when our ego lets itself *live*, when it refrains from separating its present state from its former states."[50] He adds that for this reason, the ego "need not be entirely absorbed in the passing sensation or idea; for then, on the contrary, it would no longer *endure*."[51] *La durée*, or our lived experience, is the sequence of our conscious events in which time functions as our memory of living in these events. While the past carries critical legitimacy—we can all be persuaded to believe in some historical occurrence—futurity's past is less resolute. Though they are often conflated, futurity's past is also not history.

In Bergson's understanding of time, the future is "pregnant with an infinity of possibilities." He clarifies that this idea of the future "is thus more fruitful than the future itself, and this is why we find more charm in hope than in possession, in dreams than in reality."[52] In trying to read for time outside of external measures, Bergson commits himself to understanding the very concerns of interior life that cannot easily be systematized by numbers. Lived experience, affect, and embodiment are at the apex of Bergsonian time to such an extent that in his understanding of temporality—duration in particular—feelings, sensations, and the enduring body extend the subject into the future.

Bergson advocates time for fantasy, dreaming, hoping; these unaccounted-for actions lead one into the future, even if mechanical time eliminates the importance of their tempered scores. The future, as Bergson confirms, carries the weight of endless possibility, but in *The Masses Are Asses*—a play run by fantasy—the present consumes these characters, even within a storyline that is actually set in the past. While the characters use fantasy as a temporal rejection of oppressive time, they endure the time of the play violently. The future, for these two characters, is paved with feculence, impurity, and pain. How do Lady and Gentleman arrive in the nonmechanical time of Bergson? If duration, as Bergson posits, is another word for marking existence, how does endurance offer these characters meaning, and allow them to dream in the space of despair?

It is crucial to repeat, here, that to subvert our sense of comfortable existence, Pietri creates a play run by interruption, or breaks and pauses in speech, interspliced with everyday sounds, much like the quotidian reality that interrupts history's linear progress narrative. Alongside this, he establishes a quick-paced series of events—a shooting, robbery, rape, grinding dance scene—that plays off these intervals in time. But these events are not enacted by outside characters; they are propelled forward by the voices of both Lady and Gentleman, further distressing our sense of reality. How can Lady and Gentleman be both the victims of abuse and the violent abusers? Even when we try to redeem both of these flawed personages, Pietri, through the stage directions, further criminalizes Gentleman: Gentleman's voice is the exact voice of the rapist, burglar, violent attacker, all doubling as the criminal perpetrator against Lady.

But the criminal fantasy comes to a grinding halt when Lady no longer wants to be *his lady*, and Gentleman can coexist only in his delusions, even when their world outside is falling apart, and they are contributing to its demise with Lady as the sacrificial lamb.

I want to pause here and assert that far from being the exclusive domain of the wealthy, the act of dreaming is accessible as well to the poor, for whom such an act of imagination creates a psychodynamic sense of self in a repressive world, a remaking of the rhythms of daily life. But this is also to say that dreaming is not separate from colonialism's violence; sometimes our dreaming practices are led by criminal perpetrators resembling our loved ones. Because of this, it is important to ask: what is the affective time of fantasy under colonial life, or when that fantasy is someone else's nightmare? The answer is both enlightening and agonizing; as Fanon warned, the colonized take on the properties of the colonizer. In this constant loop, time is also a protagonist in this play. Thus, it is imperative to rehearse the full range of conditions directing the perceptions of both fantasy and reality throughout Pietri's social drama.

It is in this context that I return to the doubling of space (a toilet in the South Bronx or a Parisian fancy restaurant) to question the conscious and unconscious pairing of these signifiers. These signifiers mark the fact that we all—upper class or lower class—must shit to exist. The doubling of these spaces operates as a pragmatic assessment of how bodies physiologically function in the world. We ingest and process forms of sustenance and then wait to expunge what is no longer necessary for existence. While we do not defecate as we eat, time clarifies that sooner or later, in order to survive, we must participate in the act of dejection. There's an uncanny connection between the French Dada artist Duchamp's urinal—porcelain, pristine, and signed—and this filthy brown toilet.[53] A clean urinal, even if intended to be a play on the acceptance and re-creation of an object, is still a desirable fantasy. No one wants to piss and be faced with the residue of the urine itself. Lady's toilet, filled with feces, is exactly the bad dream no one wants to smell:

> LADY: [*Lifts up her dress. Isn't wearing underpants. She sits down on toilet seat*] This toilet hasn't been flushed since the first day of our imaginary European trip a few weeks ago. The smell is unbearable.[54]

As opposed to the sanitized if also tongue-in-cheek quality of Duchamp's urinal, in this play the "unbearable" odor is in the foreground, a buried residue resurrected in plain sight. I am interested here in teasing out the ways in which Pietri performs the vulgarity of social space through a precise existential reading of time, reformulating Bergson's idea of duration against fixed time itself. The play exists in one act, one toilet, one imagined deluxe restaurant, and is given life through metered seconds—markers that the playwright deliberately repeats and refines to manipulate our lived experiences and sense of embodiment.

Pietri turns to these spaces, and their gross inseparable connection, to expose the relational ties between induced fantasy and the harsh realities of the everyday, or to show how severed this relation is when one is born into excrement, and fixed time refuses to stop ticking. The pertinent similarities between dreaming-while-rich and living-a-poor-nightmare are best ascertained in the ordinary acts we take for granted. What if Lady and Gentleman are dreaming their way through an unpaid water bill, an eviction notice just slid under their door?

In Pietri's world, these vulgar and painful scenes always meet up with the pleasant language that also maintains the energy of the characters. The banter between Lady and Gentleman continues throughout the play in a repetitive fashion: on key and in time, they never miss a syncopated beat—each compliment becoming more outlandish and sensually exciting. As they remain transfixed by the stench, in a space that is/is not French, Lady and Gentleman trade compliments and play a word game in which they mimic the rich throughout this looping one-act: "You look fantastic," "You look exciting," "You look demanding," "You look superb," "You look superber," "You look majestic," "You look majestica," "You look magnificent."[55] This charmed and charming badinage quickly relents, yielding to the reality of life in poverty; their unavoidably penniless situation is recurrently explained by Lady. For instance, she states, "We aren't all as fortunate as you whose mind lives in the suburbs while his body rots in the slums!"[56] Caged in a bathroom, Lady notes how the cruel humdrum of capitalism suppresses fantasy, consequently making us all asses in this game of laughter and condemnation.

The above superficial flatteries are interspersed with violent stretches of silence, seconds within the stage directions that redefine Lady's and Gentleman's discursive flow. They clear their throats for fifteen seconds, read the menu for seventeen seconds, and stare at one another for eighteen seconds.[57] These seconds interrupt their dialogue, creating sonic intervals that force the characters to remain still, or use the interruption as an incentive to move their bodies. For example, they sit motionless and wait as the telephone rings ten times, but never answer it.[58] Once the telephone ceases to demand stillness and silence, they proceed to compliment one another in the same fashion, the interruption just a little break to remind them that even in their unwantedness, they are still alive. Pietri, like Bergson, turns to the detail of the second to create intermissions and enliven silence, to press pause on mechanical time in a place where imperial discord and speed refashion the fervent dreams of the colonized. These incessant interruptions by Pietri clear space and demand recognition of time as the third guest at this dinner party in which the toilet has yet to be flushed and the subject has yet to be fed.

Pietri stages what philosopher Maurice Merleau-Ponty in *Phenomenology of Perception* describes as "our primordial experience" of time. Indebted to Bergson's valuation of time as duration, Merleau-Ponty argues that phenomenology itself begins from our very facticity; this is the only way we come to understand subjects and the world we live in writ large.[59] For existence is an always-already present before one begins to experience both time and space as a living entity. In order to do phenomenological work, then, as Pietri does, one must engage with the lived body, the body amid objects, and the perceptions that grow from one's very corporeality in the world. Pietri, like Bergson and Merleau-Ponty, responds to the Cartesian split, here, by capturing the full essence of experience through an understanding of the body—both its abject pleasures and its joyful disillusionments. As *The Masses Are Asses* illustrates, pieces of ourselves are not tacked onto some underlying layer called the subject; this notion called subjectivity is the dynamic interaction between all facets of our experience, including those informed by other bodies surrounding us. As Gentleman and Lady expose, our body operates as the mediator between subjectivity and the world. Or as Merleau-Ponty puts it, one can never experience existence outside of a bodily engaged subject in the world.[60] Our sense of embodiment directs our own acts of perception, and time situates us in our everyday lives, even if the body must endure against the wretched stench of feces. In this claim, we notice the intimate temporal embrace that sustains Ricanness; even in the space of heightened negation, in the place of the toilet, the future awaits.

Throughout this play, pleasure, love, aspiration, humor, and gender violence retain the rights and will to both life and death in this path toward the future. In such a claim, I am also suggesting that this existential tragifarce brings forth a countdown to existence in fully sensorial ways. As such, I labor in politically simultaneous ways: Ricanness crosses Brownness, and both work with and hit against sexualization and capitalism through ascendance and descent, a countdown to the future that resists the tendencies of living and being alive in a world where one is living dreck. The body funnels this play's countdown as Time proper, too, uses the body as carrier. And this intersubjective process is internalized through the lived body,[61] exposing temporality as an abstraction that refuses to be reduced to numerical coordinates. Like Pietri, Merleau-Ponty helps us restage the ontology of the enduring subject: "To analyse time is not to follow out the consequences of a pre-established conception of subjectivity, it is to gain access, through time, to its concrete structure."[62] That is to say that through time the subject reaches subjectivity in a world that for Pietri's personages, as for us, is always already full of obscene scenery and timeless dread.

Scatological Nightmares: Pietri's Brown Bowel Aesthetics and Gender Violence

Vulgarity, like abjection and dread, is also measured by its own time. Its temporality is expressed by Julia Kristeva in the following way: "The time of abjection is double: a time of oblivion and thunder, of veiled infinity and the moment when revelation bursts forth."[63] For Pietri, like Kristeva, the abject is neither a subject nor an object. It is also not the same as desire, or located in merely one measure of time or feeling. Abjection, according to Kristeva, reminds us of our mortality and limitations as humans. In our longing to obtain a "clean body" (or a clean toilet), we confront the very waste that escapes us. We smell the play's odor. We feel the residue of this filth, reminding us of our privilege to remove unwanted sight and smell. We are forced to listen to sexual violence, to brush up against rape in a space superimposed by duration, tight enclosure, and absolute sensual destitution. Or, as Sartre might warn, we are left feeling as if "there's no exit" and hence we must consume the Nausea of Being because the subject eventually introjects the subject—an expenditure that returns the nausea to the sender.[64] Arnaldo Cruz-Malavé, in his reading of Puerto Rican literature, reminds us not to foreclose the saturated scenes of abjection that compel the subject into being; for as he notes, the abject sits at the apex of racialized masculinity, whether or not we choose to name it as such. The abject, tragic, and existential here reveal just how human it is to be seduced by the allure of luxury while staring shit right in the face.[65]

Still, Lady and Gentleman remain escapists in a world run by capital and violence, in a world that does not want them. Every time Lady and Gentleman poke fun at the ruling classes, a "one-percenter" descends in time; with each joke, counterculture banter forces the gentry to get off their high horses, even if there are no stirrups on the way down to the commons. Their idealist hunger is also a call against the neoliberal vendor, buying and selling life, culture, and dreams at curious whim. But they, too, fall prey to the battlefield of poverty and despair, in their pretense of wealth. And in true Nixonomics fashion, Lady states, "I personally think that the only solution for poor people is suicide, since overthrowing us is out of the question and history will continue to prove it. I know it sounds inhuman but what else is there for people whose only ambition in life is to be totally miserable? This is a democratic society. If you make the decision to be rich you will be rich and if you make the decision to be poor you will be poor!"[66] Although in character for Gentleman, Lady describes the subject she wishes to expunge, and that subject is both her and her amorous other. In this deliberate act of projection and introjection, Lady consumes both the desire of suicide and the world's disavowal of her, making it unclear who owns this precious entity called life. For her impinging death, here, symbolizes the answer to capitalism's problems. As she further expresses, the poor alone are to blame for our culture of poverty; the poor alone have the power to release themselves of capital dread and despair. Gentleman, however, would rather continually deny his circumstance and live amid waste; in admitting his own reality he runs the risk of being flushed out of the world. He would rather leave the toilet unflushed than indicate to the neighbors that they are, in fact, home:

> GENTLEMAN: I prohibit you from moving your bowels again until we return from our vacation!
> *The* LADY *wipes herself. Starts to pull the chain when she is through but is stopped by the* GENTLEMAN *who leaps from his chair and rushes over to the toilet to prevent her from flushing it. He knocks her off the toilet seat.*
> LADY: This goddam nonsense has gone far enough! [*Rises from the floor, removes a blond wig from her head, throws it on the floor*] I am through playing your dumb games.[67]

Pietri presents us with a brown bowel aesthetic, here, to be somewhat playful and vulgar like the dramatist himself. Not only is this aesthetic about expunging waste, or the excess of the unwanted; it also indexes Ricanness—and, by consequence, Brownness—as disposable/unflushable ontologies with impending anticipation and pleasure, release, and exemption. Therefore, shitting is a way to modulate subjectivity: to sigh emphatically, respire in relief, and wipe away the grisly, or just to scat one's way into another time and space. It's a cathartic experience, a moment when, as Kristeva warns, epiphany mounts and surrenders, and the subject moves into a greater contemplation of self and other.

For Pietri, the bathroom is a strategic site of politics and hidden violence. Unsurprisingly, this most abject of spaces has always been a domain of both pleasure and pain, both intimacy and potential violation. For many minoritarian subjects, as Muñoz reminds us, the politics of the toilet are personally tied to a history of sexual and queer acts, regardless of visibility, and in tandem with both erotic pleasure and violence.[68] As Lady repeatedly attempts to relieve herself of her very own abjection, Gentleman demands its consumption, parrying her self-presentation with his own orientation to it. Even when she tries to pull the handle to flush the toilet (or herself of her own desperation), Gentleman knocks her to the floor—the vicious act continuing in different ways throughout the play. Lady is beaten, raped, degraded, held hostage by her husband in what amounts to the only recourse for Gentleman: attempt to bludgeon her into the submission of his own fantasy against the reality of racialized capitalism.

The play's misogyny reveals an all too familiar scene in colonial life: at the center of all drama, the female body remains the unwilling sacrificial entity. But Pietri is not the real misogynist here; instead, he forces us to provide testimony to such misogyny—not to celebrate it, but to name it, even when it masquerades as love, personal attachment, and a revolution against the capitalist state. In the 1970s, Pietri establishes his own type of feminist protocol within a Brown revolution sustained by patriarchy. His trite Gentleman represents violent masculinist offenders who oppress women as they simultaneously fight for racial justice. Pietri is intentional about the types of violence he forces the audience to experience. Without any trigger warnings and laced with ongoing humor, this play distorts our sense of reality, fantasy, and humanity. Who are we if we begin to experience the full extent of our darkest, most sadistic desires? Who are we, then, if we become both the colonizing gaze and his fist? These are the questions Pietri demands we ask ourselves as we remain locked in a space of desolation.

Although equally stock, these characters are not mutually the same: Lady brings the audience back to reality, even when Gentleman refuses to leave the location of his gross delusions. Pushing from and against these two psychic states, these characters grant us the experience of imperial dread in the domain of domestic woe. Intimacy, lest we forget, is also violent and disparaging, cutting sharply across those thin boundaries that presume to safeguard subjects. While seemingly a private affair, domesticity is not devoid of public violence; at times the dangerous tendencies of the world seep through the cracks of a closed door. Pietri's Gentleman stands in for all sadistic men, and warns Lady, "Shut up and enjoy it bitch, I don't want to hurt you, but if I have to I will!"[69] Ultimately, the audience must enter the interior life of an already intensified and vicious bathroom; with no real clock turning, the affective timer keeps ticking. Gentleman's fantasies, like that of his colonizer's, are brutal and sadistic, and even in his light and flattering rhetorical games with Lady, he is her abuser. His fantasies never release him of his violent oppression, instead they bind him to it.

Gentleman reveals to Lady, "That woman knew that man was only pretending to rape her, that's why she pretended to panic."[70] He's the rapist who refuses to confess because he does not recognize himself as the criminal offender. Gentleman, here, gives new meaning to killing time—in his torrid rendezvous in which cheap wine takes him over his edge, Lady fights for her life and reminds Gentleman that "when one woman is raped all women are raped!"[71] Such a position warrants further inquiry, and so I want to pause here and assert that women do not fantasize themselves out of poverty and despair through violent acts and acquisition of power. This behavior is an internalized colonial one that is often sustained by masculinist time and misogyny. Gentleman is the desiring colonizer, playing out his disturbed and enraged fantasies over Lady. Lady is the ethical victim of this piece, becoming the play's ultimate redeeming voice even when beaten into submission, and fighting for her life.

One might say that Gentleman's *durée*, the one that Bergson sees as the passage to a future pregnant with possibility, is in fact bearing a disturbing entity that is always violently unleashed upon the Lady. Her body and psychic life perpetually endure his violent fantasies in the very face of Rican existence. So how do these subjects, then, intertwined and consumed by so much dread and violence, make it to the future? Or, better yet, why doesn't Lady leave him in order to land in her own space of possibility? In this existential tragifarce, relegated to an odious temporal claustrophobia, we labor to imagine a future outside of mechanical time's destitution.

As Merleau-Ponty cautions, without the (self-)reflection afforded by the perceptions that subjects cocreate with others, understanding and consciousness in general would remain shrouded. In perception, even if violent, we are still in the present, going somewhere and already having been somewhere else. For without this knowledge of time, we remain stuck in the crevices of standard negation, becoming the adhesion that painfully attaches to our bodies and malignantly proliferates. This is colonialism's pathology, and Pietri offers us a snapshot of it—a recourse to the devastation of the broken subject through displeasure itself. In our shattered selves, we move to a conscious awareness of another expression of humanity, even if dread, doom, despair, and death lead the way.

I'll offer a clearer example here to expose what's at stake in such dread. In an especially pointed moment of existential advice, Gentleman lectures Lady on the meaning of the good life: "Now think, or try to think. . . . You are the pleasure of your pleasures and misery of your miseries! Doesn't that make sense? Of course it does! We may not be able to decide when we die but we can decide in between the time we are born and the time we die how well off or how bad off we want to pretend we are!"[72] At this existential breaking point we encounter another type of humanism: one laid bare in excrement, tragedy, a dark joke, a brown bowel aesthetic that remains unflushed potentially by the prospect of liberation and escape. With regard to such sentiment, Cruz-Malavé writes that Pietri's work exposes the farce of the American Dream and how the Rican subject must awaken and "withdraw from the false images of America."[73] This withdrawal is not only a political one, however, but an intimately aesthetic one. That is to say that Pietri's departure from the Young Lords Party and other political movements was not a rejection of their principles and aims, "but rather a redirection of energy into the complexity of aesthetic representation."[74] In order for Pietri to discharge a fuller conversation between class struggle and racial and gender violence under imperial precedent within the space of the aesthetic, Lady and Gentleman remain transfixed by the very stench they wish to flee. In this regard, Pietri conjoins the abject, vulgar, and absurd, and in consequence, pushes against those tight boundaries stabilizing racial representation and sexual transparency.

According to Crespy, Pietri's plays are "radical subversive absurdist psychocomedies" that are akin to the works of Ionesco and Beckett, which use language to challenge colonialism.[75] Crespy adds that his use of language explores the clash between Nuyorican and mainstream culture while moving between and around the two. It is the circular movement within the structure of his plays that Crespy identifies as the hallmark of Pietri's absurdism. As Crespy shows, Pietri highlights the "murderous inanities of the quotidian" without relinquishing attention to the structural inequalities at play.[76] Such inequalities as class and race, and even gender violence, ironically and problematically call forth the risible in life's asinine moments. This racialized existential tragicomedy is therefore not purely harrowing—it's as hurtful as it is funny, for as drama exposes, comedy is always already tragic. "Comedy does not exist independently of rage . . . rage is sustained and it is pitched as a call to social activism, a bid to take space [and time] in the social that has been colonized by the logics of white normativity and heteronormativity."[77] It's a way-of-being that is perceived as temporally incurable because of such intense desolation, unrealized desire, cruelty, and everyday dread. But as Lebrón exposed before, even death can be a welcoming smile, if we rethink the linearity of time. Pietri's parry to such existential threats reveals his deeper conversation with and commitment to experiences that might be manageable only through linguistic loops and mischievous allusions.

Unwashed Pleasures: Intersubjective Terrorist Language Games

Pietri's play is a study in linguistic subversion, twisting the rules of discourse, social space, and cultural politics. Such linguistic turns connect the various facets and philosophies of his expressive art. Called an amalgam of absurdism, surrealism, expressionism, American stand-up comedy, New York street theater, vaudeville, and circus spectacular,[78] his plays were another arsenal in his ministry. For Crespy, "Pietri's plays are built on a poet's sensibilities and a performance artist's instincts."[79] For example, lingering durations interspliced with depressing undertones seep into dialogue that is meant to engender laughter in *The Masses Are Asses*. And the play is hilarious, especially when both Lady and Gentleman speak of the masses as total asses, become paranoid of the international A.B.C.D.E.F.G.H.I. (Armed Brave Comrades Determined Efficient Fighters Gonna Humiliate Imperialism) Terrorist Group, and toast to their audacious and snobbish superiority. Underneath the hysterical, however, the audience uncovers Pietri's political analysis: his ironic critique of the upper classes also discloses his reevaluation of the political discourse of "terror" and "terrorism."

The following conversation and stage directions are worth examining in detail; they express the performativity of time and how it manages our sentiments:

A loud explosion is heard, knocking them both off their seats. The lights blink on and off rapidly. Police sirens are heard for 30 seconds. The LADY and GENTLEMAN are under the table. They snobbishly clear their throats as they cautiously rise.

GENTLEMAN: Are you okay, my dear???

LADY: Yes. And yourself???

GENTLEMAN: I'm fine . . . [*They both sit down. Refills glasses*] . . . The A.B.C.D.E.F.G.H.I. is upgrading their terrorist tactics. They have gone from bullets to bombs . . . [*They both drink up. He refills glasses*] . . . If those lunatics aren't stopped, next it will be ballistic missiles on their agenda of aggression against us.[80]

The acronym for the terrorist group unveils how anyone can—and will, as we saw with Lebrón—be named a terrorist. Gentleman voices the alarmist rhetoric often heard from those in power, particularly in times of war (as relevant for the Vietnam conflict during which the play was produced as it is for today's "War on Terror"). This tension between who is and is not a terrorist, as located in heroic descriptors such as "brave" and "determined," signals Pietri's intervention into strict dialectics. Just as someone may simultaneously be a hero and a terrorist, time may simultaneously be specific and abstract. For instance, those thirty seconds of police sirens denote a particular stretch of time. Such specific markers of time throughout the play are consistently paired with abstractions that mark arbitrary moments, such as "sometime," "will be late," "to be on time," and "to already be there." This dialectical turn between measures of time produces a phenomenological rendering of lived experience that frames how these two subjects struggle to exist in both reality and fantasy. They live in times that are simultaneously past, present, and still becoming, and this engenders a temporal disorientation that contributes to the ontology of these subjects. That is to say that we cannot understand them outside these dialectical sonic interruptions. This play's countdown to the future is accessed through the oral/aural violences of the present—sounds and silences that may have already occurred in the past. This past is also a condition of their present, shifting us all into the horizon of Bergson's endless possibility. As I see it, these dialectical encounters are emblematic of the inherent and promising contradictions found in Ricanness, openings that shatter the absolute. Pietri's lights "blink on and off rapidly," alternately illuminating and darkening these openings: shimmering ruptures that serve as escape valves from conventional negation. Ricanness is found in both the absence and the presence of this light.

Pietri is a phenomenologist on high alert, code red always sounding in his theatrical scenes of power, linguistic subversion, and temporal discombobulation. Crespy claims that "in the world of Pietri's plays, language is the key to power; the only way to control one's own destiny is through language."[81] This linguistic prerogative is wedded to subjectivity, a process in time that is inseparable from the phenomenology of life, death, and rebirth, and the symbols that represent and interweave them. Noel reconfirms this by sharing, "His poetics is not just about documenting a failure of visibility but also about occupying the space of subjection, about staging unfore*seen* encounters that demand all parties to rethink the terms of representation."[82] He adds,

> Much of Pietri's conceptual work engaged with questions of visibility/invisibility: from his use [of] performance props such as [a] begging cup that reads "Help me I can see" to textual experiments like *Invisible Poetry* (1979), a chapbook consisting entirely of blank pages, to the dada-surreal and metaphysical charge of such later works as *Lost in the Museum of Natural History* (1980) and *Traffic Violations* (1983).[83]

Such symbolic inventiveness is conjoined to dialogue in *The Masses Are Asses* in what amounts to a series of phenomenological moments that unfold around human actors. Merleau-Ponty cautions us to see language as inseparable from the speaker's lived body.[84] There is an inherent connection between the world we live in (determined prebirth), our body's choreographic movements in time and space, and language's position within our enlivened bodies. Subjectivity, here, is the dynamic and relational interaction of our experiences, in which discourse emanates from both the physical body and the voice. In the context of Pietri's world, subjectivity is not a fixed point in linear time, but the iterative unfolding of successive and self-referential moments that are meaningful in relation to social space and cultural scripts. Merleau-Ponty understands language not merely as an instrument for communication, but as an intimate disclosure of the speaker, of Being in general, and of how subjects learn to experientially relate to one another.[85] Pietri deploys this idea of language throughout his play, exposing how utterance and repetition inform our understanding of ourselves relationally through both sound and the body—a full sensorial scene that begins even before the play's opening moments.

Exceptional Listening: Reproducing Ricanness One Tape Recorder at a Time

Time is elliptical for Pietri, as a phenomenological reading will have it. Looking back in time, we move forward while still planted in the present, even as this play doubles as the past. I want to return to that moment in the play where a recording contains the voices of the two characters, and Pietri affirms their existence in sonic time. As the characters flatter one another, Gentleman secretly devises the ingenious idea to record their compliments. He whispers to Lady that he has a present, a gift "more precious than gold."[86] As she sits in anxious anticipation whispering back, he too whispers, "I have been secretly taping all the compliments we have exchanged," and pulls a "small cassette from a pocket inside his suit jacket and turns it on."[87] While they have been whispering all along in sensual buildup and exquisite tension, the recording is heard clearly. The flattery continues, "You look exciting. You look demanding. You look outstanding," until Gentleman turns it off and states, "We sound intellectually romantic. Let's drink to the sound of our voices."[88] They toast. Lady's fascination with her own voice beckons Gentleman to press play again. He concedes and the characters come into existence through documentation. There's no better place to listen for Pietri's version of tragedy and existence than in the actual recording that might be the only thing that sustains these characters, or better yet, the only way we know they were once alive:

> LADY: Please put the tape back on so we can continue listening to our interesting voices.
> GENTLEMAN: Absolutely. By all means. Listening to our voices is the most exciting event of my life.[89]

As the recording uncovers, sound redoubles their existence; on repeat, they are momentarily appeased in a world that reduces them to the very excrement they breathe in. The sonic implications of their voices restructure thought, affect, and being-with-another in such a way that Lady and Gentleman, at least for that moment in time, believe this illusion of subjectivity. It is the desire produced by their own voices that authorizes their sense of self—even if twice removed from their original utterances. The tape recorder, like Pietri's use of repetition in language, affective vulgarity, and a numerical countdown, literally retimes the play, and presents a Rican subjectivity on constant loop, in perpetual documentation. Pietri's act of looping participates in the eternal circuit of this perceived incomplete Rican subject, in which death and life continually confront one another. This tension is also seen in a pivotal stanza in "Puerto Rican Obituary," where the poet says, "From the nervous breakdown streets / where the mice live like millionaires / and the people do not live at all / are dead and were never alive."[90] In this space, where the mice pretend to be millionaires and the living are echoes in sound, Pietri reformulates the line between death and life, offering a more nuanced rendition of existence.

So then what happens when Ricanness is actualized through a tape recorder, and listening to your own voice becomes "the most important event of your life"? What happens when a recording of your own voice is the only evidence of your existence? Even as gunshots and sirens are heard outside of the South Bronx bathroom, the recording plays on until the tape malfunctions and all we hear is "You look magnificent" over and over again—without a clear indication of which character speaks. Indeed, how much does it matter who is called "magnificent" when the world is falling apart and people of color are always already dead?

The recording signifies the most important event of their lives—the moment they allow themselves the pleasure of their own voices. Offering a sonic, existential, and phenomenological transmission of the characters, the recording documents the essence of these subjects in time and space—the past, present, and future simultaneously. Pietri magnifies the audience's attention to what otherwise might appear as just an absurdist conversation, transforming its banality to reckon with the politics of ephemera for people of color. Even if they live on only with this one line, the cassette transmits an ineffable significance—one that gives these characters the will to continue living, and the audience the desire to continue remembering them as once alive, all in the tight space of a dirty toilet.

Pietri is more than a playwright. Like Bergson and Merleau-Ponty, he is that phenomenologist mixing fiction and fact, fantasy and political reality on both unconscious and conscious terrain. He rearranges time by creating a strategic interplay between the future, present, and past, all felt in the violent immediacy of the here and now. This play, as the recording proves, is set in multiple and simultaneous dimensions. "Sometime last week" is a setup for the future: the characters perform and the audience observes in the present, but the present is in overlay; these temporal proportions reveal how both the onto-political and capital's force enact one another.

This kind of temporal interpolation accentuates the intended simplicity and complication of the process of perception. One enters the world with a set of conditions already set in motion by which to perceive and be perceived. As Merleau-Ponty explains, "past time" is not erased from our experiences: it is "collected up and grasped in the present." Of the future he expresses a similar position:

> The same is true of the imminent future which will also have its horizon of imminence. But with my immediate past I have also the horizon of futurity which surrounded it, and thus I have my actual present seen as the future of that past. With the imminent future, I have the horizon of past which will surround it, and therefore my actual present as the past of that future.[91]

Similar to a Heideggerian construction of futurity, Merleau-Ponty argues above that rather than the mechanistic ticking off of automated increments, what we call "the past," "the present," and "the future" are instead constituted by how we experience their interrelationality, each made up of its orientation to the respective others. What has been exists only in our understanding of it in this here and now. Put another way, the recording of Lady's and Gentleman's voices, while "the most exciting event of [Gentleman's] life," is simply an expression of a passage of time, a crucial voice from the past that cements their existence in the present. These characters exist materially through the sound of their voices, pressing "stop," "pause," and "play" on their own lives.

Pietri is a futuristic musician keeping time. The play takes place "sometime last week," declaring a temporal particularity. It's a dialectical ambivalence in which time matters only as the weeks pass; the characters and audience members exist in the following week, but "sometime" also signifies a lack of temporal commitment. Is Pietri restaging a play from that recording in which the characters exist only in sound? The word "sometime," in this case, confirms an event, but it also diminishes a particular calendric urgency. One knows from the onset of the play that one is witnessing the past—looking back with the intention of going forward. Their recorded voices reinvite one to enter into the moment, and to purchase, through consequence, the time of futurity where their voices will wait to be played again in another week by maybe another miserable, colonized couple. Throughout *The Masses Are Asses*, Pietri both reinforces the solidity of mechanical time while also disturbing it, just as Bergson accentuates sensory and affective time.

To both provoke and capture the full sensorial essence of colonial time, I recently taught this play for an undergraduate/graduate seminar in my departmental bathroom—a toilet for one that piled in about eight. Together, we read scenes from the play with the door closed; while some students marked their spot against the shut door, others leaned against the sink or trash can, and one student perched on the edge of the toilet—all finding an object to ground themselves. As the temperature rose and time elapsed, I could feel the tension and claustrophobia mounting: in less than five minutes locked in this room, we could all sense the characters' impending doom and violence. It was clear that whether through a recording or in the flesh, Pietri determines how we experience the time of dread. All closely knit in this room, we began to smell the odiousness in *The Masses Are Asses*, and relinquish our own sensory perceptions, relieved that none of us were Lady or Gentleman in that place and time. While a perilous pedagogy indeed, it framed what's materially at stake within the temporal strictures of confined spaces. To relearn the everyday properties of colonial life, we all remained trapped in a windowless room. Time, here, recorded our sentiments, creating a documentation of our own privileged desires at the site of negation and abject residue. Alongside the play's stench and the toilet's own olfactory history, we waited to exit a scene that epitomizes the intimate gender violence perputuated by colonialism. Pietri provides the domain for the speculative drama we experienced, knowing, I contend, that a locked door, superimposed or not, is always a temporal concern, not merely a spatial dilemma. It's only a matter of time before it is opened, knocked down, or broken into.

Reflections on That Somewhere Else: Pretending for the Future

Through Lady and Gentleman, Pietri offers a critique of capital while refusing the literal address to *Brownness* or *Ricanness*; instead he calls to these ontological and ontic concerns through the immediacy of social space. Frustrating space in dark and temporal ways is Pietri's game: his plays uncover the absurdities present for oppressed subjects by taking standard tropes and disrupting them. His worlds unfurl in seemingly ordinary places—funeral home (*No More Bingo at the Wake*), living room (*The Livingroom*), bar (*Act One and Only*), factory (*Sell the Bell or Go to Hell*), and bathroom (*The Masses Are Asses*). In the latter, he forces class distinction to encounter the harsh reality of race and gender, or, as Marx might add, the war of society against the poor. Even though the claim that the masses are asses is a deliberately anti-Marxist provocation, this dramatist is engaged in a burlesque of hegemony and anticolonial theory in the tightest of abject spaces. In this case, however, "the poor" is more than a tax bracket; they are the colonized and the colonizer for one another, playing out the master/slave dialectic through sexual violence and toxic gender posturing. Pietri wants us to feel crowded, cramping our vulnerabilities, obliging us to enter into an existential crisis of perception and human worth.

With a poet's sense of rhyme and meter, Pietri uses mechanical time to congeal the characters' projects of the past and their descent into the future through these violent-scapes. The play ends with Lady succumbing to the ruse of being on vacation in Europe. The countdown clock ends at zero seconds, and the only two characters in the play descend into another recurrence, this time yielding to the next day, a Sisyphean repeat of poverty, imperialism, domestic violence, loss, and longing.[92] This eternal recurrence, however, ends with the marginalized couple snuggled up in the bathtub, waiting to repeat tomorrow. Or have they quietly submitted to the call of death? Pietri leaves us wondering and wanting, and in our shared empathy, we remain locked in the bathroom, too.

The play's final moments reveal Pietri's attachment to such discomfort as a sanction for politics, or a way to tap into our sense of humanity: "The couple finally snuggle into their bathtub wrapped in an infested old fur, repeat their opening litany of sweet nothings like a flipbook of souvenir postcards from an unspent holiday, and 'snobbishly clear their throats in zero seconds.'"[93] As they sit in their tub, closely linked, what do they really wait for in this *now's* tomorrow? If these characters fall into this tub, as descending reveals, how do they "fall out"—or is it "get out"—of the blurred lines between the tragedy of everyday life and that which is fundamentally just play? Perhaps the answers lie in our conjoined recognition as unwanted subjects, in which our relationality is as absurd as it is painful, as internal to ourselves as it is external to the world.

4

Looping Sensations

On Waiting with the Existential Ryan Rivera

Ryan was like his art: a lot of intensity, humor, a free spirit,
but not happy-go-lucky; a lot of darkness, a life worth saving, infinite promise, restlessness, and never satisfied.
—Melissa Sklarz, former president of the Stonewall Democratic Club of New York and Ryan Rivera's close friend, New
York City, 2013

As object and subject, I become the embodiment of my inner and outer realities resulting in the creation of yet another
reality, self-inflicted and projected to the world.
—Ryan Rivera, "Identity Crisis," BFA thesis, School of
Visual Arts, 2002

From 2000 until his sudden death in 2010 at the age of forty-five,
queer and Rican avant-garde artist Ryan Rivera created a body of
work that pushed the limits of technology, space, existence, and bodily
endurance—all reminiscent of durational and conceptual art of the
late 1960s and 1970s.[1] Similar to the video and performance art of
these decades by artists such as Yoko Ono, Ana Mendieta, Papo Colo,
Vito Acconci, Marina Abramović, Ulay, Dan Graham, Joseph Beuys,
and Chris Burden,[2] Rivera reacted to a capitalist world system moving
at high speed.[3] Traveling between permanency and ephemerality in
his video art, he echoed the "hostile takeover of technology over every
aspect of humanity," in his words, by pushing against the spectator's
sensorial limits. As Rivera explains, "The exploration of identity, the
tension between [the] inner and physical self and the representation
of a virtual self are extended to a certain psychological manipulation
of the viewer."[4] Virtually, Rivera accelerates the spectator's somatic

response to anguish by blurring the boundaries of empathy and antipathy within elongated temporalities.

Rivera filters through the multiple and complicated subjectivities involved in the pursuit of existence, and his philosophical spirit, expressed in the epigraph above, discloses a subject both in contradiction and direct conversation with the ineffable call of ontology. Rivera's work pulls us along his affective spectrum from lightness to darkness as emotive intensity meets the matter of time and its emotional consequences. This chapter explores the affectional depth and tension that live at the center of both the artist and his body of work, essentially moving the spectator to feel, sense, and exist alongside his temporal affectations.

These affective interarticulations in time mark the aesthetic and political spot in which Ricanness is accessed through a shared sense of endurance experienced within various scenographies of waiting. I suggest, here, that Ricanness-as-waiting, not merely a conceptual delineation, transpires within the senses in Rivera's art, informed by moments that feel longer than the actual time elapsed. Yet waiting is not a neutral act: it is a political existence for a Rican and queer subject whose intersubjective encounters are framed by states of perceived incompletion, negation, and lack. Such a claim permits a reading of Ricanness that is about a *waiting-with* but also a *waiting-on*, anchored by servility and limited control over one's labor. These shared moments of endurance unfold in Rivera's work wherein he positions his spectator directly in the seat of sensation. In my own epistemological positioning, I work to distinguish Brownness from Ricanness by conceptually acknowledging the role of racial and ethnic histories and by grounding my interpretation in the empirically conjoined elements of political, ideological, sexual, and cultural embodiments. That is to say that while analytically separable, Brownness and Ricanness are ontologically foundational and intertwined; as such, the only way through is between them, and I begin by way of Ricanness, by way of the existential artist himself.

While I work between Brownness and Ricanness in this chapter, I am fully aware of the important conceptual distinctions between specific ethnic histories and Latinx political solidarity. To be clear, then, again, I move into Brownness by way of Ricanness, just as I labor throughout this book by moving from the aesthetic to the political. That is to say that Rivera's work is discernible throughout this chapter as a queer, Rican, *and* Brown metaphor of perceived incompletion, appearing on screen incorporeally, washed out, and enclosed. I argue that Rivera's work evidences an existentialism that imagines politics not as something we arrive at, but as something that we await in our racial, sexual, and gendered particularities. Awaiting such politics is not a sedentary act, as Rivera demonstrates how waiting is in fact the condition of existence I am referring to as a kind of Brown existentialism.

Often considered exclusive to European schools of thought, existentialism has exerted a profound influence on minoritarian writers throughout the world who were already committed to and writing about meaning, consciousness, and specific Black and Brown ways of being-in-the-world. For Lewis R. Gordon, a leading scholar of Black existentialism, this philosophical movement is certainly overly concerned with the history of European thought. As such, he opts to invoke the term a bit differently: "We regard *philosophies of existence*—the specialized term that I sometimes call *existential philosophies*—as philosophical questions premised upon concerns of freedom, anguish, responsibility, agency, sociality, and liberation."[5] Or put another way, this philosophy springs from the "lived context" of Black bodies' being-in-the-world. While Black existentialism became legible at the height of existential thought in the 1940s and 1950s and historicized this way in the decades since, the term "Brown existentialism" has not been similarly documented within US philosophical traditions.[6] Instead of searching for that archive, I expand historical parameters by using existentialism as a framework to speak about both Ricanness and Brownness—that is, to turn to the situational realities that inform subjectivity, pain, despair, and liberation, intimately reframed by Blackness itself. In doing so, an appraisal of Rivera's work recuperates and reinvigorates the commonalities between Black and Brown existentialism at the site of anticolonial bodies. As a way of establishing the first pieces of a Brown, Rican, and queer existentialist archive, this chapter mainly focuses on Rivera's short experimental videos from his series *Body/Psyche* (2002), which highlight his commitment to durational and endurance art, and showcase his obsession with pushing past the limits between the physical body and interior thought, "and in exploring and expanding definitions of identity" in unconventional and less transparent ways.[7]

But *Body/Psyche* is only a small segment of his archive, so before diving into these videos, I would like to paint a more robust image of the complicated and talented artist. For example, in a video outside of this series, *Sustain*, Rivera spotlights his own mother in bra and underwear, scrubbing a pristine bathtub; for three minutes, we absorb the figure's presence in black and white, as she brushes the object's supremely clean surface. On repeat, her dark and long hair hangs above the cleaning brush, both moving back and forth in rhythmic motion as she grunts and breathes. A single earring on her right ear sparkles, the camera moving toward and away from this shimmer of light. With full force, she scours the delusion of abjection—trying to erase her own identity as a cleaning lady, or to expose the transience of her labor. Although the viewer is unable to see her face because it is covered by her hair, the repetition of her bodily movements produces the powerful sensation of Rican endurance. Once again, we are confronted with a Brown subject in a bathroom, laboring to extend herself outside the confining space of colonial life. In another poignant piece, a live performance called *Succumb* (2001), Rivera mummified himself in over "200 pounds of wire for a three hour performance during SVA Summer Residency Open Studios," allowing visitors to walk around him as he performed death, sustaining the narrow enclosure of his naked body coiled against the cold material elements of wire.[8] Whether for three minutes or three hours, the artist reorganizes linear time through the profound implications of both exertion and stillness at the edge of mortality.

Aside from making experimental videos and performances, Rivera created "site-specific installation[s] and sculptural works" to also contend with "issues of body, space, technology, and ephemerality"[9]—all common themes throughout his life's work. As an avid reader, he was highly inspired by "ancient rituals (mummification), ancient symbols (mandala), modern art (white cube), and science (string theory)," ideas making cameo appearances in *Succumb*, but also in his installations. In his site-specific installation pieces, the artist engages the body in abstract ways—an aesthetic and political interplay between string theory, light, space, and sound. Of his installation work such as *Dimensia #2* (2001), in which "more than 2000 feet of monofilament [are] randomly strung through a grid of eye screws installed on the walls and floor"; *Centrifuge* (2001), "a plastic coated copper wire (9' diameter)" consisting of "hundreds of strands of wire emerg[ing] from a central point in the wall, each strand installed in its own hole forming the diameter"; and *Wall of Light* (2001), wherein "hundreds of dowels [are] installed in individual holes in a wall," the artist states, "The very art of my art making bears a certain compulsivity and physicality, also referencing the body through the orifices made in walls for my installations." Rivera goes on to share that this work is about a type of visceral awareness with the viewer, "whether by being kept out of a space that is defined by line and dimension, or in being overpowered by the size of a piece." Consequently in these pieces, but also throughout his work, the artist calls attention to our shared sense of mortality through different kinds of bodies, openings, aesthetic holes, and "the threat of live wires." In establishing an "emotional resonance" with his audience, Rivera also comments on the relational pulls of voyeurism and the wanted violation of privacy between spectator, space, object, and artist.

Throughout this chapter, then, I suggest that all of his art performs a mode of Ricanness and Brownness that operates as a shared sense of endurance between both the spectator and artist, or an *aesthetics of mediated ontologies* in brief durations. Through a return to an engagement with Heideggerian phenomenology, I contend that Rivera's sardonic, aggressive, and histrionic videos situate the viewer directly in the seat of sensation where Ricanness unfolds as a *waiting-with* and a *waiting-on*. Violence and melodrama intensify and elongate the short time frame of each video I analyze below, enacting Ricanness-as-waiting, a kind of waiting that Rivera understands as both emotionally permanent and fleeting.

Archiving Loss, Love, and the Aesthetic Temperament

Although a prolific, multitalented, and provocative artist, Rivera is relatively unknown in the performance and media art world. Other minoritarian subjects, however, have given Rivera a tenor of life and essence post-death. Artist Yuko Shimizu provides a window into the immediacy and intimacy of Rivera's work through her sketchbook documentary *My Friend Ryan.*[10] She conceived her meditation on Rivera's different ways of being and creating art in 2002 while they were completing their Fine Arts Studio Residency together at the School of Visual

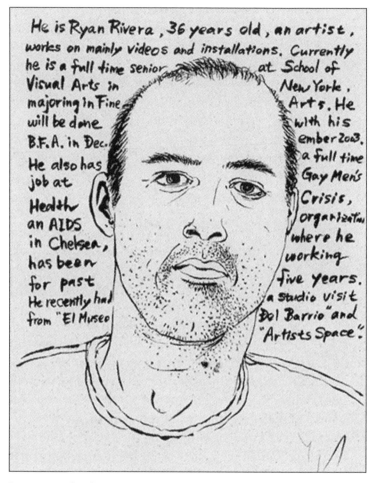

Figure 4.1. Yuko Shimizu, *Ryan Rivera*, 2002. http://yukoart.com. Sketchbook documentary image courtesy of the artist.

Arts (SVA) in New York. Upon his death in 2010, Shimizu posted her entire sketchbook online with the following address: "I know almost nobody who are [*sic*] reading this know [*sic*] Ryan, but his short precious life was worth knowing even if you didn't know him personally."[11] In thirteen sketched frames, Shimizu reveals a day in the life of the artist—with friends and his beloved dog, in class, and in his office at Gay Men's Health Crisis. Her interpretive sketches of Rivera's daring short video pieces, which were taken down from the SVA's street-level

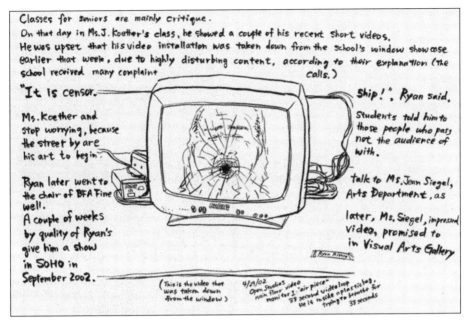

Figure 4.2. Yuko Shimizu, *Ryan Rivera: Story 3*, 2002. http://yukoart.com. Sketchbook documentary image courtesy of the artist.

window showcase "due to highly disturbing content," offer a glimpse into his visionary and censored art.[12] Shimizu's drawings invite one to consider how Rivera confronted the institution of art via his simultaneous devotion to both formal experimentation and political engagement.

Following Shimizu, one goal of this chapter is to share Rivera's archive with the reader and to place Rivera in conversation with complementary minoritarian performance and media artists committed to the experimental, such as Ana Mendieta, Félix González-Torres, Nao Bustamante, ADÁL, Freddie Mercado, and Papo Colo, to name only a few.[13] Like Rivera, these artists place pressure on both the burden of representation and the lack of attention often paid to Brown artists, particularly those who move away from folkloric aesthetics in their emerging practices of experimental art. This by no means overrides the fact that Rivera was queer and Rican but rather exposes how being both need not counterpose the experimental work often reserved for majoritarian subjects. Unsurprisingly, queer artists of color are often rewarded for rehearsing racial and sexual narratives of compliance, unadulterated pleasure, and amenability—a type of posturing that mediates their value and aesthetic currency. However, not all Brown subjects are jovially singing, gesturing, and dancing—as is the case in Rivera's disturbing artwork. In this challenging genealogy of work, new temporal possibilities are discovered and not merely recovered—even if one must wait in anxious anticipation, and labor diligently against the burden of liveness, the politics of identity, and fabricated narratives of joy and pleasure.

So as a way to lay bare how waiting is both the torment and pleasure of existence in Rivera's work, I specifically focus on five of his short experimental videos, all produced in 2002: *Bash, Reflex, Hand Play, Breath Piece,* and *Goodbye Piece.* In every video, less than a minute each, Rivera subjects himself to various cruelties: bashing his head until bloody against a piece of plastic, stuffing his fist down his throat, punching and slapping his face, holding his breath, and sobbing histrionically. With the videos tightly shot from the shoulders up, a frame in which he is both subject and mise-en-scène, he dares the viewer to endure the monstrous in his desire to be seen, heard, and felt in the colonial sites of art and postcolonial social spaces.

These heady and controversial videos earned him a spot in El Museo del Barrio's *The (S) Files 2002: The Selected Files,* a biennial survey of emergent Latina/o artists; the museum featured several of his videos from the series *Body/Psyche,* a set of ten short pieces characterized by brief duration combined with extreme emotional intensity.[14] In each piece, Rivera exaggerates quotidian practices "to the point of obsession," as he explains, through which "the actions themselves reveal the humanity in overindulging, overdoing, and pushing ourselves to the limit, containing an emotional resonance we can all identify with." In this interplay between artist and viewer, "physical self-consciousness" meets the complicated allure of "compulsivity and mortality through everyday rituals."[15] Through a "scenography of waiting," Rivera drives his spectator as arduously as he labors.[16] And as I suggest throughout this chapter, his provocative videos create exchanges of sensory endurance, or what I see as a shared sense of waiting in which the viewer stays, suffers, feels, loves, and worries alongside Rivera. If waiting, as per Roland Barthes's meditation on this dimension of time, is a "delirium," "a minor mourning," and "an enchantment" followed by "orders not to move," then Rivera fixes the viewer in the very space of affliction and seductiveness.[17] This paradox of sentiment—of both pain and pleasure—does not disengage from a full range of affect; in fact, remaining with sensation deepens affective exchanges through prolonged instances of intersubjectivity.

Eternal Recurrence of the Rican Subject

Endurance is often seen as labor maintained over linear time, but in Rivera's work the intensity of the recorded acts stretches the brief duration of the video into a cyclical, looping eternity for the spectator. In these moments of sufferance, the videos transgress the boundary between subject and object as the spectator assumes the bodily effects of Rivera's violence. This is achieved through editorial techniques that speed up, overexpose, and loop the video frames, effectively enveloping the viewer with a similar affective ferocity that Rivera sustains. Of the technicality imbued in these videos, Rivera shares, "Limited to less than sixty seconds, each video piece becomes a concentrated moment played on a relentless loop; a hyper-reality that I like to compare to the replaying of moments in our lives over and over again."[18] That is to say that a sensorial interchange between the performer and viewer transcends mediation, making the screen more than just a barrier between bodies: it creates a sort of eternal immanence.

Just as we saw with Colo, Rivera's performance also invokes Nietzsche's notion of the eternal recurrence, a concept that is summarized when he exclaims the following, displacing his own voice into that of a "demon" who arrives into one's "loneliest loneliness" to disclose, "The eternal hourglass of existence is turned over again and again, and you with it, speck of dust!"[19] Although Nietzsche was not concerned with Ricanness, extrapolating from his insights provides significant purchase on Rivera's oeuvre. In the same aphorism from which the "hourglass" metaphor above is drawn, Nietzsche—quoting again the demon hovering above us all—shares, "This life as you now live it and have lived it, you will have to live once more and innumerable times more; and there will be nothing new in it, but every pain and every joy and every thought and sigh and everything unutterably small or great in your life will have to return to you, all in the same succession and sequence."[20] The return of "every pain and every joy," for Nietzsche as for Rivera, redounds through an enduring body, "all in the same succession and sequence." In typical Nietzschean form, he questions us to complicate the cycles of both time and emotion:

> Would you not throw yourself down and gnash your teeth and curse the demon who spoke thus? Or have you once experienced a tremendous moment when you would have answered him: "You are a god and never have I heard anything more divine." If this thought gained possession of you, it would change you as you are or perhaps crush you. The question in each and every thing, "Do you desire this once more and innumerable times more?" would lie upon your actions as the greatest weight. Or how well disposed would you have to become to yourself and to life *to crave nothing more fervently* than this ultimate eternal confirmation and seal?[21]

For Rivera, "the greatest weight" is lifted again and again—similarly to the Sisyphean ontology we witnessed in Lebrón's affirming actions, Colo's belabored cape, and Pietri's tragic characters—in order to transcend violence through resilient repetition.

Working from these philosophical concepts, Rivera explores the psychic ramifications of focused endurance pieces violently enacted upon Brown bodies. While Rivera's head is isolated in each frame, the disappearance of his body manifests the full sensorial corpus of the spectator. Curator Deborah Cullen comments on this disappearance by informing us that Rivera's videos are "short, looped enactments of aggressive and sardonic behaviors," videos that operate as "psychological windows onto naked emotion, challenging the viewer to watch what the artist presents publicly."[22] It is here, in this metaphorical and corporeal amputation, that the viewer wears his phantom limbs, immersed in both virtual noise and visual discord. In this visual and sonic pathos the spectator experiences what Rivera calls "hyper-reality," which he describes above as a kind of phenomenological looping, that is "replaying moments in our lives over and over again."[23]

Paralleling Rivera, Guy Debord expresses how sociality is framed by spectacle and mass media and saturated with representations of a commodified life. The abstraction of the commodity leaks into human existence, making the copy the placeholder for being. In uncovering modernism's consumerist project, Debord recycles the spectacular images used to impede culture and creates a type of being-with that inverts the dominance of the commodity over social interaction. By exploring this colonization of human existence, Debord reroutes our ways of seeing. He also redirects the colonization of time, in part through an exploration of historical chronology and mechanical time, in contempt of the alienating force of labor. Such technological alienation is a defining feature of Rivera's embodiment, which he elaborated in a letter to Margarita Aguilar, the curator of El Museo del Barrio at the time in 2001, four days before September 11. Disclosing his concern for technology's superimposition over the daily activities and sentiments of the human, Rivera boldly wrote, "It is the supplier, the connector, and the conveyer of communication, power, and information hidden behind our walls, in our machines, and under our feet."[24] He expresses here a focus on the mediated ontology of technical reproduction and quotidian rhythms that inflects his project with a Debordian accent. The varying temporal meters for Debord generate a worldview that is always in conversation with mediation. Foreshadowing a point expressed by Rivera, Debord states, "Spectacle cannot be understood either as a deliberate distortion of the visual world or as a product of the technology of the mass dissemination of images. It is far better viewed as a *weltanschauung* that has been actualized, translated into the material realm—a world view transformed into an objective force."[25]

Made anxious by media culture's rising ability to tarnish authentic human connection, a fear akin to Heidegger, Debord presents a worldview that disidentifies with the spectacular and mimetic in order to subvert the image's inherent deception. This mediatized *Da-sein*, to be playful here, is similar to but different from the claim I explain later in this chapter of an *aesthetics of mediated ontologies*. While I am aware that objects, beings, things disappear, I essentially believe that the image has its own life filled with endless potentiality, and that reproduction, not disappearance, is the guiding force behind all mediations. Debord rightly points out that "the spectacle is not a collection of images; rather, it is a social relationship between people that is mediated by images."[26] For some of us not included in that original, authentic heteronormative archive of both circulation and knowledge—Rivera essentially—media "gives us life" as a type of being-with that informs our personal subjectification and subjectivity in a way quite reminiscent of Lebrón's recitation for existence. That is to say that this kind of being-with reminds us that we still exist some place that wants us, even outside of the cultural storehouses that preclude our worth. Debord's *détournement*—the rerouting of an original work or technology for antithetical ends—meets recuperation in this chapter in which a translation of Heideggerian phenomenology is both a contextual and situational endeavor. Put another way, by conversing with and relooping phenomenology so that it accounts for queer Rican and Brown existence, I hope to tenderly rub together discordant epistemological, genealogical, and ontic-ontological realities that Rivera weaves together in his own performances.

A deeper, keener viewing of—or rather listening to—Rivera's videos presents more than an ocular hyper-reality, a whole that is far greater than the sum of its Debordian parts. Spectators are asked to stand in *for* as they stand *by* Rivera's absent body in his videos; all the while, both inharmonious and natural sounds such as gagging, abrasive banging, and crying resonate bodily responses. But what does it mean politically when a queer Rican subject conceals his body only to lend the viewer his psyche in spaces filled with dissonance? And how does sound, in concert with the full force of the senses, engender a type of queer and Brown intimacy?

Mediated Ontologies: The Spectator *Contra el Tiempo*

In spite of our independence, Rivera intimately entrances us with the exploitation of our senses and perception, producing an *aesthetics of mediated ontologies*. That is to say that real time is so disturbed that the dialectic of subject and object—Rivera and the spectator—creates a vortex that sucks in the object and subject to such an extent that the dialectic becomes the scene of the exchange, one that cannot exist outside of waiting. The full force of ontology, here, is witnessed in the plural, where to sit with the artist means to transcend the screen, object, and ultimate essence of self. In this virtual exchange, Rivera apprehends the existential with profound implications for our understanding of Ricanness, Brownness, queerness, and racial ontology. His project mediates three key elements that span his oeuvre and are central to our discussion here: (1) Rivera is interested in the viewer's sense of *being-in-the-world*; (2) Rivera invites the viewer into *being-within* the scene of aesthetic encounter; (3) Rivera does so in order to disclose how Ricanness is about a *being-toward-death*. To best explain the significance of these modes of existence, I return to Heideggerian phenomenology as both a methodological and conceptual framework. Rivera's work, I suggest, demands an engagement with this philosophical tradition precisely because the conditions of possibility of Ricanness—as a waiting with, for, or on— are guided by ontological and not strictly epistemological concerns. Waiting is a practice of existence that is attuned to both Ricanness and Brownness as a projection into that which is not yet here. That is to say, following Heidegger's construction of *being-in-the-world*, that Ricanness waits in the simultaneity of what is now and what may only ever come. Like *Da-sein*, which is undetermined even in various temporal shifts, Ricanness rests alongside the path of incompletion, in which the present continuous sustains Being.

Within such assertions I also claim that Rivera performs a translation of Heideggerian phenomenology in which being *futural* mandates the development of a present always already laced with reproductions of the past.[27] It isn't a far stretch to add, analogously, that the practice of being an artist in the world is always already an exercise of projection; in this case study, Rivera labors diligently to realize his full potential through a sense of projectile relationality. If *Da-sein* is also about a *being-there*, then Rivera drives the point that in his movement toward death in video life, the spectator must surpass the emptiness of the flat screen; in doing so, they enter multiple sensorial dimensions in time. By situating the spectator in the very face of death—through acts like slapping and punching, for example—the subject confronts the authentic condition of being in the world. Heideggerian authenticity demands a full acceptance of one's mortality, one that does not deter from the expansive potential of the *futural*, or promote linearity.

It is imperative to understand Rivera's work and its significance for a Brown existentialism in concert with Heidegger's philosophical meditations on anticipation, and so I'll re-rehearse the implications below. In the Heideggerian sense, waiting as anticipation is the symbol of its being in time, toward death and the *futural*. In other words, "thrownness" (existence as thrown into the world) is itself a projection into futurity for any and every existential object or being.[28] That is to add that waiting outside of projection would mean waiting outside of time. It is here, right after the possible impossibility of existence, that I would like to argue once again for ontologies (plural) in which Ricanness-as-waiting, a waiting-with or even on and for, speaks to *Da-sein* as a political and aesthetic gesture in time. Temporality, for Heidegger, "is experienced as a primordial phenomenon in the authentic being-a-whole of *Da-sein*, in the phenomenon of anticipatory resoluteness."[29] This means that *Da-sein* does not lie within one isolated agency of time such as the past, present, or future, but links these states together in pursuit of the transformation of the subject.

Rivera's spectator experiences this alliance of past, present, and future in their being-as-waiting-for, waiting-with, and waiting-on, all within a circumscribed temporality. I submit here again that being-in-waiting is always already tied to the Heideggerian being-toward the possible impossibility of *Da-sein* that mobilizes death as an authentic potentiality in the world. Coming to terms with one's mortality, as Rivera does violently and depressingly in each video, is an act of existence motivated by a different type of authenticity—one measured not by an essentialism of difference, but by a sense of approaching life in death. *Da-sein*, for Heidegger, will always be "something that is not yet at an end" because if it "has reached the end, it precisely no longer is."[30] Herein lies the ultimate potential: Brown bodies always wait in the durational aesthetics of politics, even if in heightened velocity; to be Brown means to *wait-with*, but also to *wait-on*. To be Brown also means to gently hammer through the conventional philosophical wall that refuses to account for difference in questions of Being, and Rivera exposes such Brownness through his Rican queerness, offering somewhat of a corrective to Heidegger's pale account of existence.

The sound for such a corrective plays out for twenty-seven seconds in *Hand Play*, in which Rivera repeatedly slaps and punches his face. These forceful repetitions thrust us toward nothingness in a space of openness; the viewer understands that the video will end soon, and yet still lingers emotionally in expectation, and on loop. Waiting becomes warped and time extends, making each hand movement feel like a condition of forever. In this particular video, the viewer experiences the potential for real time, a type of duration that exists outside the artist's molesta-

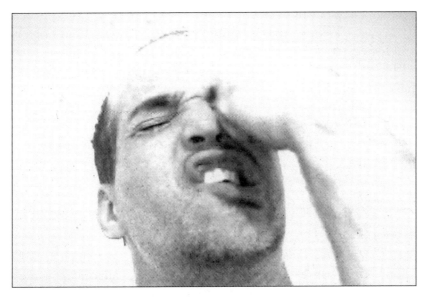

Figure 4.3. Still from *Hand Play*, 2002. Photo courtesy of Rebecca Rivera.

tion of frame upon frame. Mechanical time meets Bergson's *durée* in this piece, in which the latter accounts for affective experiences, giving time a profound type of ontological relevance, immeasurable in its intersubjective possibilities. As expressed in my analysis of Pietri's work, endurance sustains the play, actors, and audience, simultaneously engendering an affective concurrence between all three, a Bergsonian endeavor that makes space beholden to time and affective particularities.

These kinds of spatial-durational-emotional constellations appear prominently in *Hand Play*—in which the less-than-thirty-second video is sped up and spliced with relentless looping, and in which Rivera's face and the entire background of the screen are overexposed. Blending the object with the background floods us with a semblance of whiteness in a contained place of Rican endurance. Rivera's face, arms, and hands become decontextualized by speed and light in a flurry of fragmentation; one is moved by occasional grunting, blows to the face, and heavy breathing. And each breath feels more dire and urgent as time proceeds, gripping one in the lingering possibility of his final breath. These dissonant sounds and actions bind one to Rivera in a psychic space of conflict. Simultaneously, the spectator waits in distaste for the brutal-ity to end, takes vicarious pleasure in the various sensations of pain, and remembers their own limited existence. Heidegger might explain such a description of despair as one's inability to continually face the full extent of one's freedom. Ryan Rivera might call it something else: his ultimate desire for "the viewer to experience a certain physical self-consciousness" at the hands of his troubling work. For in the face of all that is existential anxiety, his Ricanness and queerness map out ways to move in the world, even without one's visible and transparent body.

Phenomenological Cadences: Ontologies of Finitude and Infinity

The historical reality of Ricanness evolves and moves in the passage between affective valences and somatic experiences, with an eye cast upon the endurance of the always-in-waiting Rican subject. This ontol-ogy of race and understanding of authenticity cuts past "the bad present of the everyday" into the "fundamental phenomenon of time [as] the future."[31] A key component of Heideggerian ontology is that it "is possible only as phenomenology" in its quest to consider the transfigu-ration of the subject. In this case study both Rivera and the spectator are embroiled within the world of the video, facing the vibrant horizon it avows. This engulfment is marked by spatial expansion through a sped-up capitalistic rhythm that is evidenced in Rivera's videos. At the same time, Rivera lingers in our connected bodies and skillfully plays with the notion of duration as experience, holding himself and the viewer captive in pain and violence with no sense of narrative finality, except through cinematic form. That is to say that the video *ends*, but the experience it produces lives on despite its formal denouement. The artist helps us understand this phenomenon as a performance of exhaustion in the anticipatory and insurgent location of waiting.

Rivera's affective mapping through the maze of exhaustion occurs by manipulating "the very part of the body where thought and creativity originate," different from but similar to the move made by Colo in his act of superhero depletion.[32] As Rivera conceals his body on screen, he manipulates the viewer's own. The "subversion of this focal point is fol-lowed through to the molestations of time, space, and linearity creat-ing a counterbalance between illusion and reality, between a real self, false self." I would add that in this performance of mediated ontologies, a *spectator self* is also produced in phenomenological and existential crisis.[33] The relentless looping in the work is meant to create alternate realities "self-inflicted and projected to the world." It is here that performance, rituality, and technology conjoin to produce a kind of Brown aesthetics, informed by queer and Rican temporalities.

I would be remiss if I did not place Rivera's work alongside that of queer Cuban artist Félix González-Torres—that is, within a trajectory of Brown and queer aesthetics. Both artists operated in the space between contemporary art and queer Brown life in New York City, sharing an all-too-real awareness of life's fragility in the throes of the AIDS crisis. Time, for both, was always already in conversation with the tangible threat of premature death, and the racialized materiality embedded within the project of being-with anything and anyone. In placing Rivera within a genealogy of Brown and queer aesthetics, I am reminded of González-Torres's *"Untitled" (Portrait of Ross in L.A.)*, an installation of 175 pounds of candy representative of the artist's partner Ross Laycock, who died of complications from AIDS that same year (1991). In an intimate embrace with both the spectator and his lover, González-Torres invites his spectator to walk away with a piece of candy. As the Art Institute of Chicago notes, "The diminishing amount parallels Ross's weight loss and suffering prior to his death."[34] The artist demanded that the pile be "continuously replenished, thus metaphorically granting perpetual life." The pile of candy, while not a performance for video, is nonetheless perpetually on loop. In this loop, however, the spectator is arrested by a pivoting silence and slowness that lingers in her personal ingestion, sense of taste, and possible return for another piece of the amorous subject. Here again, the audience participates in a corporeal amputation; yet, in the case of González-Torres, such severing is also a form of transubstantiation that is composed of his lover's deadly virus—a looping ingestion that makes us metaphorically accountable to a diseased life.[35] Both performances dwell within the terrain of projection and transference whereby introjection begins via the consumption of a melancholic subject. The viewers, driven to internalize their existential strife, unconsciously weave their loss and pain into their own sense of despair.

In González-Torres's project, specifically, unwrapping the candy instantiates a temporal action in which the loved object is a reminder of mortality—gradually and instantly one devours the signifier that situates death as always near. While death circulates in the eternal looping of both artists' work, the rotation changes between multiple viewers, rendering waiting unique in its extended anticipation. In this mediated ontology as spectators in Rivera's project, we serve as bodily supplements: Rivera "uses" us to funnel chaos, love, pain, and empathy through the affective and visceral barriers we wish to sustain. Waiting functions as a form of resistance, as a way to authentically and jointly sense, feel, love, and be of the world relationally. That is to say that our senses drift in discordance in the narrow space where the screen is the interlocutor and time brushes against and negotiates our relationalities and singularities.[36]

This particular sensibility of the Brown aesthetic, advanced by both González-Torres and Rivera, is embodied in *Bash*, another video performance in the vein of *Hand Play*. Exhibiting a tactile going-beyond in this thirty-eight-second video, Rivera partakes in reflexive self-injury, hitting his head against a sheet of plexiglass placed in between his face and the camera. The "unbreakable" glass functions as a mediator in this experience. Rivera "interpret[s] the head as representative of a catalyst, of sustenance, and the very definitions of 'I.'"[37] He goes on to share that this interpretation is aligned with a certain kind of subversion: "My subversion of this focal point is followed through the manipulation of time, space, and linearity creating a counterbalance between illusion and reality."[38] But how does reordering—or smashing—this "I" extend or limit the parameters of being-with? This piece works in the tradition of conceptual artist Bruce Nauman's 1994 *Poke in the Eye/Nose/Ear 3/8/94 Edit*, an hour-long video consisting of slow-motion footage of the artist poking himself in each orifice.[39] While Nauman slows down time and Rivera animates it, both contribute to durational aesthetics and present us with a screen made flesh. I turn to Nauman here as a way to evince the aesthetic tradition in which Rivera was steeped. In Nauman's case, however, the spectator is never worried about his corporeal wholeness, whereas Rivera's bodily integrity is always already tenuous, reminding one of how waiting is about the performance of both aesthetics and politics in the space of racialization and sexualization.

In my interpretive sketch, following the artist's visual and written lead, Rivera challenges space's often restrictive takeover of time. The artist manipulates time as a way to address the limited space allotted for Brown bodies in everyday places and locations of art. I want to believe that Rivera is our aesthetic schema for Rican, Brown, and queer life, and in this way, he demonstrates how to temporalize Ricanness, queerness, and Latinx studies more generally, so that spatial concerns aren't the primary frameworks for all conscious events in Latinidad. A purely spatial analysis dominated by borders and nationalism delimits the importance of traversing epistemology and durational aesthetics. Time gives us space in these linked traditions, and refuses heteronormative chronophobia by returning us to the abstracted body. Consideration of the temporal (as we see in Rivera's attention to string theory, for example) restages a conversation between Euro-American conceptualism, colonial life, and Brown aesthetics. This attention to temporality is also evident in Rivera's turn to abstraction as a transgressive force. While it appears that the right to abstract and be abstracted is a purely majoritarian concern, queers and people of color have always used these aesthetic tools as conscious political endeavors.

Rivera's clever use of abstraction is seen in his appropriation of the Cartesian split. This split, an antecedent to philosophical constructions of embodiment, informs the artist's exploration of the boundaries between the mind and body. Rivera destabilizes the (in)famous phrase by the "father" of modern philosophy: "I think, therefore I am." In this egocentric claim, pertaining only to the mind thinking it, Descartes imagines himself as a singular thinker without a body; any bidirectionality between the two is nullified by the fact that *he* alone thinks—and, well, the body cannot, for the body may not even exist. Nonetheless, his reliance on "this one firm and immovable point," as he puts it in his meditation on doubt, is for him a way to uncover the existence of God. But in playing God, Descartes disappears the body, superimposed by a thinking mind.[40] It is Rivera himself who provides an antidote to this philosophical paradigm of the erasure of the body when he claims to reinterpret "the very definition of 'I'" and bring to light "the crisis of identity, the tension between my inner and physical self."[41] While Rivera is disembodied throughout his videos, he desperately tries to smash through the first person, asking the spectator to retrace the specter of his queer Rican body—there, but visually not there. There's an intimate bodily interaction happening in Rivera's work as he engages the body and mind, and disrupts such a split by trusting the spectator to also hand over their body, feel their body in a space mediated by a screen and his prospective death. Alas, Descartes's aesthetics of mediated ontologies is only a singular affair—there's no room for the relational moment between bodies. For Rivera, his absent Brown body is his response to the call for a transparent Rican subject, imparting to us an abstracted way of visualizing constructions of race, gender, and sexuality.

To consider another take on this Cartesian and iconic phrase, we might note Judith Butler's essay "How Can I Deny That These Hands and This Body Are Mine?"[42] This is a phrase directly dislocated from the "hands" of Descartes, and so Butler imagines the performativity enclosed in this phrase—a discrete hand wrote that phrase, a disjunct body enabled a hand to compose a speech act. Butler attempts to discursively access the body's hand that creates an incorporeal claim, pushing the limits of time and space in a way that is thoroughly queer and nonlinear. In Rivera's case, his hands become part of the suspended spectator's body, albeit frenetically; in elongated moments they comprise the moving nexus of queer, Rican, and Brown temporality and the expanse of his missing, but "visible" body, "extended to a certain psychological manipulation of the viewer."[43] In such a claim, I am also suggesting that "these hands and this body" are equally mine, jointly ours.

Corporeal-Temporal Affections: In Recognition and Absence

Adjoined to this context of theatrical ephemera that frames the entire corpus of Rivera's work is the fragmentation of his on-screen body, which produces a sense of disembodiment that, in turn, compels one to redeem one's own body. Tempered but determined, the spectator plays artist by fantasizing various extensions of Rivera's truncated videos: we imagine the denouement, create the climax, and stage our own scenes of catharsis, since his experimental video pieces offer none of these formal elements. This leads one to wonder about the sensual properties of our physical consciousness: while our somatic responses and feelings are mimetic, they are also very much our own; and so, in this encounter with the other, projection and transference necessarily appear. Barthes would say that "wherever there is waiting there is transference" and that he "depend[s] on a presence which is shared and requires time to be bestowed" because "to make someone wait" is "the constant prerogative of all power."[44] There is profound administrative violence in forcing one to wait, yet enduring the uncertainty of waiting is also a sign of love.

There are stages of love evinced in the production of aesthetics: Rivera's affair with his own art is one such affection, one eventually adjoined to the spectator through his labor; this love is then emotionally consumed and harbored by the viewer as they watch his videos in order to return the tenderness, and confirm such entanglement. In this ritualistic repertoire of love, the question of violence and possible death meets the event of also being alive, being able to be enough to love. This commitment, as Barthes suggests in A Lover's Discourse: Fragments, is an event sometimes irresponsible, not always benevolent, but invariably inevitable and worthy. Barthes's analysis of the term love, in the vignette "I-love-you (je-t'-aime)," therefore, is both an affective and a semiotic one. He states, "The word (the word-as-sentence) has a meaning only at the moment" it is spoken—a speech act that is formulaic, full, and sometimes unabiding. Barthes entertains this inevitable and "metalinguistic" I-love-you by responding to it with "mundane answers."[45] For example, we see a similar move in his section on waiting (attente): scenes that may or may not actually happen, but certainly do exist in language—acts that contain a sort of choose-your-own-adventure quality to them.[46]

In this discourse on love, Barthes extends a tableau of obsession, affection, mourning, and, in terrifying honesty, an object of love that exists only in discourse. This absent yet present object is a construction of the one who waits and, in waiting, loves. Barthes's other is a consequence of fabricated scenes, torturous adventures, and temporal anxiety in which waiting is transference, subjection, and projection; recognition—that thing Barthes wants so badly—becomes the fulfillment of the senses in the circuit between performer and audience. For Barthes, this scene of unrequited love unfurls through the creation of a play that has two endings. The first option ends in grief—the lover never appears, or as Barthes states, "the other is as if dead."[47] In the second option, on the other hand, the lover arrives, but it is the time of the lover's arrival that marks the performativity of his existence. Barthes states, "If the other arrives in Act I, the greeting is calm; if the other arrives in Act II, there is a 'scene'; if in Act II, there is recognition, the action of grace."[48] I refer to this section in Barthes because when I think of the word "love" and its scenic entanglements in connection to aesthetics, at least in my reaction to and reception of it, I always want to say "I love you" to the object, artist, subject, experience—all intricately intertwined on screen, onstage, or in the everyday. It's a Bergsonian temporal affection, one that takes time to feel and utter, even if the answer to such a phrase is an internal abeyance located in the dislocations of language itself.

This is all to say that I will wait with and for Rivera because *I-love-him* and the art that reveals both him and itself to us. Put another way, this process of love is perpetually framed by stealing sideways glances at art, the artist, and then directing such intense observation and affection inwardly and back out again in the name of closeness and aesthetic sense. Perhaps it's like an aesthetic ménage à trois begun at the moment Rivera presses record on his camera. The French phrase *la petite mort* elegantly captures this erotic/death relation: in eros as in death, a larger unconsciousness swallows the individual. And, such administration is the project of art: "The object of art is to put to sleep the active or rather resistant powers of our personality, and thus to bring us into a state of perfect responsiveness, in which we realize the idea that is suggested to us and sympathize with the feeling that is expressed."[49] These feelings provoked by Rivera lead the viewer into the projection of the future that eventually returns them to Barthes's lamentation on waiting, Heidegger's obsession with temporality, and Bergson's promising *durée*. Through this eternal return, Rivera's artwork sets the stage for our boundless reengagement with Ricanness.

In an especially dramatic example of such engagement, I'd like to return to Rivera's *Bash*, which translates Heideggerian phenomenology into Rican aesthetics. Let us recall that *Bash* presents one with more than thirty frames per second of repeated cruelty: Rivera's lips curl under his smashed nose, and his eyes open and close in a space of negativity and corporeal tightness. These hits, like a drum, keep time and measure the absent-but-present narrative of the anticlimactic object. A bodiless reservoir of intensity crashes against the screen: this is Rivera quickly moving backward and forward within each frame, unable to transgress the border between spectator and artist. Although unyielding and permanent, this border does not deter Rivera from wanting to break free, to be both against the screen and closer to the viewer. For this queer and Rican subject, such a desire resembles that existential freedom that keeps one seconds away from death and minutes into life. My contention, here, is not that only those queer, Rican, Brown subjects struggle to break free or wait in anxious anticipation, but that under the colonization of time, every hit against the glass is a step closer to the anticolonial for these sexualized and racialized citizen-subjects. One can imagine Rivera's head as a failing postcolonial one: where is his anticonquest narrative? To invoke Spivak here, does this subaltern subject speak, or is Rivera's missing body the ultimate sign of staged muteness? Throughout these videos, Rivera refuses to utter a word; a head that remains freighted with symbolic weight and makes noise only with heavy breath. He lends us sound instead of conventional language, a practice cultivated by oppressed and colonial subjects in the face of the regimented discourse of social and economic power.

By dramatizing these symbolic confrontations, Rivera prepares a way out of this miasma. He uses the editing process repeatedly to time the affective-sensory schema; our "authentic" emotional experience is contoured by his representation of "linear" affectivity. He demonstrates how to feel and when to shut off emotional excess by queering the straight line and splicing through the parameters of horizontality. But when will the last blow to his head take him out? Without definitive end, he offers one timelessness (an expressive sign of Ricanness) and a place to wait interminably. In this limited space of injury and confrontation, the viewer *lives* Ricanness. Just as Barthes's other lives in discourse and the feelings he accords his amorous subject, Rivera's head offers one a dialogic encounter framed by endurance that holds the potential for real duration. It is through the experimental that Rivera links politics and aesthetics and bestows upon the viewer an alternative way to confront and map out their own complicated subjectivity.

Futural Affectations in Those Ephemeral Tears

Waiting with Rivera is about confronting one's own disgust, nausea, pain, angst, desire, love, and pleasure. These modes of waiting suggest that Ricanness is not something that can be completed or avowed, as Rivera's work is both anticathartic and antinarrative. At the same time, such waiting resists the subjectivating discourse of Brownness as a "dead" subjectivity,[50] one positioned by Viego when addressing the temporal dimensions of Brownness in its immediate proximity to Latinidad: "*Latino* as a term is resignifying temporality, not just race and ethnicity; it should affect how we will tell the time and the history of the Americas in the future."[51] Brownness, here, is the enactment of waiting; it is both a project and a projection, ongoing and existing beyond taxonomies of race and ethnicity. In Viego's understanding, as in my own, these "dead subjects" proliferate against their given ontological validity and alongside their own facticity. Rivera's videos illuminate this idea by interrupting the spectator at the intersection of retrospection and prospection, extending his head to our bodies for the potential of the *futural*, against our own conjoined deadness. This shared corporeality operates in the time of experimental aesthetics and performs the politics of Ricanness in the form of a shared sensorial waiting. Beautifully and painfully, Rivera probes us to see ourselves through the eyes of the other via the sonic interplay of dissonance and resonance. Confronting the self through someone else's eyes initiates an uncoordinated vulnerability sprung from the limbs of Rivera's involuntary muscle movements and unconscious remembrances. In these recollections of discomfort, the parameters of endurance sustain us in Rivera's deferred ending. As Rican subjects, then, we learn to wait-on one another in a space of consensual servitude and projective identification, which is to say a process of identification deferred or displaced onto the *futural*.

Rivera directs our waiting even as the clock stops, lending us a sample of eternity—one miniature window with a view toward past, present, and future, or Heidegger's "ecstatic"—the necessary conjunction of past and present with the *futural* holding the utmost promise.[52] "This ecstasy makes it possible for *Da-sein* to be able to take over resolutely the being that it already is" and the conditions of possibility of what it might become.[53] Let us recall that time's greatest expanse is realized in Heidegger's assessment of death as the authentic potential of existence. Pausing in our shared waiting, we learn how to organize Rivera's video frames in order to access finitude. For one, the spectator waits for Rivera's own death by auto-affliction. Two, that same spectator recalls the illusory nature of immortality sparked by the acceptance of mortality— which Heidegger claims is the ultimate test of living an authentic life. Three, Rivera's disembodiment invites the viewer to join his "body" via the intended guarantee that perception will generate wholeness. Rivera labors against the viewer's emotional and sensorial freedom in his deliberate engagement with *arte de sufrimiento*, calling one to consider one's own existential and phenomenological condition in a mediatized colonial world. As the spectator frowns in disgust, nervously laughs from displeasure, or shakes from distaste, they engage with the limits of freedom as witness of Rivera's art practice. And the artist is the resistant object of these violent and sad acts; he exercises complete authorial control over the space of the video image, while marking the relative vulnerability of being queer and Rican in a hostile, colonial world. His performance of Ricanness generates a momentary sense of wholeness, even if fleeting, shortly staged, fragmented, and unruly.

This ephemeral quality of the existential condition is what impels Rivera's *Goodbye Piece*. In this video, Rivera delivers a gentler and less conventionally masculine affectivity, which might be read as a more tempered sort of waiting. His eyes are shut, his cheeks distended, pushing up against the crevices of his eyelids. Rivera's smile lines, those parenthetical markers of feeling, surround his mouth, and the viewer remembers what crying looks like. His halfway-open mouth implicates our ears, and spectators are called into the phenomenology of the cry. Working from a particular performance tradition of the 1970s, this piece is reminiscent of the European conceptual performance and video artist Jas Ban Ader and his piece *I'm Too Sad to Tell You* (1971). In this piece, Ader silently cries with indirect purpose, leaving us waiting and wanting for a revelation that will never arrive: he is too sad to share his pain. Or as Jennifer Doyle asserts in her own meditation on the phenomenology of the cry, or the "strange theatricality of tears," in *Hold It Against Me: Difficulty and Emotion in Contemporary Art*, "The title reminds us, we do not know why Ader is crying; his sadness is cited as the very thing in the way of explanation, and so it registers as expression itself."[54] Although unaware of the source of these tears, we remain implicated in this emotive composition, feeling deeply with the artist. Doyle says that "how we read emotion, and how emotion circulates, depends very much on the location and identity of the bodies shedding the tears."[55] In like but dissimilar fashion, Rivera emotionally labors against the grain of machismo, showing how Ricanness can be a sobbing act of resistance in exercises of racialized masculinity, or that face-to-asphalt that Colo renders in contempt of brute force.

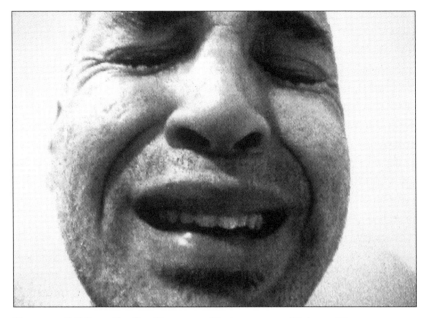

Figure 4.4. Still from *Goodbye Piece*, 2002. Photo courtesy of Rebecca Rivera.

Similarly but uniquely, artist Nao Bustamante's stunning piece of histrionic crying, entitled *Neapolitan*, speaks particularly to the affective performativity of queer Latina femininity (2003). In her video installation, she sits intimately with the film *Fresa y chocolate* and cries profusely over a love scene. Repeatedly watching a video that is already on a loop highlights the social and political nuances embedded in a spectatorial embrace of depression. Muñoz claims, "Repetition is the piece's most obvious depressive quality. It describes the ways in which subjects occupy and dwell within the depressive position."[56] For Muñoz, the aesthetic details of the piece—lighting, weeping, etc.—contribute to "the artist's comments of the complicated choreography of introjection and projection."[57] But waiting in Bustamante's Brown and queer embrace is more than a mimicry of her depressive position; transference surpasses the screen in an act of repetition with the slightest difference. Here, Brownness and "queerness become the site of emotional breakdown and the activation of the melodrama" in Bustamante's piece.[58] And Bustamante and Rivera become conduits for Brown existence in spaces often closed off to minoritarian subjects.

Adding to the emerging discourse of what I call Brown existentialism, Ann Cvetkovich, like Muñoz, views Bustamante's depressive embodiment as "what it feels like for people of color to live in the context of racism."[59] She adds that an action like crying "is a necessary method in order to capture affective experiences that aren't always publicly visible, especially to white observers."[60] Let us recall that Fanon ends his essay "The Fact of Blackness" by saying, "I wanted to rise, but the disemboweled silence fell back upon me, its wings paralyzed. Without responsibility, straddling Nothingness and Infinity, I began to weep."[61] On Fanon, Nelson Maldonado-Torres, in an insight that recalls Lebrón, claims that the cry is "a revelation of someone who has been forgotten or wronged," or that resounding exhale that accompanies the failure and collapse of self.[62] It is also, for Maldonado-Torres, "a call for the Other," a hailing also made audible by Barthes's extended anticipation for something, someone unreal, and yet "real" in any space of waiting.[63] In Rivera's case, the spectator responds to the intensity of his videos and experiences a unique temporal space determined by video aesthetics and their own response to Rivera's self-inflicted violence. The spectator waits *with* Rivera, *within* the aesthetic dimension, and *for* the phenomenology of the cry to mark its moment in resolution.

For the Love of Waiting

In El Museo del Barrio's *The (S) Files* (2002) exhibition catalogue, Rivera's video stills from *Goodbye Piece* and *String Piece* are introduced with an existential passage (in both English and Spanish) from Fyodor Dostoyevsky's *Notes from the Underground*. Considering Rivera's philosophical preoccupations, I'd like to reproduce the passage, signaling its temporal performativity:

> I will explain; the enjoyment was just from the too intense consciousness of one's own degradation; it was from feeling oneself that one had reached the last barrier, that it was horrible, but that it could not be otherwise; that there was no escape for you; that you never could become a different man; that even if time and faith were still left you to change into something different you would most likely not wish to change; or if you did wish to, even then you would do nothing; because perhaps in reality there was nothing for you to change into.[64]

Dostoyevsky's words paired with Rivera's stills outline the artist's Brown-Rican existentialist intention. In Dostoyevsky's description we learn to accept some of the predetermined components of life; even if we desire to transform, there is no guarantee that we will. By turning to Dostoyevsky, Rivera reveals his commitment to the existentialist tradition, imparting new ways to transcribe a sense of being in the world as a Brown man. Transformation of the self remains a ubiquitous cultural and psychological holy grail, yet here one witnesses Rivera channeling one of the most eminent authors in the Western canon to undermine the unconscious devotion to "change" as an end in itself. As a result, genuine acceptance of oneself paves the way for a type of metamorphosis that might actually deliver freedom—even if only on screen, or in a catalogue. In like manner, Rivera's stills visually signal a subject morphing into multiple abstract versions of his interior self. Refusing to speak in the first person, the artist instead turns to Dostoyevsky's words to explain his own work. For Rivera, word and image are linked by a relational signifying chain—denying his personal "I," he compels us through the author's "I" to join our bodies to his bodiless form. In such a pursuit, we are left with Dostoyevsky's hopeless words and two images: one in which the artist contorts his face mid-wail (*Goodbye Piece*), another in which he performs a bloodless self-mutilation by wrapping string repeatedly around his head, his swollen skin rising between the lines (*String Piece*). Both word and image, while communicating pain, also lay open the possibility of connection. Maybe there is "nothing for [us] to change into," but there is a relation for us to *enter* into with the artist—one in which the screen metaphorically shatters and our bodies conjoin.

While Dostoyevsky is resigned to his fate, Nietzsche and Rivera provide the counterpoint to such passivity. In a manifestation of Nietzsche's *amor fati* (literally, love of one's fate), Rivera's videos assert the ultimate embrace—albeit violent and saturated with angst—of what it means to be Brown, Rican, and queer.[65] In *On the Genealogy of Morals*, Nietzsche proclaims, "My formula for greatness in a human being is amor fati: that one wants nothing to be different, not forward, not backward, not in all eternity. Not merely bear what is necessary, still less conceal it—all idealism is mendaciousness in the face of what is necessary—but love it."[66] Nietzsche here is exhorting us to love our lives, not in spite of but because of their painful complexities. Rivera's text, in spite of itself, recognizes the lure of the impossible; the viewer is seduced by the imagined possibility of transformation even though there is little, as Dostoyevsky explains, for us "to change into." But it is Rivera who deliberately engages those philosophical questions often barred for people of color—either because existentialism and phenomenology are types of thinking already "owned," or because they constitute an intellectual luxury far removed from everyday minoritarian struggles. In creating this Brown existentialism, Rivera refashions the Rican self into the domain of both philosophy and fate.

Taking ownership of one's fate both challenges conventional notions of minoritarian life and offers an alternative modality to being, being-with, and waiting-with that allows for different ways to conceptualize Rican subjectivity in conversation with philosophy. This is what it means to wait-with and wait-on Ricanness, even if one must press against transparency and the anticipation of death, where death marks not only the end of the self but the anticipation of the dissolution of race tout court. Another way of expressing the above is by reiterating Rivera's representation of time paired with the spectator's perception of time: this produces an alternative vision of the incomplete Rican subject as a relational entity. The spectator's ability to perceive the world in different meters of nonlinear time allows them to access the full complexity of subjectivity through enduring time itself.

The interplay between different ways of "being-with" one another is neatly sealed in Rivera's *Breath Piece*. In the span of twenty-three seconds, the artist psychologically prepares himself to stop breathing momentarily, then physically withholds his breath against time for the viewer. Rivera exaggerates the process of respiration, taking in an extensive gulp of air at six seconds to vigorously expel it from his lungs at twenty-two seconds. In between the space of the first five seconds before he takes in the exuberant breath and that last second of releasing it all, we wait with the artist. We wait with and for him, against our own state of negation, because holding in air is both primordial and an ephemeral renunciation of life. Rivera enacts both, inviting us to play a part in his existential, masochistic, and sadistic physical/psychological experience.

It's one of the few videos in the collection that showcases the color of his natural flesh. His brown and breathless face intrudes the frame, resembling a recently blown-up balloon in a close-up shot that challenges

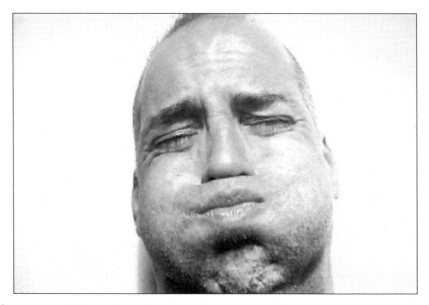

Figure 4.5. Still from *Breath Piece*, 2002. Photo courtesy of Rebecca Rivera.

our own visceral desires and rules of voyeuristic engagement. While the video is brief, the sensation of holding in air extends into the domain of finality, turning compression into conspiration in a conjoined space of air. Breathing, even if mediatized and mediated, is a relational adventure; we conspire to respire together.

It's crucial to specify that in his performance, Rivera splices the video frames, creating cuts and overlaps between visual segments. In doing so, the artist makes it appear as if he has edited a longer effort to hold his breath into a shorter expression of endurance. This, however, does not erase the sensation of claustrophobia, or the emotional tension embedded in running out of oxygen. As the piece progresses, his head and neck move at an increasingly frantic pace, appearing to grow in size and causing the quotidian ritual of breathing to appear larger than life itself. And on the other side of the screen, we listen to the inhalation filling his lungs: Rivera's dynamic face leading us to conspire—or is it respire?—against the postcolonial grain in our shared unwantedness. The way in which Rivera holds his breath and moves his head/neck rapidly simultaneously stops and speeds up time, and doubly disrupts the viewer's sense of temporality.

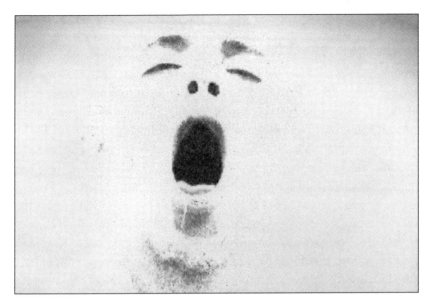

Figure 4.6. Still from *Reflex*, 2002. Photo courtesy of Rebecca Rivera.

Endurance takes on many forms, faces, and sounds in the artist's body of work. For example, in Rivera's *Reflex*, vomiting reveals the full sensorial endurance practice that the subject must undergo to reach completion: first there is nausea, an uncomfortable psychical condition and experience; then, retching or dry heaving, spasmodic respiratory movements; and last, emesis or vomition. In this video, Rivera is almost completely washed out, his Ricanness even more self-erased in this video than in the others, his face glowing with bright white light. But as we have seen in previous chapters, even in the space of overexposure, such glimmers of light are deliberate political openings, visual pathways into the futural. In contrast to the blinding glow, his open, abysmal, and dark mouth takes center stage as Rivera repeatedly places his fingers down his throat and gags. Between the deafening and percussive heaving, we hear Rivera catching his breath before and after each time his fist enters his mouth; a melodic gasp invaginating the space between utmost abjection and pleasure, the sound is a cut—a break in time, in the eternal loop. Such a sound ruptures space and enables Ricanness to whisper in the sonic enterprise of hetero-whiteness.

This eternal loop is also erotic: there's something to be said about an *aesthetics of mediated fellatio* in which giving head is not just about going in and pulling out, but a gagging for pleasure—a desirable and acutely anticipated sound. Rivera's hand, like that featherless cock in one's mouth, is a persistent act of endurance working the throat to finally expire from pleasure and psychological incapability. There's an art to fellatio—a call and response that requires a resilient and abiding opening even in the act of auto-fellatio. Vicariously experiencing this rhythmic sensation, the spectator undergoes the accentuated respiration in the interstices between masochistic pain and ecstatic elation. The orality and aurality of Rivera's action brings a symmetry of time and space, as the repetition heralds the reliable reproduction of a domesticated scene, thus granting both the artist and viewer a portal to visceral and visual desire.

Throughout this sonic reciprocity the viewer waits for vomit, but instead Rivera just retches. Frustrated in our anticipation of the moment of possible expulsion, Rivera stops at forty-one seconds, leaving one visually vomitless, and suspended in the sound of an overworked mouth and larynx wheezing repeatedly amid overexposure. We wait for the unwanted, vile material to land on our laps, but Rivera leaves us at empty. The potential expulsion, I suggest, makes touch between the colonized possible, for in this wretched way we feel ourselves simultaneously existing. The vile meets the vital in the following state of remembrance: every finger down his throat, every gag, all those heaving sounds prefigure the redemptive quality in vomiting—the subject will return its body to its natural state; an existential resolution meets a physiological conclusion. Equilibrium always follows the abject, even if they violently resist the bodily baseline.

Appearing to be merely a vessel for morose agitation here, Rivera instead loops us back to our inner vitalism.[67] Such vitality is immanently bound to both erotic euphoria and degraded abasement, because "the sexual" is a "tangled enactment of psychic encounters that promise ecstasy and abjection."[68] In Rivera's video, the haptic joins an unpleasant gagging sound: both intimately tied sensorially. Even in the face of filth, the spectator touches the raw viscerality of Rican existence and, in effect, is equally touched by it. Expulsion, then, becomes just another reminder of the elusive nature of immortality in a heteronormative, colonial world. And self-induced vomiting, in this case and point, produces an intersubjectivity within the self, enacting the boundary between self and not-self, and the internal conflicts and resolutions between queerness, Ricanness, and Brownness as embraced by Rivera.

Like crying, banging, punching, or holding one's breath, vomiting redirects the viewer to the path of the not-yet-here, a version of a *futural* paved in Brown, and far beyond a linear idea of Ricanness. Through the "intensity," "darkness," and "humor" of his self-presentation, Rivera's work interrogates the taken-for-grantedness of Rican, Brown, and queer lifeworlds. In doing so, his art provides a way forward for other Rican subjects to disrupt and upend the dominant-dominated relationship between the oppressor and the colonial subject, filling space and time that was erstwhile incomplete. In yet another loop, another act of waiting and enduring through time, Rivera's existential art calls upon both finitude and infinity in pursuit of the horizon. For this artist, endurance is not about giving up, but about keeping on—even with the ambitious task of sustaining the experimental within postcolonial promises. All of this, every ounce of Rivera's darkness and emotional intensity, is interwoven into a "life worth saving" both in spirit and on the page.

Epilogue

A Few More Scenes on the Unwanted, or a Pause for the Rican Future

I find myself suddenly in the world and I recognize that I have one right alone: That of demanding human behavior from the other. One duty alone: That of not renouncing my freedom through my choices.
—Frantz Fanon, *Black Skin, White Masks*

Sadness merges with the earth.
The fruit is born with love and sorrow.
That's why the child when he cries, laughs,
and man when he suffers, he dreams.
Suffering is oil of the earth:
set to the image of a beautiful pathway.
—Dolores "Lolita" Lebrón Sotomayor, "La Crisis"

The colonial history of Ricanness ontologically forbids conclusion. Always working against linear time, Ricanness's looping nature suggests that both endings and beginnings are similar entities in continuous conversation: an ending, in this case, is often an opening across an impasse. In the present state of a slow and ongoing Rican death, this temporal loop is profoundly felt in the everyday acts of Rican existence post–Hurricane Maria, compelling one to ask: How (de)colonial is the colonial? And what's the ideological time behind this critical analysis?

The indexical power of the narrative is figured to establish closure, a temporal move to secure resolution. Under colonialism, however, this gesture toward completion is impossible, an act forgone the moment it begins.

Throughout *Ricanness*, then, I have unearthed promising openings within the impasses of negation, rather than negligently valorizing abjection, failure, and violence as the only lenses through which to read for the oppressed subject. Aware that the fallacy of "subject wholeness" would loom over this incomplete project, through the aesthetic I discovered apertures in the tight place of foreclosure. That is to say that I found new holes within this construction of a Rican completion and began to fill them, empty them out again, and rebuild against their familiar narrative structures. But, in the face of the chronic slow death of Ricanness, why purchase theories in which pain, violence, and suffering communicate a significant understanding of humanity? Or, how do we critically locate the value in negation when life's tempo is set to terror?

Interested in how disorder, revulsion, incompletion, and violence spur the subject into forward action, I disclose what moves the Rican subject, accessing a form of perceived completion through endurance, sometimes at the expense of death. *Ricanness* has imparted such a politic through the aesthetic as intervention, or at least has illustrated what happens when the social and psychic meet within the space of performance. In shifting perspectives, I have laid out how working through incompletion—even in the space of unrealized revolution—shifts us beyond dread and despair, reorienting subjects often lost in history. In other words, a move against failure, negation, and abjection will not replace the beastly tendencies of oppression; in fact, this maneuver makes certain subjects more vulnerable and susceptible to death. Recognizing oneself in complicated ways materializes through an "image of a beautiful pathway," as Lebrón explains, in which suffering sustains the earth we stand on. Or, endurance is set to the pulse of dreaming and "demanding human behavior from the other." If one endures these emotional states, then one can also imagine a more "beautiful" tomorrow, traveling a prosperous path into the *futural*.

How does this ideological vision of endurance remain germane amid the continual death of Ricans? This "slow death" is not something new; it was always already part of existence for the colonial subject, born somewhat already deadened by lack of sovereignty and resources. To try and understand this question I'll rehearse another relentless death scene again in a broad pause for the Rican future.

On September 20, 2017, Hurricane Maria ravaged Puerto Rico. The Category 5 hurricane left most of the archipelago without power or water and forced the residents to deal with colossal flooding. Homes and families were destroyed, and Ricans were urgently dispossessed.[1] As they were unable to leave the island immediately or receive the necessary emergent aid under Trump's authority, this slow death accumulated. For nearly a year after the event, the US government maintained and documented only sixty-four total deaths, but this number is now estimated to be *forty-six* times higher—close to three thousand.[2] While the colonizer turns a blind eye, the living burn their dead, deal with disease and contamination, and die daily. This ongoing death, coupled with the growing debt crisis of the island now exceeding seventy-four billion dollars,[3] has invigorated colonial practice, unmasking how it is still on active loop. In this case, the language of debt reveals the imperial implications of this silent death. Ultimately, the language of debt is as terrorizing as the end of life—both recycled from colonialism to permeate a *non-future* for Ricanness under the neoliberal enterprise.

Let us pause again for the Rican future to clarify what we mean in this deliberate engagement with crisis, debt, and death in the current state of emergency. I understand that my attention to the death embedded in Hurricane Maria may appear insensitive, but my intention stems from a desire to continue dreaming within the call of endless finality. Like Fanon and Lebrón, I command the condition of the human in my own resilience, never "renouncing my freedom through my choices" by living the decision to endure, demand, and dream. In writing this book under the specter of Maria, I have constantly addressed my own political and cultural impotence. As I write from a place of privilege and stasis in this *here* and *now*, lives are lost, families torn to pieces, and a restoration of colonial law enacted. While I am part of this lineage of Rican unwantedness, this sense manifests differently for various enduring subjects. It's harrowing to write about this disaster precisely because of its temporal location: it's occurring in the present continuous, and the emotive experience is an everlasting quotidian violence—one we have seen differentiated in repetition, but always looping.

Chronological, linear, and historical time depend upon the emergency of the here and now to trap us within this ominous present; in this way, the manipulation of emergent time prevents us from landing in the future, and dreaming lifeworlds beyond ultimate despair. Without this option of time travel, we remain transfixed by a constant and immediate dread, one that precludes us from processing existence itself, and locks us tightly into the pessimistic-optimistic dialectic. Although we are terrorized by a steady state of emergency, the aesthetic helps us slow down and *do* our time in life differently, within varying velocities. Frequently when we recycle painful events we create the opening through which to imagine a superior future—one not impervious to suffering, but pushing against its stagnant saturation.[4] A crisis is not meant to be everlasting—its *foreverness* exists within the transformation of the subject, a nation, and/or an onto-ideological cause. That is to say that I hope this pause redirects our temporality and docks us in a *futural* formed by our own cycles of freedom. For Ricanness is not an insular construction; it extends outward, and as a theorization may be used to understand other sites under siege. Ricanness affords us a relational way to imagine, dream, and construct alternate forms of living under colonialism, across bodies of water.

ADÁL's photographs of Ricans drowning in debt, aesthetic acts foreshadowing Maria, call attention to the predetermination of events: the aftermath clearly exposes everyday abuse within colonial life. Or there's nothing like a "natural" disaster—and the world's lack of response—to remind us just how much the future doesn't want us in it. Certainly uncanny, ADÁL's visual acts of endurance are a manifestation of pain, suffering, holding one's breath to be able to exhale again in spaces of both growing engulfment and stasis.

If Ricanness is also an expression of suffering—in both lyric and body—as Lebrón confirms in her poem "La Crisis," then this economy of atonement is a method of endurance used to stop mechanical time. If the body endures *into* negation as a response to colonial rule, then time proper modifies the specificity of sacrificial time. What remains sacred, in this here and now, is our reconceptualization of endurance as an exercise in not giving up, but in keeping on, in finding the light.[5] In an act of eternal recurrence, Lebrón's poem, written while doing her own time in prison, delineates the distinction between her gift of death in 1954 and what one owes in the space of another temporal debt. If in one case Lebrón offers something "freely," what does it mean to owe everything against one's constant will, especially after an "unnatural disaster"? A possible answer to this question lives in a line of her poem that manifests the synchronous and productive interplay between these dialectical feelings: "That's why the child when he cries, laughs, and man when he suffers, he dreams." Or, the ability to dream, to be curious, to suffer with desire, belongs to the unwanted, even—perhaps especially—under colonialism. The dreams of the unwanted are always the most potent, urgent. They live in the future of the future, looking back to exit finitude. Or, as Fanon reminds himself (and us), "the real *leap* [of faith] consists in introducing invention into existence."[6]

Fanon, Lebrón, and the cultural workers of this book—ADÁL, Papo Colo, Pedro Pietri, and Ryan Rivera—reimagine a future beyond a looping colonial obligation. If when we suffer we also dream, then *Ricanness* is proof that we are "part of Being to the degree that" we move "beyond it," thinking worlds outside of linearly conceived planes.[7] And if "suffering is oil of the earth," then it is also an act of dreaming, which we must embrace in this global economy that perpetually clocks in our dreams, and clocks out our lives.

ACKNOWLEDGMENTS

This book has been a collective and community effort, reconceptualized under a looming specter of death. There have been many brilliant thinkers who have helped shape the following pages. I am eternally grateful for great minds and even bigger spirits.

I am indebted to many compelling scholars who helped turn an idea into a book: three are still here shaping this world—Karen Shimakawa, André Lepecki, and Licia Fiol-Matta—and two are now creating worlds elsewhere—José Esteban Muñoz and Randy Martin. Their lasting breaths are aesthetic gems, revealing, too, the material limits of existence. Luckily for me, the dead are always living. José, your visionary spirit is always an incredible presence, guiding me through all those details filled with meaning, rigor, and love.

For my students, my mentees, you make this profession worth every obstacle. You are my most prized interlocutors and I thank you for pushing me to think harder, to love greater. From JHS 45 and NYU, to Pratt and Wesleyan, to the University of Illinois—I'll keep listening for you wherever I end up. The following list is certainly incomplete, but these students at Illinois have shaped the ideas of this project during the last six years: Durell, Michelle S., Ethan M., Evan D., Amy H., Eric P., John M., Mark, Xuxa R., Brenda, Mike, Angelica, Flor, Mayra, Javi, Carlos, Mateo, Jess, Melody, Adonis, Peter, Brian, Gaby, Helena, Sarah, Meghan, Chris W., Adrianna, Andrea, Gustavo, Moises, Cindi, Victoria, Jema, Monica, Gabyliz, Iris, Letty, Chloe, Laura, Hilary, Bea, Catalina, Valeria, Jayel, Melissa, Stefany. And to all of the students in Theories and Methods in LLS and Latinx Performance, thank you for pushing me to relearn teaching. Thank you, Dan Sickles and Sam Dash, for making teaching lessons into scores for friendship. Ten years after we first crossed paths at NYU, you continue to educate me about life, love, and art. Mateo Hurtado and Angelica Sánchez, you're the lights that never go out, and

I'm privileged to call you collaborators and friends. Brenda Garcia, you have provided valuable research support and friendship.

This project was assisted through various forms of internal institutional support. Scholars at Illinois have been staunch supporters of my work. As a recipient of an IPRH Fellowship, I was granted time off from teaching and the honor of workshopping my ideas. A special thank-you to the College Campus Research Board for a Humanities Release Time Award for another semester off and research funding. The Unit for Criticism and Interpretive Theory, under the guidance of the wonderful Susan Koshy, has been instrumental in helping me complete this project. I served as the Unit's Junior Fellow from 2016 to 2018, and during this time Susan organized and led a transformative manuscript workshop, inviting my in-house scholar-mentors Lisa Marie Cacho and Siobhan Somerville, and outside readers Jennifer Doyle and Ramon Rivera-Servera. All scholars provided invaluable insights, pushing this book forward.

I am lucky to be in two encouraging departments. Thank you Department of English, for supporting my ideas, particularly JB Capino, Irvin, Justine, Trish, Susan, Siobhan, Chris Freeburg, Andrea Stevens, Vicki Mahaffey, Derrick Spires, Bob Parker, Gordon Hutner, and Jodi Byrd. My colleagues in the Department of Latina/Latino Studies have given me the space and time to write, think, and explore. Thank you Lisa Marie Cacho, Jonathan Xavier Inda, Julie Dowling, Isabel Molina-Guzmán, David Coyoca, Edna Viruell-Fuentes, Rolando Romero, Gilberto Rosas, Natalie Lira, and to those who have gone on to other institutions, such as Ricky Rodriguez. Ricky, thank you for your incredible mentorship and long-standing support of this project. I am also grateful to be an affiliate faculty member with fantastic colleagues in Latin American and Caribbean Studies; Comparative and World Literature; the Unit for Criticism and Interpretive Theory; and Holocaust, Genocide, and Memory Studies.

To my Illinois writing buddies Rana Hogarth, Samir Meghelli, and at some points Irvin Hunt and Toby Beauchamp, thank you for sharing ideas, resources, and for all of the laughter. To the Illinois Chancellor's postdoc crew—Isa, Samir, Rana, Chris, Joyce—we made it out alive by working collectively.

My editor, Eric Zinner, has been a staunch advocate for this book. Thank you, Eric, for believing in the philosophical scope of this book and encouraging its creativity. Thank you to Dolma Ombadykow for all of your diligence and care. The three NYU readers for this book have been precious sources of rigor and inspiration.

Lisa Marie Cacho, your beautiful and powerful mind is all over this book, found in the details for both the reader and concepts. Thank you for reading every page with care, intellectual rigor, and enthusiasm, and for spending months cheering me on when I thought I couldn't finish this book. You're an incredible teacher and mentor—wise and untouched by linear time—and I am a better writer and thinker because of you. Your heart is large, my friend. Siobhan Somerville, for so many of us on the margins you make academia a breathable place, showing us how to both walk lines and read between them. This profession needs a million more versions of you. You're a beautiful force, my dear friend and mentor, and I am better for being touched and led by your magic. I could not have completed this journey without your incredible acts of love. Isabel Molina, you've been a great mentor and *amiga*, encouraging me from the moment I landed at Illinois. I am eternally grateful for extraordinary women like you, who spend their lives guiding those coming up with tenderness, wisdom, savvy, and strength.

Fiona Ngô, you're my collaborator and the fork to my spoon. I've been so lucky to create aesthetic worlds with you, always impressed by your bold ideas and creative vision. I appreciate how you perpetually refuse the call to be a dream killer; instead, you ask, in your week-of-the-genius style, how can we mess shit up in beautiful ways? And you do, wise one. Jennifer Monson, my otherworldly creature friend, who helps make life so joyful, thank you for our walks, laughing fits, and dream sessions. I want to keep walking this world next to you because you help me believe it's all possible, and show me that dance is always the most serious. Ruth Nicole Brown, I told you once, but I'll say it again, they ain't ready for you. You are of the future of the future. Thank you for sharing your big and beautiful brain with me.

To my brother, Joshua Chambers-Letson, thank you for being by my side through all of this: I have lived for our long FaceTime chats where we explore all things undercommons and shower each other with laughter, silliness, and love. Jessica Kadish-Hernández, you've been an incredible research assistant, copy editor, listener, reader, and image collector for this project. I am honored that this book has helped us develop a beautiful friendship and many aesthetic collaborations. Thank you for the long hours, late nights, extra care, and for your critical attention to every detail of every detail. I'm really privileged to know you. Thank you, Alexandra T. Vazquez, for providing pivotal feedback on this book and for being a fabulous *hermana*. You're insightful, and my book is better because of your ideas. Jennifer Doyle, I appreciate all of the insights you've provided, and I am beholden to our time together during the Unit workshop. Thank you for investing in this work and sharing your genius with me. Ramón Rivera-Servera, I have benefited greatly from your guidance and mentorship over the last few years. This, plus your commentary on my book, has been instrumental in my career. Tavia Nyong'o, thank you for your insights and for laboring alongside the manuscript until its very end. I am indebted to your kindness, ideas, and commitment to this work. I hope that one day I can return the gesture.

To Antonio Viego, thank you for providing extensive feedback on the Lebrón chapter and for complicating the field of Latinx studies. To my lovely friend, and a brilliant scholar, Jackie Loss, who offered great feedback on many chapters, gracias. Larry La Fountain-Stokes, thank you for reading earlier drafts of this book, for your attention and labor.

To all of my fabulous Illinois colleagues and friends who make life on campus so bright, I thank you. Soo Ah Kwon, I benefit greatly from your radical, compassionate spirit. Edna Viruell-Fuentes, thank you for looking out for me with powerful grace and tenderness. Natalie Lira, your generosity and thoughtfulness always enliven work life. Ellen Moodie, Martin F. Manalansan IV, Naomi Paik, Becky Maybee-Ferrell, Cynthia Oliver, Valleri Robinson, Lilya Kaganovsky, Karen Flynn, Chantal Nadeau, Maryam Kashani, Dara Goldman, Ghassan Moussawi, Vincent D. Cervantes, Mark D. Steinberg, Jon Seydl, and Brett Kaplan, I appreciate your vision for a better world. To Amy Powell, let's keep dreaming. To Regina Garcia (my special *pana pana*) and Anderson (book title master and fierce-soul-friend), thank you for watching over me since the postdoc year. And for those now at other places, Robert Ramirez, Mireya Loza, Marla Ramirez, Sarah Quesada, Jose de la Garza-Valenzuela, Michael Rothberg, thank you for sharing love and immeasurable wisdom.

To the beautiful M. Laura Castañeda, I always benefit from your compassion, love, and tenderness. I am lucky to call you a friend and *comadre*. Alicia Rodriguez, my co-conspirator, I am always moved by your stunning heart and open mind. Thank you for holding one hand during the darkest of times and for holding the other through light and vision.

To my sharp friends across schools, institutions, and spaces, thank you for your wisdom and affection: Karen Jaime (homie since grad school, breaking the rules of presentations with Goya props!), Deb Vargas (a mentor to so many of *los yuniors* and my *pana pana*), Lucia Cantero (my twin), Ricky Lutz Abisla (your love is always so near), Adrian Jonas Smith (your big mind has helped shape these pages), Shane Vogel (thank you for your brilliance), Wilson Valentín-Escobar (keeping our time in the Rican avant-garde), Christina León (la *Leona* of the Leo enterprise), David Lojkovic (always the Pisces to my Taurus) and Long Bui (my Taurean occult brother). To Uri McMillan, Ricardo Montez, Christine Balance, Beth Stinson, Katie Brewer-Ball, Youmna Chlala, Carlos Sandoval DeLeon, Dusty Lynn Childers, Sujay Pandit, Tracie Morris, Serap Erincin, Ronak Kapadia, Leticia Alvarado, Roy Perez, Iván A. Ramon, Joshua Guzmán, John Andrews, Jesus Hernandez, Alberto Laguna, Leon Hilton, Chris Loperena, Zoraya Garces, Natalie Belisle, Kenneth Pietrobono, Antonio Santini, Long Bui, Michelle Rodriguez, Autumn Knight, Erica Gressman, Lauren Berlant, Vijay Iyer, Fred Moten, and Anne F. Harris: thank you for your incisive minds and creative spirits.

I am tremendously grateful to the artists who have shared their work and aesthetic vision with me. You've helped me tell a story, one guided intimately by your talent. Thank you Papo Colo, Máximo Colón, ADÁL, Jacob Burckhardt, and friends and family of Ryan Rivera, especially Rebecca Rivera, Yuko Shimizo, Melissa Sklarz, and Sarah Wolfe.

Earlier drafts of this book received critical attention and care from friends such as Julia Steinmetz, Fares Alsuwaidi, and Vanessa M. Rodriguez—thank you for your trust in this project. Luis Martos also provided editing feedback on earlier drafts, and I am thankful for his work and mind. To the Brown Theatre Collective, I look forward to traveling the world with you, my vibrant collaborators. I am very grateful to El Museo del Barrio, especially Noel Valentin for his diligence; SVA; City Without Walls; Exit Art; and all other aesthetic sites that have helped see this project to its end.

Thank you, Feinberg, for showing me that one can begin new chapters later in life by emptying the internal cup, refilling it with generous acceptance.

To my given family, I am grateful you've taught me to fight for what's rightfully mine. May we always find peace and more love, Mom, Bebe, Jeanette, Edgar, Tony, Yasi, Niko, Cristian. Eloisa, *mi querida abuelita*, rest in expuisite peace. Dad, thank you for teaching me how to manipulate time. Keep staging scenes of revolution and justice in the elsewhere.

Thank you to the Brandariz Nuñez family, Marisol, Carlos, and David, who took me in as their own. I am forever grateful for all of your love and compassion.

Alberto, you make me a better human every day; your heart is golden, your mind that vision for a better world. Thank you for your love; it's an honor to love you. And Gali Lolita, *chusma* of my heart, you're the most wonderful dog-child I've ever been privileged to hold.

NOTES

INTRODUCTION

1   The title of this chapter is a deliberate riff on Frantz Fanon's 1959 book *A Dying Colonialism*. While the book specifically addresses the Algerian War of Independence from France and is not a reflection of PR/US colonial history, it beautifully elucidates the temporal concerns of anticolonial want and the covert strategies used by the colonized against their oppressor. It also exposes the complicated relationship between national liberation movements and the social, cultural, and political transformations that the colonized must endure to understand themselves anew—that is, within a different system of both freedom and subjugation.

2   Molly Hennessy-Fiske and Curtis Lee, "After Hurricane Maria, 'Puerto Rico Isn't Going to Be the Same,'" *Los Angeles Times*, September 20, 2017, http://latimes.com.

3   The Spanish-American War of 1898 resulted in the US control of Puerto Rico, Guam, and the Philippines, and the eventual independence of Cuba.

4   Fanon, *Wretched of the Earth*, 35.

5   The Foraker Act (the Organic Act of 1900), a law that established Puerto Rican citizenship, declared that Puerto Rico was under US federal law and created a civilian government with a governor and executive council, an elected House of Representatives, a Supreme Court, and a nonvoting representative to Congress. The Jones-Shafroth Act of 1917, a law that replaced the Foraker Act, imposed citizenship on Puerto Ricans and called for the creation of a legislative and executive branch similar to those of the United States, with the exceptions that the president picked the governor and that the US Congress needed to approve all cabinet members and could veto any legislation. See Morales Carrión, *Puerto Rico*.

6   The history of sterilization in Puerto Rico has been traced to the late 1930s. The procedure was available at little cost to women when other forms of contraceptives were unavailable. Clarence Gamble, a wealthy leader in the eugenics movement, helped make sterilization widespread in Puerto Rico. See Silliman et al., *Undivided Rights*, 220. See also Lopez, "Ethnography of the Medicalization of Puerto Rican Women's Reproduction," 240–241.

The 1902 Language Law made English and Spanish the official languages of the island, but English was the official language of instruction in schools until 1947. See Muñiz-Argüelles, "Status of Languages in Puerto Rico," 457–472.

7   The gag law (or *la ley de la mordaza*), formally known as Law 53, was enacted by the Puerto Rican legislature in 1948 to make a felony the organization of or

association with any groups that advocated "by force or violence" the overthrow or destabilization of the Puerto Rican government. This law, modeled after the US Smith Act, was passed after a university strike that protested the quelling of nationalist activities. See Friedman, *Citizenship in Cold War America*, 135–136.

The year 1952 marks a crucial yet not entirely decisive moment in US/PR relations. After many internal deliberations and demands from the US Congress, two important and apparently promising laws for the island were passed. Public Law 600, passed in 1951, enabled Puerto Rico to draft their own constitution under the stipulation that it must contain language for the formation of a democratically elected government and a Bill of Rights. Public Law 82-447, a law approved by Congress in 1952, amended the Constitution of the Commonwealth of Puerto Rico to include compulsory elementary education, but it removed recognition of certain human rights and prevented additional amendments that would potentially alter the power structures between the United States and Puerto Rico. President Truman and the US Congress, after these amendments and deletions to the original document, declared the island an Estado Libre Asociado de Puerto Rico. This was translated in English as the Commonwealth of Puerto Rico, instead of the literal Free Associated State of Puerto Rico. This status, which was intended to establish a sense of freedom from US rule for Puerto Rico, meant the following: that the newly created constitution, done by Congress, defines Puerto Rico as a territory, provides a Bill of Rights, and scripts some alterations to the structure of the legislative branch of government. See "50 Years of Commonwealth."

8 Operation Bootstrap, or La Operación Manos a la Obra, was the economic development program that converted Puerto Rico from an agrarian economy to an export-led industrial one. With a resulting shortage of employment, the government encouraged Puerto Ricans to migrate to the mainland, resulting in a million people leaving the island between 1950 and 1965. See Berman Santana, "Puerto Rico's Operation Bootstrap."

9 In 1950, two Puerto Rican Nationalist Party members, Oscar Collazo and Griselio Torresola, attempted to assassinate Truman with an attack at Blair House, which was his temporary residence at the time. They did not reach their intended target, but Torresola was killed, as was a Secret Service agent. See McCann, *Terrorism on American Soil*, 88–92. With this event, along with the Jayuya Uprising, Nationalist Party leader Pedro Albizu Campos and approximately one thousand other people were detained and arrested. During this sentence, claims of Albizu Campos's torture first appeared alongside press releases from the federal government that he was suffering from dementia. In late September 1953, Governor Luis Muñoz Marín pardoned Albizu Campos, although the latter rejected the pardon, through the intervention of the president of Costa Rica, as well as for concerns about his age and health. After his release, scientific investigators from Cuba determined that he had been subject to radiation. These claims were never fully investigated by other authorities. See Tovar, *Albizu Campos*.

10 Jackson, "Powerful Photo Series 'Puerto Ricans Underwater.'" Previously known as Adál Maldonado, this Rican artist uses the name ADÁL professionally; I honor his request to use this name as I reference his work throughout this book.

11 Prior to the recent natural disasters hitting the island, Puerto Rico was already facing over seventy billion dollars in debt, which led to the creation of the Puerto Rico Oversight, Management, and Economic Stability Act in 2016, with the goal of creating a repayment plan that would still allow the government to function. As of May 1, 2017, a plan had not been implemented, causing Governor Ricardo Rosselló to begin bankruptcy-like measures in addition to calling for cuts to schools, universities, health care, and civil service jobs and pensions (see Vicens, "Puerto Rico Files for Bankruptcy"). This financial crisis coexists alongside population loss: the Pew Research Center estimates that almost five hundred thousand Puerto Ricans have migrated to the mainland within the past ten years; as of 2017, there are now more Puerto Ricans living on the mainland than on the island (see Arelis R. Hernández, "Exodus from Puerto Rico Grows as Island Struggles to Rebound from Hurricane Maria," *Washington Post*, March 6, 2018, www.washingtonpost.com).

12 President Donald J. Trump asserted that US federal government aid was slow to arrive in Puerto Rico "because it's an island . . . sitting in the middle of an ocean. And it's a big ocean; it's a very big ocean" (see Philip Bump, "The 'Very Big Ocean' between Here and Puerto Rico Is Not a Perfect Excuse for a Lack of Aid," *Washington Post*, September 26, 2017, www.washingtonpost.com).

13 ADÁL's images, and the current excessive neoliberal state of Puerto Rican politics, remind me of Grover Norquist's infamous remarks about wanting to shrink government "to the size where [he] can drag it into the bathroom and drown it in the bathtub" (see Mara Liasson, "Conservative Advocate," *Morning Edition*, NPR, May 25, 2001, www.npr.org).

14 For an in-depth analysis of the Rican avant-garde, and the aesthetic and political relationship between Pietri and ADÁL, please anticipate the forthcoming work of curator, musician, and scholar Wilson Valentín-Escobar in his comprehensive book *Bodega Surrealism: Latina/o/x Activists in New York City* (New York University Press).

15 "Loisaida Figures"; Estrin, "Puerto Rican Identity"; Noel, *In Visible Movement*.

16 Ramon Nuez, "An Interview with Adal Maldonado on the Identity of Photography," *Huffington Post*, October 15, 2013, www.huffingtonpost.com.

17 Ibid.

18 Jackson, "Powerful Photo Series 'Puerto Ricans Underwater.'"

19 Barthes, *Camera Lucida*, 97.

20 Grosfoguel, Negrón-Muntaner, and Georas, "Introduction," 2. Puerto Rican scholars Grosfoguel, Negrón-Muntaner, and Georas attempt to free themselves of this apprehension, too, by thinking past the "nationalist/colonialist dichotomy"—a binaristic analytic that represses other directions in Ricanness (2). Placing pressure on this dichotomy, they curate essays that position the Puerto Rican situation as an ethno-nation, translocal nation, postcolonial space, beyond the space of

colonial despair and nationalist rhetoric. In thinking Puerto Rican studies past its own past, however, the authors land on the crux of colonial time. They ask: "How can a postcolonial politics be imagined as a basis for a political practice without falling into the trap of altogether ignoring the fact that Puerto Rico is a colonial configuration?" (33). As the editors try to move beyond the debate, the question of the island's status survives at the center of the anthology—like a ghost who refuses to transfer over.

21 Duany, *Puerto Rican Nation on the Move*, 284.

22 Ibid., 284. Duany rethinks the nation "not as a well-bounded sovereign state but as a translocal community based on a collective consciousness of a shared history"—that is, a "postcolonial colony" (4). The Puerto Rican nation "is no longer restricted to the Island" but interlaced by spatial incompletion: Puerto Rico, the Caribbean island, and "the diasporic communities settled in the continental United States" (5). These two fragments are actually differently articulated models of incompletion. In this conjoined state of being, Duany produces "a postcolonial colony," yet without the liberatory moment, the "post" in postcolonial remains undetermined. Incompletion is bearable and productive because it *is* temporal and always already colonial, even—and indeed especially—if subjects move around the globe. By refiguring geographical diffusion and spatial politics, Duany moves from different forms of nationalism—cultural, social, and political—in order to link cultural migration and existence under the inadequacies of unsovereignty. Duany locates the "completion" of the Rican subject within the potentiality of the hybrid state. Concepts such as ambiguity and ambivalence become activated positively through the dispersal of the subject, or what Duany calls the Rican subject on the move, creating alternative acts of existence in different geographical locations. It is through these bodily movements within different spaces that he shares a historical consequence: the island's performances of nationalism have often been reactions to colonialism. Consequently, the movements of el vaivén are often enacted to preserve Puerto Rican culture itself. Duany argues that this has positioned national identity against a construction of American culture, industrialization, and homogeneity, rather than acknowledging fluidity as an inevitable result of colonial and imperial practice. He importantly adds that the nation is a place where "all forms of identity are imagined, invented, and represented—but not necessarily arbitrary, immaterial, and irrelevant" (8).

23 Negrón-Muntaner, "Introduction," 6.

24 Ibid., 12.

25 See Fiol-Matta, "Forget '98." Fiol-Matta, in the special section "Forget '98," plays with the terms "forgetting" and "remembering" to mark the hundred-year anniversary of the Spanish-American War. Fiol-Matta contends that on the island, "remembering is an ideological exercise fraught with consequence, a not so innocent process of alignment with imaginaries and the exercises of power they abet" (99). The process of remembering, like forgetting, is always selective and political. Her deliberate use of an apostrophe before 98 signals all that is remembered and

potentially lost in the processes of commemoration, of over a hundred years. It also signals the slippery nature of time. How do we remember in a present state when time appears to have been intimately still? How does time move, advance, progress in Ricanness when it appears to be standing still? I move throughout this book deliberately, then, staging time across dates like 1898, 1954, 1977, 2016, to name a few here, in order to rehearse the looping and elliptical nature of colonial time, and its forbearance against Ricanness.

26 Jones, *Body Art*; Goldberg, *Performa*; Gonzalez Rice, *Long Suffering*.

27 Heathfield, "Durational Aesthetics," 140.

28 Ibid., 140.

29 Gonzalez Rice, *Long Suffering*.

30 Césaire, *Discourse on Colonialism*, 39.

31 Schechner, *Performance Theory*.

32 Fanon, *Black Skin, White Masks*; Fanon, *Wretched of the Earth*.

33 Fanon, *Black Skin, White Masks*, 109–140.

34 Ibid., 109.

35 Ibid., 109.

36 There are many variations and meanings of this word in English translations of Heidegger: *Da-sein, Dasein, dasein, da-sein*. Throughout the text, I use *Da-sein*, as Joan Stambaugh does in her translation of *Being and Time*, but also maintain each author's version when quoting them directly.

37 Heidegger, *Being and Time*; Nietzsche, *Thus Spoke Zarathustra*; Hegel, *Phenomenology of Spirit*; Sartre, *Nausea*; Lacan, *Seminar of Jacques Lacan*; Merleau-Ponty, *Phenomenology of Perception*.

38 Turner, "Fanon Reading (W)right."

39 Muñoz, *Disidentifications*, 9–11. Muñoz discusses how disidentification actually works when reading through Fanon's ideas on colonial subjectivity: "Fanon dismisses the possibility of a homosexual component in such an identic formation. This move is not uncommon; it is basically understood as an 'it's a white thing' dismissal of queerness. Think, for a moment, of the queer revolutionary from the Antilles, perhaps a young woman who has already been burned in Fanon's text by his writing on the colonized woman. What process can keep an identification with Fanon, his politics, his work possible for this woman?" (9).

40 Bergson, *Time and Free Will*; Heidegger, *Being and Time*; Merleau-Ponty, *Phenomenology of Perception*; Maldonado-Torres, *Against War*; Fanon, *Black Skin, White Masks*; Spivak, "Time and Timing."

41 Heidegger, *Being and Time*, 217.

42 Heidegger, *Concept of Time*, 6E.

43 Heidegger, *Being and Time*, 111; Blattner, *Heidegger's* Being and Time, 73–76.

44 Heidegger, *Being and Time*, 22–23.

45 Heidegger, *Being and Time*, 7.

46 Heidegger, *Concept of Time*, 7E.

47 Heidegger, *Being and Time*, 311.

48 Ibid., 311.
49 Ibid., 236.
50 Ibid., 371–398.
51 Heidegger, *Concept of Time*, 5E.
52 Ibid., 5E.
53 Ibid., 5E.
54 Ibid., 10E.
55 Ibid., 12E.
56 Ibid., 12E–13E.
57 Ibid., 13E.
58 Ibid., 14E.
59 Ibid., 15E.
60 Ibid., 19E.
61 Ibid., 16E.
62 Ibid., 14E.
63 Blattner, *Heidegger's* Being and Time, 23.
64 Ortega, *In-Between*.
65 Ibid., 1.
66 Ibid., 1.
67 Ibid., 5.
68 Ibid., 5.
69 Fanon, *Wretched of the Earth*, 41.
70 Fanon, *Black Skin, White Masks*, 229.
71 Ibid., 231.
72 Du Bois, *Souls of Black Folk*.
73 Fanon, *Black Skin, White Masks*, 112.
74 Paget Henry explains the limits of philosophy by exploring the Du Boisian and Fanonian contribution to an Africana existential thought. By turning to an evaluation of different types of conscious splitting in reference to the racialized subject, Henry rethinks the normative codes embedded in existential thinking. He argues that Fanon's trenchant "psycho-existential analysis" of multiple states of consciousness and the "psychopathological and philosophical explanation of the state of being other" help him best understand existence and racial construction (see Henry, "Africana Phenomenology").
75 Camus, "Myth of Sisyphus," 3.
76 Viego, *Dead Subjects*, 4.
77 Gherovici, *Puerto Rican Syndrome*, 29.
78 Ibid.
79 Khanna, *Dark Continents*. In offering a corollary to a purely Lacanian understanding of the subject, Khanna highlights the significance of psychoanalysis as a reading exercise, while also remaining suspect of its colonialist past. Khanna reads psychoanalysis, as a discipline that has been used to render colonies and their subjects immobile through pathological universalisms, "against the grain"

(5) in order to create a dialogue between this reading practice, colonialism, and postcolonialism. According to Khanna, "The rescripting of psychoanalysis manifested colonial melancholy" (29). Melancholia as affect, then, may be used to rethink, as she claims, a new way of imagining an ethical and political system for the colonial being. Melancholia allows the postcolonial subject political validation under a system of loss. By turning to Freud's "Mourning and Melancholia," Khanna locates melancholia in the remnants of colonial subjectivity: "Melancholia becomes the basis for an ethico-political understanding of colonial pasts, postcolonial presents, and Utopian futures" (30). Turning to Lacan does not provide much tractive force for Khanna, unlike Gherovici and Viego. "What the future holds for Lacan is, perhaps, a whited out notion of political context, in which the death drive and the Other are without color" (190). She claims that Lacan misses the mark on the importance of "social antagonisms"; although she is clear that "psychical antagonisms and social antagonisms" are contingent upon one another, in the former a commitment to the self overshadows a critical involvement with the social (186). It is through the social that Khanna locates the conditions of possibility for the colonial and postcolonial subject.

80 Aparicio, "Exposed Bodies," 166.

81 Muñoz, "'Chico, What Does It Feel Like to Be a Problem?'"

82 Muñoz, *Cruising Utopia*, 1.

83 See Ahmed, *Queer Phenomenology*; Halberstam, *In a Queer Time and Place*; Nyong'o, *Amalgamation Waltz*; Ferguson, *Aberrations in Black*; Luciano, *Arranging Grief*; Freeman, *Time Binds*.

84 Freeman, *Time Binds*, 3.

85 Ahmed, *Queer Phenomenology*.

86 Heidegger, *Concept of Time*, 12E.

87 Fanon, *Black Skin, White Masks*, 229.

88 Lawrence La Fountain-Stokes's important *Queer Ricans* focuses on sexuality as a critical component of the US-Puerto Rican migration experience. His contention is that sexuality is equally important as immigration, debt and capital accumulation, and politics. Through the aesthetic—performances, literary works, and film—he exposes how queer Ricans have negotiated sexuality within ethnic and national identities throughout generations. La Fountain-Stokes's book addresses lives often unnoticed in the larger expanse of Ricanness. He collects the uncollectible in the face of constant erasure. For La Fountain-Stokes, this is located in queerness's ability to be disruptive and transform into "something new and different" (xi). Conversely, Juana María Rodríguez's *Sexual Futures* turns to racialized queer female subjects in sites between performance and the law, reviving alternative conceptions of sex, pleasure, and desire. Her turn to the gestural opens up new citational pathways that allow deviant acts to enter queer futures. At the space of the detail, Rodríguez resets time, showing us how ephemeral our ambitions often are and how the pulse of mechanical time, policy, and institutional demise assuage intimacy. She, too, displays the hard work of Ricanness, especially

at the limit of the law, always apprised by colonial rhetoric. Similarly, Ramón Rivera-Servera's commitment to choreography highlights the "utopian performative" found in bodily movements, which I will detail in chapter 2 (see *Performing Queer Latinidad*). Subjects participate in Latinx queer spaces, such as concert dance and the dance club, through the level of affect, rather than an identity marker. He claims that Latinx queer performances provide opportunities for "new social formations and modes of being in the world" that can lend themselves to the utopic (18).

89 Here, I am reminded of Nyong'o's "Little Monsters," in which he offers a sharp re-encounter of the sovereign and the beast in the aforementioned film. As the author notes, the film takes place on an island called the Bathtub—"often described as a post-Katrina allegory" (256). Dealing with this excess of water, the author offers a close reading of this island/the Bathtub by turning to Denise Ferreira da Silva's theory of "the strategy of engulfment" from her 2007 magnum opus, *Toward a Global Idea of Race*. From da Silva to the film, he brilliantly asks, "How might the racial other be engulfed by the extension of a transparent and universal reason, even under the guise of fabulated machines of cinematic dreaming?" (261). In such a question, I am immediately transported to ADÁL's scenes of photographic engulfment, wherein Rican subjects hold their breath within their own allegorical bathtub.

90 Lopez, "Ethnography of the Medicalization of Puerto Rican Women's Reproduction," 240–241.

91 Pietri, *Masses Are Asses*.

92 City of New York, Department of City Planning, www1.nyc.gov.

93 I want to thank Lisa Marie Cacho for helping me rethink the political implications of impotence and the ramifications of violence under colonial time. Her brilliant *Social Death* has been instrumental in my thoughts about violence, but also our conversations about these painful themes have helped shape many moments in this book.

94 In making this claim, I am also thinking of Licia Fiol-Matta's *The Great Woman Singer*, in which she asks us to consider the "thinking voice" of great Puerto Rican female singers like Lucecita Benitez. This "thinking voice," according to Fiol-Matta, harbors the full and conscious capacity to conceptualize, to think strategically about sound, image, and the complete performance persona that creates the Rican singer writ large.

CHAPTER 1. LIPSTICK REVOLUTIONARIES

1 This chapter's epigraph was uttered by Lebrón upon her arrest in Washington, DC, in 1954. In full, she is reported to have said, "Yo no vine a matar a nadie, yo vine a morir por Puerto Rico!" (see "Lolita nos dijo adiós," *El Nuevo Día*, August 1, 2010, www.elnuevodia.com). The abbreviated version of her declaration, painted in a community mural on a New York City wall, is included in an essay by Elsa B. Cardalda Sánchez and Amílcar Tirado Avilés, "Ambiguous Identities!," 274.

2   While this chapter is devoted to Lebrón, I remain cognizant of the fact that she operated under a history of Puerto Rican female revolutionary activity and, whether written into popular script or neglected after such actions, provides a temporal base that fuels the legacy of revolution in heteronormative time. I would now like to engage with some of the Puerto Rican female revolutionaries before her. The three women I will be highlighting—Mariana Bracetti, Lola Rodriguez de Tió, and Blanca Canales—have all contributed to the evolution of the Puerto Rican Nationalist Party and the flag as a symbol in and for frontal attacks against colonial rule, whether against Spain or the United States. During the Puerto Rican independence movement of the 1860s, in which *independentistas* endeavored to seek sovereignty from Spanish rule in the revolution known as El Grito de Lares, Mariana Bracetti was a leading patriot and revolutionary. Bracetti has been attributed with designing and knitting the first flag of the future Republic of Puerto Rico. Before September 23, 1868—the date of El Grito de Lares—Bracetti participated as one of the leaders of the Lares Revolutionary Council, whose members convened to strategize and wage war against Spain. On the day of the revolution, Bracetti's flag was placed over a picture of Spain's Queen Isabel. While Bracetti was not on the front line, her creation of the flag, as both a national symbol and a revolutionary gesture, was instrumental in attempting to reclaim space—albeit the revolution ended on Spanish terms. Puerto Rican female revolutionaries and their relationship to the flag as a signifier of independence extend beyond Bracetti. The first Puerto Rican poetess to garner widespread Latin American appeal during the mid- to late 1800s, Lola Rodríguez de Tió, was inspired to write the lyrics to "La Borinqueña" (Puerto Rico's anthem for the independence from the Spanish regime). Her lyrics ask the islanders to "wake up" from colonial rule and demand sovereignty by all means necessary. In one of the most profound lines of this anthem, Rodríguez de Tió asserts, "Le dará el machete su libertad" (the machete will give you your liberty). Along with the creation of this anthem, Rodríguez de Tió has been credited with suggesting that the Puerto Rican flag model the Cuban flag by reversing the colors as a form of allegiance to a similar national struggle. Finally, Blanca Canales, the leader of the Jayuya Uprising in 1950, physically led a group of Puerto Rican nationalists in taking over the town of Jayuya for three days as part of a plan to liberate Puerto Rico from US rule. During this revolution, Canales raised the Puerto Rican flag on a flagpole designated only for the American flag. In the 1950s, it was illegal to display the Puerto Rican flag as a national symbol. As well, the tradition and the importance of the flag as a national symbol of protest and cultural affirmation are linked to the performative act undertaken by Lolita Lebrón on March 1, 1954. See Jiménez de Wagenheim, *Puerto Rico's Revolt for Independence*; "Lola Rodríguez de Tió," *El Boricua*, August 13, 2017, www.elboricua.com; Juan Antonio Ocasio Rivera, "Puerto Rico's October Revolution," *New York Latino Journal*, n.d., www.nylatino-journal.com (site now discontinued).

3   Manuel Roig-Franzia, "A Terrorist in the House," *Washington Post Magazine*, February 22, 2004, W12.

4 The failed assassination attempt on President Truman was actually carried out by two Nationalists, Griselio Torresola and Oscar Collazo. However, it is widely accepted that party leader Pedro Albizu Campos, a seminal and iconic figure in the Puerto Rican independence movement, planned the event. Born in 1891, the Harvard-educated lawyer joined the Nationalist Party in 1924 and quickly rose through its ranks, becoming president in 1929. In 1936, under charges that fell under the wartime Sedition Act of 1918, Albizu Campos was arrested and convicted for "conspiring to overthrow the United States government." In December 1947, he was released and resumed his leadership of the party until 1950, when he was arrested again after the assassination attempt and rebellion of *nacionalistas*, known as the Jayuya Uprising. He was sentenced to fifty-three years in prison but was pardoned in 1953 because of his health. It was only six months later that Albizu Campos was again removed forcibly from his home after the US Capitol attack in 1954 by Lebrón. This time, his pardon was revoked and he spent another ten years in prison until his deteriorating health—which some allege was the result of malicious radiation tests by prison authorities—led to a final release by the governor. The leader died on April 21, 1965, at a home in Hato Rey, Puerto Rico. For more information, see Tovar, *Albizu Campos*.

5 I have chosen to use the name Lebrón, not Lolita, throughout this book to take a deliberate stand on the representation of this iconic figure.

6 Clayton Knowles, "Five Congressmen Shot in House by 3 Puerto Rican Nationalists; Bullets Spray from Gallery," *New York Times,* March 2, 1954, 1; Alvin Shuster, "Shooting Blasted Day of Routine," *New York Times*, March 2, 1954, 18; "The Nation," *New York Times*, March 7, 1954, E1; "The Capitol: Puerto Rico Is Not Free," *Time*, March 8, 1954.

7 "The Capitol: Puerto Rico Is Not Free."

8 While no one was killed during the attack, five congressmen were injured and rushed to hospitals. None of the five men—Ben Jensen, Alvin Bentley, Cliff Davis, George Fallon, and Kenneth Roberts—suffered life-threatening injuries, although Bentley was seriously wounded in the chest.

9 Carlos Ventura, "Lolita lebron ataca el Congreso 1954" (filmed March 1954), YouTube video, 3:51, posted September 29, 2009, https://youtu.be/Pom5iJlVLrk; Newsreel footage, "News of the Day: Vol. XXV No. 254," begins at 0:50 of the video.

10 Ibid.

11 On the morning of March 1, 1954, the first American hydrogen bomb (code-named Bravo) was tested on Bikini Atoll in the Pacific Ocean. The explosion was stronger than expected and caused radiation sickness for 264 natives, including 23 Japanese fisherman near the area at the time (see Dibblin, *Day of Two Suns*). In the House of Representatives, at two thirty the same afternoon, on the agenda was the discussion of the "wetback" bill on the admission of Mexican farm labor ("The Nation"). Operation Wetback was a plan designed by the US government to remove illegal aliens that resulted in the deportation of over three million Mexicans

during the 1950s. As one can see, the conflict on the congressional floor on March 1 incarnated the geospatial politics reverberating around the world. The historical moment thus embodied several parallel valences of revolutionary agency and US expansionist ideology. These lateral events illustrate the dominant force of time, for while national leaders either consented or were coerced in far-reaching jurisdictions around the globe, specific localities were coordinated temporally.

12 Knowles, "Five Congressmen Shot."

13 As the post-9/11 discourse and the USA PATRIOT Act have made clear, the term "terrorist" invokes the global geopolitical theater of which the United States has been a dominant director, positing attacks not merely as criminal transgressions but as existential threats.

14 Ramos-Zayas, *National Performances*, 93.

15 Ibid., 92.

16 Nabokov, *Lolita*, 1.

17 Ramos-Zayas, *National Performances*, 95.

18 "The Capitol: Puerto Rico Is Not Free"; C. P. Trussell, "Witness Describes Shooting, Capture: Reporter Sees Firing in House," *New York Times*, March 2, 1954, 1.

19 Roig-Franzia, "Terrorist in the House."

20 During the Puerto Rican independence movement of the 1860s, El Grito de Lares was a major event in which *independentistas* rebelled against Spanish rule. See Jiménez de Wagenheim, *Puerto Rico's Revolt for Independence*.

21 Despite being a member of the Liberal Party of Puerto Rico—a proindependence political party—Lebrón became fervently interested in politics only after police—at the instruction of US-appointed governor Blanton Winship—shot and killed nineteen peaceful protesters (and wounded an estimated two hundred) in a march in Ponce on Palm Sunday, March 21, 1937. The march was organized by the Puerto Rican Nationalist Party, receiving a legal parade permit, to protest the US government's imprisonment of the party's leader, Albizu Campos, on sedition charges. "Immediately after the massacre, Governor Blanton Winship blamed it on the 'Nationalist Terrorists,' and his Insular Police followed the wounded to Trioche Hospital in Ponce, arresting them in their stretchers and hospital beds" (Denis, *War Against All Puerto Ricans*, 50). Since one of the major points of this book is the relationship between Ricanness and death, I'd like to say the names of those killed on that day: Irvin G. Rodríguez Figueras, Juan Torres Gregory, Conrado Rivera Pérez, Georgina Maldonado (seven-year-old girl), Jenaro Rodríguez Mendez, Luis Jiménez Morales, Juan Delgado Cotal Nieves, Juan Santos Ortiz, Ulpiano Perea, Caferino Loyola Pérez (Insular Police), Eusebio Sánchez Pérez (IP), Juan Antonio Pietrantoni, Juan Reyes Rivera, Pedro Juan Rodríguez Rivera, Obdulio Rosario, María Hernández del Rosario, Bolívar Márquez Telechea, Ramón Ortiz Toro, Teodoro Vélez Torres. Saying their names is a popular political speech act. It is also a way to continue archiving the "unarchivable." Endnotes, as I argue throughout the book, are pregnant with possibilities—stories and lives missing from dominant discourse. Oftentimes it is the perpetual endnote that

becomes not only the text, but the paratextual. Saying their names is a recognition of their necessity as historical subjects.

22 Jiménez de Wagenheim, *Nationalist Heroines*, 246.

23 Ruiz and Korrol, "Lebrón, Dolores 'Lolita' (1910–),"380.

24 Ibid.

25 Friedman, *Citizenship in Cold War America*, 139.

26 It is notable that this occurred after the United States had dropped the two atomic bombs in Japan and the United Nations had been formed.

27 Jiménez de Wagenheim, *Nationalist Heroines*, 248.

28 Silliman et al., *Undivided Rights*, 220.

29 Briggs, *Reproducing Empire*, 115.

30 Ibid, 110.

31 Ibid, 149. It has been reported that by 1965, 35 percent of Puerto Rican women were sterilized (Lopez, "Ethnography of the Medicalization of Puerto Rican Women's Reproduction," 240–241).

32 Ibid.

33 Friedman, *Citizenship in Cold War America*, 153.

34 Ibid.

35 Roig-Franzia, "Terrorist in the House." Lebrón claims "she spoke little on the ride down," instead calmly gazing out the window: "It was an enjoyable trip. . . . I looked at the animals, the vegetation. I was going to give my life for my country. . . . I was going to give the shout of liberty." It "would be her own Grito de Lares."

36 Knowles, "Five Congressmen Shot." Another version of the "suicide note" is reproduced in McCann, *Terrorism on American Soil*, 95.

37 "The Capitol: Puerto Rico Is Not Free."

38 Maldonado-Torres, *Against War*, 122–123.

39 Whereas Melanie Klein approaches suicide as a fundamental expression of self-condemnation, Camus and Émile Durkheim highlight the act of offering death as embedded in sociopolitical and religious relationships. For Durkheim, the act of suicide cannot be thoroughly examined without looking at its relationship to society and can be classified into three different categories: egotistic, altruistic, and anomic. The latter two concern us here: altruistic suicide results when the individual takes their life or attempts to for religious conviction and political reasons, whereas anomic suicide results from "the regulation of the individual from society" whereby the individual is forced to uphold beliefs, systems, and behaviors he or she cannot possibly endure. Lolita's handwritten note can be read as sacrificial—an example that Durkheim might call anomic—written by a being that can no longer endure; but what if her note was the self-realization that death could be experienced only with the inscription of said note? In this incantation for being, Lolita rewrites and affirms her death. See Durkheim, *Suicide*; Klein, "Contribution to the Psychogenesis of Manic-Depressive States."

40 Rodríguez, *Sexual Futures*, 4.

41 Ibid., 4.

42 Althusser, "Ideology and Ideological State Apparatuses," 175–176.

43 Foucault, *Discipline and Punish*, 170–194.

44 Hegel, *Phenomenology of Spirit*.

45 Fanon, *Black Skin, White Masks*, 109.

46 See Fred Moten's discussion of "the resistance of the object" (*In the Break*, 1–24).

47 Fanon, *Black Skin, White Masks*, 218.

48 Austin, *How to Do Things with Words*.

49 Biopower and biopolitics have been among the most influential—and controversial—topics in social and cultural theory over the past two decades, addressing a diverse range of scholarly debates from war and genocide to natural disasters and postindustrial/immaterial labor. First formulated by Michel Foucault in *The History of Sexuality*, biopower describes a type of institutional power concerned with the optimization of life itself, "a power to foster life or disallow it to the point of death." As it emerged in the late eighteenth century and early nineteenth, biopower represents the state's control of the subject through bodily means. Foucault's theory is apt for describing a kind of government that manages the lives of subjects through political practices. Simultaneously supplementing and reversing Foucault's analysis, postcolonial theorist Achille Mbembé analyzes the ontology and politics of death in order to underscore what it means to be perpetually subjugated to the limits of life as a colonial other. "Necropolitics," according to Mbembé, is predicated on "power and the capacity to dictate who may live and who must die." Foucault emphasizes the forms of governmental power aimed at enhancing and maximizing the life of populations; Mbembé insists that colonial and postcolonial governance involves not only the administration of life (as described by Foucault) but also a determination of how, when, and who will die or be killed. In this account, life and death become close companions, blurring distinctions of colonial power as benevolent on the one hand (e.g., economic development, provisions of political stability, public health) and exploitative and oppressive on the other—including the always-present threat of the colonized being killed. This basic political uncertainty complicates the colonial subject's everyday life since (as many theorists of colonialism including Mbembé contend) that subject's temporality is fundamentally propelled by the Other. See Mbembé, "Necropolitics."

50 Heidegger, *Being and Time*, 223.

51 Paul Ricœur's elegant meditation on death, or what he calls *Living Up to Death*, is a project in incompletion. Ricœur, while taking on one of the most important philosophical quandaries, is depleted by mortality. Unable to fully extend such introspection, his book "lives up" to and leaves one with the fragment—that discursive "thing" lingering and figuring as half of something, something missing, but also so pregnant with possibility and potential even in its disappearance. But Ricœur pauses in the Heideggerian construction of death and wonders:

what about life? According to Ricœur, Heidegger's obsession with death neither elongates life nor lingers within it; instead it fast-forwards, missing the living and existing in Being. His presentation of death is beautiful and parsimonious, lingering alongside an investigation of the onto-theological.

52 Lebrón's enigmatic nature, like the typology of death that Jacques Derrida rhetorically constructs in *The Gift of Death*, is relevant in her embodied dialectic of dearth and surfeit. Part of her allure and complexity is the fact that she can't be unhinged, figured out; she does not speak to the legible gender body politic—the body of the US civic sphere that reduces questions of life and death, masculine and feminine to skeletal and juridical linguistic oppositions. In examinations of her, the life she almost gave becomes part of her representational stature. Derrida considers the linguistic specificities embedded in death by showing how death is also an act of reciprocity, even in its singular execution. By describing the intricate differences between *donner la mort* (to give death), *la mort donnée* (the gift of death, or putting to death), *se donner la mort* (to kill oneself), *de la mort donnée* (gifts of death, or literally translated, of given death), he challenges the parameters of sacrifice, suicide, and "the possibility of death" (3–10). The gift of death is a different type of rebirth in that the subject must confirm her unique possession of her own death, a self-gift that cannot be taken away, and that is the locus of both freedom and will. Coming to terms with one's mortality, an obsession of Derrida's that stems from his long-standing engagement with Heidegger, is a journey through authenticity. To know and own one's death is to know and believe in the illusory and subtle nature of immortality.

53 Fanon, *Wretched of the Earth*, 313.

54 Gherovici, *Puerto Rican Syndrome*, 21.

55 Ibid., 38.

56 This has been translated in English as "nervous attack" or "nervous breakdown." According to the *Diagnostic and Statistical Manual of Mental Disorders*, *ataque de nervios* is categorized under "Culture-Bound Syndromes" as an "idiom of distress principally reported among Latinos from the Caribbean but recognized among many Latin American and Latin Mediterranean groups."

57 Gherovici, *Puerto Rican Syndrome*, 134.

58 Lacan, *Seminar of Jacques Lacan*, 29.

59 Ibid., 20, 223.

60 Bruce Fink, *Lacanian Subject*, 36.

61 Ibid., 9–10.

62 Ibid.

63 "Aftermath," *Time*, March 15, 1954, 23.

64 Ibid., 23.

65 Gherovici, *Puerto Rican Syndrome*, 132.

66 Ibid., 134.

67 Nelson, "Lolita Lebron Would Rather Die in Prison." The article was written before Lebrón's release that same year after being pardoned by President Jimmy Carter.

68 Ibid.

69 Ibid.

70 Ibid.

71 Sewell, *Encyclopedia of U.S. Military Interventions.* According to Irene Vilar in *The Ladies' Gallery*, the day symbolized Puerto Rico's refusal to die under imperial rule. Notwithstanding this resistance, the conference featured Secretary of State John Foster Dulles proposing a joint action program to twenty Latin American countries against "the menace of international communism" (93).

72 As discussed previously, the Foraker Act (the Organic Act of 1900), a law that established Puerto Rican citizenship, declared that Puerto Rico was under US federal law and created a civilian government with a governor and executive council, an elected House of Representatives, a Supreme Court, and a nonvoting representative to Congress.

73 Two years prior, not on but near March 1, after a 1950 authorization for a local constitution, PL 600 was ratified through a popular vote on March 3, 1952. According to Pedro A. Cabán in "The Colonial State and Capitalist Expansion," while it appeared that the Commonwealth provided Puerto Ricans with their own autonomy to shape policies, it served only to maintain the colonial state and make the island a more efficient and profitable land (89). In order to do so, the local government worked to increase industrialization as well as social order, which it did through the encouragement of migration and sterilization as well as the brutal suppression of unions, leftists, and nationalists. In a matter of four years (1950–1954) thousands of Nationalist Party members had been arrested, which, according to Andrea Friedman, "decimated" the party in Puerto Rico and on the US mainland (*Citizenship in Cold War America*, 120). Additionally, around the same date, President Wilson signed the Jones-Shafroth Act on March 2, 1917.

74 McCann, *Terrorism on American Soil*, 93. Contrary to Lebrón's idea of revolution, McCann argues, "Definitions of terrorism are complicated by the fact that many forms of violent action—such as war, guerilla activity, and related forms of political violence—overlap with terrorism" (7). In his chapter on Lebrón's attack on Congress, he tendentially asserts that she is a "convicted terrorist" who was able to triumphantly return to her native home "to continue to support [her] original cause." But for Ronald Fernández, in *Prisoners of Colonialism*, Lebrón is a revolutionary who attempted to eradicate the hold of American imperialism and colonialism.

75 Vilar, *Ladies' Gallery*, 94.

76 Ibid., 94.

77 Ibid., 94.

78 Ibid., 95.

79 Viego, *Dead Subjects.*

80 Ibid., 134.

81 Viego, "Unconsciousness of Latina/o Studies," 335.

82 Ibid., 335.

83 Freud, "Mourning and Melancholia," 249–250.

84 De Kesel, *Eros and Ethics,* 214.

85 Freud, "Mourning and Melancholia," 246.

86 Butler, *Gender Trouble,* 177; and reference to conceptualizations in *Bodies That Matter* (1993), *Excitable Speech* (1997), and *The Psychic Life of Power* (1997).

87 Butler, *Excitable Speech.*

88 Saldaña-Portillo, *Revolutionary Imagination in the Americas,* 4.

89 Ibid., 7.

90 Ibid., 79.

91 Through a postcolonial and postmodern lens, Emma Pérez faces history against the grain by tracing historical events and accounting for the footnotes in all of the unsung tales of historiography. She poignantly contends, "As a historian, I have been trained . . . to trace continuities and changes, and to unify that which seems out of synchronicity, to categorize words and facts which seem to be 'lost in space,' lingering alone. . . . On the other hand, if one studies history only from a Foucauldian stance, to rupture totalities and dispute origins, one can become disillusioned; yet disillusion may be essential in order to interrogate differences and subjectivities in different ways." See Pérez, *Decolonial Imaginary,* 32.

92 Barthes captures a simulacrum of life, giving one life beautifully: "What matters to me is not the photograph's 'life' (a purely ideological notion) but the certainty that the photographed body touches me with its own rays and not with a super-added light," a transcendence that, as he accounts, is what one adds to the image "and what is nonetheless already there" (*Camera Lucida,* 81, 55).

93 Spivak, "Time and Timing." Time proper or "Time" is elicited as an abstraction in postcolonial theorist Spivak's very first line: "Time is a word to which we give flesh in various ways." She introduces European constructions of "Time" to produce a distinction between "Time" and "timing."

94 Lebrón, *Antología de la Poesía Cósmica de Lolita Lebrón.* While Lebrón's collection of poems has been published in Spanish, it remains to be translated into English, a project I am currently undertaking with Dr. Jacqueline Loss.

95 Ibid., 38.

96 Ibid.

97 I appreciate Luis Martos's sociological renderings of religious life, which we discussed in earlier versions of this chapter. These renderings helped me rethink the social spaces of poetic verse.

98 Lebrón, *Antología de la Poesía Cósmica de Lolita Lebrón,* 248.

99 Ibid., 49. When initially translating this poem, I translated "la Patria" into "motherland," I suppose unconsciously keeping with the theme of Lebrón-as-Mother-

of-the-Rican-nation, but in most Latin American contexts this complicated word might be translated as "fatherland" and not necessarily even "homeland." I'm intrigued by these translational slippages, but not at all surprised by my desire to undo the inherent gendered constructions of the nation that reify ideas of the revolutionary herself. Thank you Jackie Loss for noting this slippage and for compelling me to share more of the unconscious desires laced within translation work.

100 Both before and after her time in prison, Lebrón advocated for violent resistance; however, the direction of her call to violence shifted by 1975. Whereas in 1954 she aimed her gun at the ceiling, in 1975 she wrote of targeting the oppressor more directly.

101 Nelson, "Lolita Lebron Would Rather Die in Prison."

102 Here, I engage in Lacanian play, turning the Law of the Father into the Law of the absent Mother.

103 I am using the term "modernity"—and the chronological and developmental qualifier "high"—to refer to the "multidimensional array of historical phenomena" characterized especially by the emphasis on scientific and political rationality, which reached its peak during the Cold War of the mid-1950s to early 1960s. For a more detailed analysis of the complicated intersection between this historical narrative of progress and its gendered ramifications, see Rita Felski's extremely erudite *Gender of Modernity.*

104 Vilar, *Ladies' Gallery,* 6.

105 Ibid., 2.

106 Shakur, *Assata,* 256.

107 Nelson, "Lolita Lebron Would Rather Die in Prison."

CHAPTER 2. RUNNING OUT OF TIME

1 Moten, *In The Break,* 1.

2 Cullen, *Arte ≠ Vida*; "Papo Colo," MoMA PS1, 2015, http://momaps1.org; "Papo Colo," Museo de Arte de Ponce, n.d., http://www.museoarteponce.org; "Papo Colo," Radical Presence NY, 2013, http://radicalpresenceny.org. According to Radical Presence, in *Supernman 51,* "written on each of the sticks was the name of a state as well as that of Puerto Rico."

3 Striff, "Introduction," 11.

4 Stoler, *Carnal Knowledge and Imperial Power,* 7.

5 Pasquini, "One Last Word on Puerto Rico."

6 Freeman, *Time Binds,* 7.

7 Bhabha, "Signs Taken for Wonders," 42.

8 Spivak, "Time and Timing," 99. Regarding the deliberate and subtle interarticulations between temporality and colonialism in her read of Hegel's read of the *Srimadbhagavadgita,* Spivak offers the difference between time and timing.

9 Ibid., 99.

10 Colo, "Hybrid State."

11 According to Colo, "the hybrid form" is "the expression of a postcolonial aesthetic" or "utopia as possibility." "The art of the postcolonial mind must be a paradox between the penetration of the masters and the syncretism of their origins."

12 Ibid.

13 Colo, "Endurance Art," 69.

14 For more about Abramović, Stelarc, Athey, and other endurance performance artists, see Jones, *Body Art*; Goldberg, *Performa*; Gonzalez Rice, *Long Suffering*.

15 Colo, "Endurance Art."

16 Wilson and Colo, "'Oh Colo How You Perform Contradiction?'" Colo's full description of *Superman 51* in the conversation with Wilson:

   SUPERMAN / running dragging lumber 51 sticks of wood tied to my body on the West Side Highway till exhausted / bound in ropes / premeditated act of defeat / a way Americans sometimes make sacrifices / to show poetics / symbolism to express a theatre without an audience I no one can follow you / they can see you but they have to run to follow you / also about sports / endurance / pushing my body to the limit / extreme way to achieve ecstasy / psychology of force / culture and language dissolve / culture is irrelevant

17 Mbembé, *On the Postcolony*.

18 Ibid., 3.

19 Bhabha, Spivak, and Mbembé are useful to turn to as scholars of postcolonial theory; even in these modest passages, they explicate the profundity of the colonial subject's choreography in time and space. But none of them is directly speaking of the special situation of Puerto Rico or this place as one of exception; thus I am aware that invoking the problems that "Africa" and "India" face, for example, may appear as a conflation of geographies, people, and even time. Yet the turn to these authors and spaces is not to appropriate the internal logic from which they write, reprove, and rethink, but to place the situation of Puerto Rico within a larger framework of the rhetoric and practice of colonial subjectivity and its direct relation to Being.

20 Mbembé, *On the Postcolony*, 9.

21 Hegel, *Hegel's Science of Logic*.

22 Viego, *Dead Subjects*.

23 Ibid., 4.

24 Roger Stern, *Superman: Sunday Classics: 1939–1943* (New York: DC Comics, 2006).

25 Muñoz, *Disidentifications*, 42–43.

26 Simonini, "William Pope.L," *Interview Magazine*, January 20, 2013, www.interviewmagazine.com. Simonini notes that the work took place in installments, with "each installment lasting as long as Pope.L could endure the knee and elbow pain (often about six blocks)."

27 Lepecki, *Exhausting Dance*, 100; Thompson, "Afterbirth of a Nation," 67; Sweeny, "'This Performance Art Is for the Birds,'" 142. Some authors cite *The Great*

White Way as beginning in 2002 (Lepecki); others identify its start date as 2001 (Sweeny), "well before the events of September 11" (Thompson), or even as early as the late 1990s (Simonini).

28 Thompson, "Afterbirth of a Nation," 69. A special thank-you to Jessica Kadish-Hernández, a former student of William Pope.L at the University of Chicago for her insights on the intricacy of this piece, explaining precisely the feat of endurance undertaken by the artist for almost a decade.

29 Lepecki, *Exhausting Dance*, 97.

30 Ibid., 97.

31 Fanon, *Black Skin, White Masks*, 109; Lepecki, *Exhausting Dance*, 88.

32 Heidegger, *Being and Time*, 216.

33 Blattner, *Heidegger's* Being and Time, 128.

34 Ibid., 128.

35 Lepecki, "Stumble Dance."

36 Ibid., 51.

37 Ibid.

38 Rivera-Servera, *Performing Queer Latinidad*.

39 Ibid., 139.

40 Ibid., 139.

41 "Artist Papo Colo Is Spending 400 Days of Solitude in the Puerto Rican Jungle," *Creators*, February 13, 2017, https://creators.vice.com.

42 Biesenbach, "My Trip to the Puerto Rican Rainforest with Papo Colo."

43 Krogstad, "Historic Population Losses Continue across Puerto Rico."

44 Biesenbach, "My Trip to the Puerto Rican Rainforest with Papo Colo."

45 Papo Colo intended to spend four hundred days in El Yunque; he began on January 7, 2017. On day 256—September 20, 2017—Hurricane Maria struck.

46 Wilson and Colo, "'Oh Colo How You Perform Contradiction?'"; "Digital Mural Project: Papo Colo."

47 Monica Uszerowicz, "'I Am an Invented Character.'"

48 Ibid.

49 Nietzsche, *Thus Spoke Zarathustra*.

50 Ibid., 3.

51 Ibid., 5.

52 Ibid., 12.

53 Miklowitz, *Metaphysics to Metafictions*, 117.

54 Ibid., 119.

55 Ibid., 120.

56 Papo Colo, *Coronation* (1976, gelatin silver print, New York, MoMA PS1).

57 "Papo Colo," MoMA PS1.

58 "Papo Colo," Museo de Arte de Ponce.

59 *Playing with Fire: Political Interventions, Dissident Acts, and Mischievous Actions,* El Museo del Barrio, n.d., www.elmuseo.org.

60 Quiles, "Bearing Witness," 112.

61 Ramírez, "Passing on *Latinidad*."

62 In 1977, El Museo del Barrio's third director, Jack Agüeros, moved the museum from a series of storefronts in El Barrio to its current location on Fifth Avenue (Ramírez, "Passing on *Latinidad*," 8). Although El Museo moved closer to institutions such as the Metropolitan Museum of Art and the Guggenheim, for almost twenty years afterward, the museum's mission remained clearly defined as an institution that was dedicated to the art of the Puerto Rican community in El Barrio. But between 1994 and 2000, the museum's mission statement changed three times. In 2000, the statement read, "The mission of El Museo del Barrio is to present and preserve the art and culture of Puerto Ricans and all Latin Americans in the United States" (Ramírez, "Passing on *Latinidad*," 4).

63 According to Yasmín Ramírez, over the six years between the first and third mission revisions, the museum was met with protest campaigns from the Puerto Rican community in the guise of the following collectives: Next Millennium (1997–1999), We Are Watching You (2001–2002), and Nuestro Museo Action Committee (2002). Ramírez writes that arguments from these groups claimed that El Museo del Barrio was a testament to the survival of the Puerto Rican diaspora and struggles in the 1960s and 1970s by Puerto Ricans for equal rights and self-representation. The community saw the move by the board as one that rejected US Latinx art for what Arlene Dávila argues as art from the "open-door" countries that have strong European ties (Dávila, *Latinizing Culture,* 14). As one community member commented in 2002, "There is too much focus on Eurocentric Latin American artists. The board wants to eliminate its Nuyorican identity, which to them means lower class" (Lee, "A 'Museo' Moves Away.").

On the other side of the debate were the Board of Trustee members who felt that El Museo del Barrio needed to become a Latin American art museum that would benefit from entering the "better-respected" and financed network of the Latin American art market. Justifications were also made through the changing demographics of El Barrio: the museum exhibited Latinx work since 1977, increased the funding pool, and created a version of Puerto Rican identity as essentially Latin American (Ramírez, "Passing on *Latinidad*," 3). The board director, Tony Bechara, echoed this sentiment to the *New York Times*: "If the criticism is that we're not an ethnocentric gallery, then that's fair, but our ambition and our mission demand that we become a world-class museum, open to all people" (Lee, "A 'Museo' Moves Away"). But why isn't an ethnocentric museum world-class and open to all? Does this opposition implicate another understanding of class? By world-class, does he really mean a stratification of art that repositions the binary of high art and low art, and its inherent connection to race and racialization?

In 1994, the mission statement added the idea of the museum as a "forum" for cultural exchange. Susana Torruella Levál, director, organized a three-part exhibition, Artists Talk Back: Visual Conversations with El Museo, which invited Puerto Rican, Latinx, and Latin American artists to speak to visitors about art and works from the museum's collection (Ramírez, "Passing on *Latinidad*," 4). In 1996, a newly constituted Board of Trustees created a Mission Task Force Committee, which defined the purpose of the museum in terms of collecting and exhibiting art rather than a forum. They also attempted to shorten the name of the museum to El Museo. While they were not successful, they were able to remove mention of Puerto Ricans from the mission statement (Ramírez, "Passing on *Latinidad*," 4).

In 2002, Julián Zugazagoitia, a Mexican, became the first non–Puerto Rican director of the museum. Speaking with *Hispanic* magazine in 2006, Zugazagoitia, who spent years at the Guggenheim Museum as well as in Europe, stated in justification of his hiring, "You don't have to be Egyptian to be a great Egyptologist" (Caballero, "El Museo on Fifth Avenue," 56). The problem with this example is that an Egyptologist studies an ancient culture far removed from present-day Egyptian culture, while a Puerto Rican director of a Puerto Rican institution is a member actively living and participating in that culture. His example conflates history, people, culture, and a field of study. For Zugazagoitia, the progression of the museum to an institution that showcases Latin American artists and not solely Puerto Rican artists is natural, as "no institution can survive in a multicultural world focusing only on one culture" (57). The island itself has become bound by incompletion: if they are not presented with their dutiful attachments as necessary to remain whole, then they are excluded. The selection of Zugazagoitia as the museum's director above community protest represents the distancing of El Museo del Barrio from the Puerto Rican community under the guise of "legitimizing" the institution in the art world. Arlene Dávila, in "Latinizing Culture," 187, argues that Puerto Rican artists are not accepted as Latin American artists and are more likely to be subject to political and economic criteria when included in exhibitions. While El Museo del Barrio attempts to alter its conception as a "minority" institution, Latinxs are faced with marginalization not only from the majoritarian establishment, but from the Latin American art world that rejects US-based Latinxs. Caballero affirms Zugazagoitia's belief, writing, "Appointing an individual with such a distinguished background represents a significant milestone in the development of El Museo as an institution with a broader and more relevant mission on a global scale" (56–57). Zugazagoitia himself adds, "El Museo was never only Puerto Rican. Even the earliest exhibits featured art from other Hispanic cultures. Raphael Montañez Ortiz, El Museo's founding force, would say exactly the same thing" (ibid., 57). The Puerto Rican activists who have worked to keep the museum focused on El Barrio would surely challenge this claim, from the evidence of community protests.

64 Bennett, *Birth of the Museum*, 5.

65 Ibid., 90–91.

66 Tony Bennett, "The Exhibitionary Complex," in *New Formations*, 4 (Spring 1988): 73–102.

CHAPTER 3. COUNTDOWN TO THE FUTURE

1 "Guide to the Pedro Pietri Papers," Centro de Estudios Puertorriqueños, Archives of the Puerto Rican Diaspora, Hunter College, City University of New York, April 2007, http://centropr.hunter.cuny.edu.

2 By the great Fornés, here, I am referring to the feminist, queer, Cuban American prolific playwright, director, and pedagogue Maria Irene Fornés. A leading figure in the avant-garde Off-Off-Broadway movement, which began in New York City in the 1960s, she wrote over forty plays and directed the INTAR Hispanic Playwrights in Residence Laboratory for nearly fourteen years, beginning in 1981. See "Maria Irene Fornés," *Encyclopedia Britannica*, May 10, 2018, www.britannica.com; "María Irene Fornés: 1999–2000 Residency 1 Playwright," Signature Theatre, n.d., www.signaturetheatre.org; "History," INTAR: Producing Latino Voices in English since 1966, n.d., www.intartheatre.org.

3 Pietri, *Masses Are Asses*. It is important to note that the geographical details in the text are revealed over the course of the play. On page 6, Pietri first establishes the setting as "a fancy restaurant or an empty apartment." Soon after, on page 8, Gentleman locates the fancy/fantasy restaurant in Paris, then shares the apartment's South Bronx location in a line on page 36. Finally, on page 37, Lady reveals the true nature of the "closet size apartment": it "used to be a toilet and is still a toilet and will always be a toilet!"

4 Ibid., 7.

5 Ibid., 6. Through this use of Arabic numerals, "30 or 93 / 93 or 30," Pietri wants to distort our understanding of linear time through numbers as a way to expose how the countdown prefaces the looping nature of time itself.

6 Ibid., 17.

7 Ibid., 43, 72.

8 Ibid., 18.

9 Noel, *In Visible Movement*, 19.

10 Ibid., 19.

11 Pietri, *Masses Are Asses*, 37.

12 Virilio, *Aesthetics of Disappearance*.

13 Pietri, *Masses Are Asses*, 6.

14 In the text, Pietri uses Arabic numerals rather than spelling out numbers (e.g., 15, not fifteen) to visually guide how we understand the play's tempo. The reader's visual experience contributes to the play's affective experience.

15 Pietri, *Masses Are Asses*, 25.

16 Ibid., 28.

17 Ibid., 31.

18 Ibid., 10.

19 Ibid., 11.

20 Pietri, *Pedro Pietri: Selected Poetry*, 3.

21 Ibid., 12.

22 Pietri, "In His Own Words," 173–174.

23 Pietri, *Pedro Pietri: Selected Poetry*, 3.

24 "Guide to the Pedro Pietri Papers."

25 Márquez, *Puerto Rican Poetry*.

26 David González, "Pedro Pietri, 59, Poet Who Chronicled Nuyorican Life," *New York Times*, March 6, 2004, www.nytimes.com.

27 Hernández, *Puerto Rican Voices in English*, 116.

28 "Guide to the Pedro Pietri Papers."

29 Pietri, "In His Own Words," 174; Hernández, *Puerto Rican Voices in English*, 116.

30 Pietri, "In His Own Words," 173; "Guide to the Pedro Pietri Papers."

31 "Guide to the Pedro Pietri Papers."

32 For a beautiful exploration of the New Rican Village alongside the aesthetic components of political life in Puerto Rican revolutionary politics, research Wilson Valentín-Escobar's curated show at Loisaida Inc., part of the 2015 three-part exhibition "¡Presente! The Young Lords in New York" (see Holland Cotter, "When the Young Lords Were Outlaws in New York," *New York Times*, July 23, 2015, www. nytimes.com). Valentín-Escobar's exhibition, which also included a video homage to trans activist Sylvia Rivera, highlighted "the cultural legacy that the Lords left, a populist activism that produced vivid images and had the imaginative lift of performance art" (ibid.).

33 Roseman, "New Rican Village," 139.

34 De La Roche, *Teatro Hispano!*, 18; "Guide to the Pedro Pietri Papers"; Hernández, *Puerto Rican Voices in English*, 108.

35 "Pedro Pietri," *Playbill Vault*, n.d., www.playbillvault.com.

36 Pietri, "In His Own Words," 174.

37 Ibid., 173.

38 "Guide to the Pedro Pietri Papers."

39 In the 1990s, Pietri and the artist ADÁL (then known as Adál Maldonado) developed *El Puerto Rican Embassy* from the ashes of Eddie Figueroa's performance space New Rican Village; this mobile collaboration, which included creating gallery installations, passports, and a national anthem as well as award ceremonies and performances, continues on in the form of an Internet archive maintained by ADÁL. See Noel, *In Visible Movement*. ADÁL and Pietri would also organize Viequethon 2002: Poetry and Concert for Peace, an event on the island of Vieques to protest the United States' use of it for bomb testing. See Caronan, *Legitimizing Empire*.

40 Hernández, *Puerto Rican Voices in English*, 116.

41 Pietri, "There Was Never No Tomorrow."

42 Ibid.

43 Goffman, *Presentation of Self*.

44 Pietri, *Masses Are Asses*, 41.

45 Ibid., 39.

46 Ibid., 44.

47 Ibid., 41.

48 Crespy, "Nuyorican Absurdist," 41.

49 While Einstein affirmed some place for psychical time, he rejected an affective and intuitive one, following to a large degree that Parmenidean frame against duration in favor of a rigorous and horizontal past, present, and future. Bergson argued against Einstein's theory of relativity. See Einstein, *Relativity*.

50 Bergson, *Time and Free Will*, 100.

51 Ibid., 100.

52 Ibid., 10.

53 Marcel Duchamp, *Fountain* (1917/1964, ceramic, glaze, and paint, 15 × 19 1/4 × 24 5/8 inches [38.1 × 48.9 × 62.55 cm]), San Francisco Museum of Modern Art, www.sfmoma.org. Research suggests, however, that Duchamp did not in fact create this piece. Groundbreaking Dada artist Baroness Elsa von Freytag-Loringhoven may have originally created it under the pseudonym Richard Mutt; it was rejected from its first exhibition and later attributed to Duchamp, following Freytag-Loringhoven's death. See Josh Jones, "The Iconic Urinal & Work of Art, 'Fountain,' Wasn't Created by Marchel Duchamp But by the Pioneering Dada Artist Elsa von Freytag-Loringhoven," *Open Culture*, July 5, 2018, http://openculture.com.

54 Pietri, *Masses Are Asses*, 40–41.

55 Ibid., 12–14.

56 Ibid., 48.

57 Ibid., 8–9.

58 Ibid., 9.

59 Merleau-Ponty, *Phenomenology of Perception*, viii.

60 Ibid., 215.

61 Ibid., 478.

62 Ibid., 477.

63 Kristeva, *Powers of Horror*, 9.

64 Sartre, *Nausea*.

65 Cruz-Malavé, "'What a Tangled Web!': Masculinity, Abjection, and the Foundations of Puerto Rican Literature."

66 Pietri, *Masses Are Asses*, 22.

67 Ibid., 42–43.

68 Muñoz, *Cruising Utopia*.

69 Pietri, *Masses Are Asses*, 45.

70 Ibid., 52.

71 Ibid., 53.

72 Ibid., 49.

73 Cruz-Malavé, "Teaching Puerto Rican Authors," 48.

74 Rossini, *Contemporary Latina/o Theater*, 28.

75 Crespy, "Nuyorican Absurdist," 26.

76 Ibid., 28.

77 Muñoz, *Disidentifications*, xi–xii.

78 Matilla Rivas, "Algunos Aspectos," 91. Translation to English is my own.

79 Crespy, "Nuyorican Absurdist," 27.

80 Pietri, *Masses Are Asses*, 21.

81 Crespy, "Nuyorican Absurdist," 30.

82 Noel, *In Visible Movement*, 22.

83 Noel. "On *Out of Focus Nuyoricans, Noricuas*, and Performance Identities," 2.

84 Merleau-Ponty, *Phenomenology of Perception*, 210.

85 Ibid., 228.

86 Pietri, *Masses Are Asses*, 11.

87 Ibid., 12.

88 Ibid., 12.

89 Ibid., 13.

90 Pietri, "Puerto Rican Obituary," in Pietri, *Pedro Pietri: Selected Poetry*, 4.

91 Merleau-Ponty, *Phenomenology of Perception*, 215.

92 Pietri, *Masses Are Asses*, 79.

93 Killian and Brazil, *Kenning Anthology of Poets Theater*.

CHAPTER 4. LOOPING SENSATIONS

1 A shorter version of this chapter, titled "Waiting in the Seat of Sensation: The Brown Existentialism of Ryan Rivera," can be found in "Lingering in Latinidad: Theory, Aesthetics, and Performance in Latina/o Studies." This special issue of *Women & Performance*, edited by Christina León and Joshua Guzmán, highlights emergent experimental aesthetics in Latinidad (*Women & Performance* 25, no. 3 [2015]: 336–352). Prior to publication, the central theoretical strands of this piece were first presented for the panel "Feeling Time in the Lower East Side: Shifting Narratives of Ricanness" at the "Haciendo Caminos: Mapping the Future of U.S. Latina/o Literatures" conference at John Jay College, City University of New York, March 2013.

Through the generous support of the School of Visual Arts, El Museo del Barrio (especially Noel Valentín), City Without Walls, the Queens Museum of Art, Exit Art, artists Yuko Shimizu and Sarah Wolfe, Stonewall Democratic Club of New York City former president Melissa Sklarz, curator Deborah Cullen, Ariana Ruiz, Joshua Chambers-Letson, Jessica Kadish-Hernández, and Mateo Hurtado, I have been able to acquire and house most of Rivera's work, including self-published novels, emails, letters, and other personal information. I also want to thank Rebecca Rivera, who graciously shared the rights to her brother's impressive archive, helping this project to take on its fullest shape. I want to also add that the job of any Brown existentialism is to capture those personages often only relevant for a moment in a specific spatial context. Specks of Ryan Rivera were waiting in the world to be forms of evidence. In fact, waiting to matter in the world is the business of Brownness and Ricanness, of all colonial lifeworlds.

2 For an exquisite look at these performers, see Warr with Jones, *Artist's Body*.

3 Working from this provocative tradition, informed by both Euro-American and minoritarian conceptualism, landed Rivera in evocative exhibitions at SVA Eastside Gallery (2002), El Museo del Barrio (2002), Exit Art (2002), New Jersey's City Without Walls (2006), and the Queens Museum of Art (2008).

4 Rivera, "Identity Crisis," 2.

5 Gordon, *Existentia Africana*, 10.

6 Some authors identified as Black existentialists include Richard Wright, Frantz Fanon, Ralph Ellison, William R. Jones, Lucius T. Outlaw, Naomi Zack, and Lewis R. Gordon. It is necessary to reiterate that the height of every movement, as we know, always already harbors an historical antecedent. For many of the aforementioned authors, it was impossible to advance a theory of existentialism and race without considering the important work of W. E. B. Du Bois—a prolific body of work dating back to the late 1800s that expresses an ontology of race and Being.

7 Rivera, "Identity Crisis," 2.

8 Ryan Rivera, letter to Margarita Aguilar, attached slide list, September 7, 2001, courtesy of El Museo del Barrio.

9 Ryan Rivera, letter to Margarita Aguilar, September 7, 2001, courtesy of El Museo del Barrio. All quotations in this paragraph come from this letter.

10 Shimizu, *My Friend Ryan.*

11 Ibid.

12 According to Shimizu, the administration of the School of Visual Arts (SVA) declared his work too disturbing to continue displaying.

13 One take on Brown experimental work, "Puerto Rican *Rasanblaj,*" comes from Lawrence La Fountain-Stokes. In this article, La Fountain-Stokes restages a conversation with Gina Athena Ulysses's concept of *rasanblaj* in order to consider the complex aesthetic traditions of Puerto Rican performance artist Freddie Mercado. He argues that Mercado's performance of drag must be looked at through concepts such as *translocura*, or a state that explores "transgender, translocal, and transnational phenomena," disidentification, archival drag, and *relajo* to account for his "project of staging and rearticulating a complex trans-Caribbean identity." Importantly, La Fountain-Stokes reshifts the aesthetic narrative here, providing Brownness with a way to transcend the boundaries of location, post–Latin American art, and folklore.

14 El Museo del Barrio, *(S) Files 2002.* El Museo, founded in 1969 during the height of the Nuyorican and civil rights movements, was the first Puerto Rican museum of New York City, located in the heart of El Barrio. El Museo is known as an important cultural site in which community concerns are central to the presentation of art. In 2000, two years before Rivera's reveal, the museum began a major expansionist project that included a more global take on Puerto Rican and Latin American art. Rivera's work was featured during a critical ideological time for El Museo, one of which included a more inclusive understanding of Ricanness and Brownness. The expansion was both welcomed and rejected. Community members felt that the move away from primarily Rican concerns would diminish the political and aesthetic importance of the space.

15 El Museo del Barrio, *(S) Files 2002*.
16 Barthes, *A Lover's Discourse*, 37.
17 Ibid., 37–39.
18 Rivera, "Identity Crisis," 3.
19 Nietzsche, *Gay Science*, 194.
20 Ibid., 194.
21 Ibid., 194.
22 El Museo del Barrio, *(S) Files 2002*, 2.
23 Rivera, "Identity Crisis," 3. This Nietzschean recurrence is also reminiscent of Guy Debord's theory of the spectacle.
24 Ryan Rivera, letter to Margarita Aguilar, September 7, 2001.
25 Debord, *Society of the Spectacle*, 2.
26 Ibid., 12.
27 Heidegger, *Concept of Time*, 14.
28 Heidegger, *Being and Time*, 131.
29 Ibid., 131.
30 Heidegger, *Concept of Time*, 10E.
31 Ibid., 14E.
32 Rivera, "Identity Crisis," 2.
33 Ibid., 2.
34 Félix González-Torres, *"Untitled" (Portrait of Ross in L.A.)* (candies individually wrapped in multicolor cellophane [endless supply], 1991), Art Institute of Chicago, www.artic.edu.
35 For a more robust reading on this installation, González-Torres's body of work, and the law that frames the conditions of the Brown and queer subject, please turn to Joshua Takano Chambers-Letson's beautiful essay, "Contracting Justice: The Viral Strategy of Felix González-Torres."
36 In *Being Singular Plural*, Jean-Luc Nancy elucidates the intricate interplay between being and being-with. He states that "being cannot *be* anything but being-with-one-another, circulating in the *with* and as the *with* of this singularly plural coexistence" (3).
37 Rivera, "Identity Crisis," 2.
38 Ibid., 2.
39 Bruce Nauman, *Poke in the Eye/Nose/Ear*, Art21, December 27, 2013, https://art21.org.
40 Descartes, *Meditations on First Philosophy*, 24.
41 Rivera, "Identity Crisis," 2.
42 Butler, "How Can I Deny That These Hands and This Body Are Mine?"
43 Rivera, "Identity Crisis," 2.
44 Barthes, *A Lover's Discourse*, 40.
45 Ibid., 147–149.
46 Ibid., 37–40.
47 Ibid., 38.

48 Ibid., 38.
49 Bergson, *Time and Free Will*, 14.
50 Viego, *Dead Subjects*.
51 Ibid., 121.
52 Heidegger, *Being and Time*, 333.
53 Ibid., 311.
54 Doyle, *Hold It Against Me*, 87.
55 Ibid., 89.
56 Muñoz, "Feeling Brown, Feeling Down," 418.
57 Ibid., 418.
58 Ibid., 418.
59 Cvetkovich, *Depression*, 122.
60 Ibid., 122.
61 Fanon, *Black Skin, White Masks*, 140.
62 Maldonado-Torres, *Against War*, 13.
63 Ibid., 136.
64 Fyodor Dostoyevsky, *Notes from the Underground*, quoted in El Museo del Barrio, *(S) Files 2002: The Selected Files*, 66.
65 Luis Martos's philosophical insights on the concept of *amor fati* in the earlier stages of the writing process helped pave the way for valuable philosophical journeys.
66 Nietzsche, *On the Genealogy of Morals*, 122.
67 Ngai, *Ugly Feelings*, esp. chap. 5, "Anxiety."
68 Rodríguez, *Sexual Futures*, 2.

EPILOGUE

1 Robinson Meyer, "What's Happening with the Relief Effort in Puerto Rico? A Timeline of the Unprecedented Catastrophe of Hurricane Maria," *Atlantic*, October 4, 2017, www.theatlantic.com.
2 See Leyla Santiago, Catherine E. Shoichet, and Jason Kravarik, "Puerto Rico's New Hurricane Maria Death Toll Is 46 Times Higher Than the Government's Previous Count," *CNN*, August 28, 2018. www.cnn.com. This article reports the current definitive estimate of 2,975 deaths, the result of a study conducted by the Milken Institute School of Public Health at George Washington University in collaboration with the University of Puerto Rico Graduate School of Public Health. Over the course of the year following the disaster, this number fluctuated substantially—at one point nearing 5,000—as multiple studies were conducted. This fluctuating death toll exposes the constant loss of life for colonial subjects and the ways in which data are manipulated to enable and disguise genocidal acts and can never fully capture the essence of loss. For an earlier estimate, see Nishant Kishore, Domingo Marqués, Ayesha Mahmud, Mathew V. Kiang, Irmary Rodriguez, Arlan Fuller, Peggy Ebner, et al., "Mortality in Puerto Rico after Hurricane Maria," *New England Journal of Medicine*, May 29, 2018, www.nejm.org. December 2017 inde-

pendent estimates initially were closer to 1,000 (from the *New York Times*, 1,052; from Puerto Rico's Center for Investigative Journalism, 1,065; see Patricia Mazzei, "Puerto Rico Orders Review and Recount of Hurricane Deaths," *New York Times*, December 18, 2017, www.nytimes.com). From December 9, 2017, through August 28, 2018, the official government death toll remained at 64.

3   Nathaniel Parish Flannery, "Will Puerto Rico Require Substantial Debt Forgiveness?," *Forbes*, October 9, 2017, www.forbes.com.

4   Since Hurricane Maria, the aesthetic has played a prominent role in helping reimagine all components of recovery. Centros de Apoyo Mutuo (mutual support centers) sprang up across the island in the wake of the storm, offering theater, dance, music, and other performative avenues alongside food, clothing, shelter, and medical aid; for example, offerings at Centro de Apoyo Mutuo Bucarabones Unido include Theatre of the Oppressed workshops (May 2018), art classes for children and adults (November 2017), live music (December 2017), and more (see www.facebook.com/cambupr). Projects such as Teatro Rodante's "¡Ay María!" provide a theatrical, comedic outlet for performers and spectators to process their experiences with Hurricanes Irma and Maria (see www.facebook.com/aymariaporfavor).

5   It is evident that Lebrón's political and moral philosophical positions, expressed through her poetry, were based on Nationalist Catholicism. Nationalist Catholicism privileged the defense of the nation against tyranny because of the Catholic supposition that if a nation was being suppressed then an immediate uprising was a means of "just war." This particular ideological state was inhabited by Lebrón to advance the subject in favor of the sacrifice of a national culture.

6   Fanon, *Black Skin, White Masks*, 229.

7   Ibid.

BIBLIOGRAPHY

"50 Years of Commonwealth: Part I: Establishing the Commonwealth Constitution, 1950–1953." *Puerto Rico Herald*, July 2, 2002. www.puertorico-herald.org.

"Aftermath." *Time* 63, no. 11 (March 15, 1954): 23.

Ahmed, Sara. *Queer Phenomenology: Orientations, Objects, Others*. Durham, NC: Duke University Press, 2006.

Althusser, Louis. "Ideology and Ideological State Apparatuses: Notes toward an Investigation." In *Lenin and Philosophy and Other Essays*. London: New Left, 1971.

American Psychiatric Association. *Diagnostic and Statistical Manual of Mental Disorders*. 4th ed., text revision. Washington, DC: American Psychiatric Association, 2000.

Anzaldúa, Gloria. *Borderlands/La Frontera: The New Mestiza*. San Francisco: Aunt Lute Books, 1987.

Aparicio, Frances R. "Exposed Bodies: Media and U.S. Puerto Ricans in Public Space." In *None of the Above: Puerto Ricans in the Global Era*, edited by Frances Negrón-Muntaner. New York: Palgrave Macmillan, 2007.

———. "On Sub-versive Signifiers: U.S. Latina/o Writers Tropicalize English." *American Literature* 66, no. 4 (December 1994): 795–801.

Arendt, Hannah. *The Life of the Mind*. Boston: Houghton Mifflin Harcourt, 1981.

"Artist Papo Colo Is Spending 400 Days of Solitude in the Puerto Rican Jungle." *Creators*, February 13, 2017. https://creators.vice.com.

Austin, J. L. *How to Do Things with Words*. Cambridge, MA: Harvard University Press, 1975.

Bakhtin, Mikhail. "Forms of Time and of the Chronotope in the Novel." In *The Dialogic Imagination*, edited by Michael Holquist, translated by Caryl Emerson and Michael Holquist. Austin: University of Texas Press, 1982.

Barthes, Roland. *Camera Lucida*. Translated by Richard Howard. New York: Hill & Wang, 1981.

———. *A Lover's Discourse: Fragments*. Translated by Richard Howard. New York: Hill & Wang, 1978.

Bennett, Tony. *The Birth of the Museum: History, Theory, Politics*. New York: Routledge, 1995.

Bergson, Henri. *Time and Free Will: An Essay on the Immediate Data of Consciousness*. Mineola, NY: Dover, 2001.

Berman Santana, Déborah. "Puerto Rico's Operation Bootstrap: Colonial Roots of a Persistent Model for 'Third World' Development." *Revista Geográfica* 124 (1998): 87–116.

Bhabha, Homi K. "Signs Taken for Wonders." In *The Post-colonial Studies Reader*, edited by Bill Ashcroft, Gareth Griffiths, and Helen Tiffin. New York: Routledge, 1995.

Biesenbach, Klaus. "My Trip to the Puerto Rican Rainforest with Papo Colo." *Artsy*, January 12, 2017. www.artsy.net.

Blattner, William. *Heidegger's* Being and Time. London: Continuum, 2006.

"Board." *ExitArt.org*. www.exitart.org/ (site discontinued).

Briggs, Laura. *Reproducing Empire: Race, Sex, Science and U.S. Imperialism in Puerto Rico*. Berkeley: University of California Press, 2002.

Butler, Judith. *Bodies That Matter: On the Discursive Limits of "Sex."* London: Routledge, 1993.

———. *Excitable Speech: A Politics of the Performative*. London: Routledge, 1997.

———. *Gender Trouble*. New York: Routledge, 1999.

———. "How Can I Deny That These Hands and This Body Are Mine?" In *Material Events: Paul de Man and the Afterlife of Theory*, edited by Tom Cohen et al. Minneapolis: University of Minnesota Press, 2000.

———. *The Psychic Life of Power: Theories in Subjection*. Palo Alto, CA: Stanford University Press, 1997.

Caballero, Ana María. "El Museo on Fifth Avenue." *Hispanic* 19, no. 3 (2006): 56–59.

Cabán, Pedro A. "The Colonial State and Capitalist Expansion in Puerto Rico." *Centro Journal* 2, no. 6 (1989): 87–100.

Cacho, Lisa Marie. *Social Death: Racialized Rightlessness and the Criminalization of the Unprotected*. New York: New York University Press, 2012.

Camus, Albert. "The Myth of Sisyphus." In *The Myth of Sisyphus and Other Essays*, translated by Justin O'Brien. New York: Vintage Books, 1991.

"The Capitol: Puerto Rico Is Not Free." *Time* 63, no. 10 (March 8, 1954): 21.

Cardalda Sánchez, Elsa B., and Amílcar Tirado Avilés. "Ambiguous Identities! The Affirmation of Puertorriqueñidad in the Community Murals of New York City." In *Mambo Montage: the Latinization of New York*, edited by Agustín Laó-Montes and Arlene Dávila. New York: Columbia University Press, 2001.

Caronan, Faye. *Legitimizing Empire: Filipino American and U.S. Puerto Rican Cultural Critique*. Champaign: University of Illinois Press, 2015.

Carter, Holland. "At Museum Born of Politics, New Chief Faces Economics: El Museo del Barrio, Stabilized, Expands Its Mission." *New York Times*, June 6, 2014, C21.

Centro de Estudios Puertorriqueños. "Guide to the Pedro Pietri Papers." Archives of the Puerto Rican Diaspora, April 2007. http://centropr.hunter.cuny.edu.

Césaire, Aimé. *Discourse on Colonialism*. Translated by Joan Pinkham. New York: Monthly Review Press, 2000.

Chambers-Letson, Joshua Takano. "Contracting Justice: The Viral Strategy of Felix González-Torres." *Criticism* 51, no. 4 (Fall 2010): 559–587. https://doi.org/10.1353/crt.2010.0002.

Colo, Papo. "Endurance Art." *Performing Arts Journal* 18, no. 3 (September 1996): 66–70.

———. "The Hybrid State." *Papo Colo Concept Plus*. www.papocolo.com (site discontinued).

Crespy, David. "A Nuyorican Absurdist: Pedro Pietri and His Plays of Happy Subversion." *Latin American Theatre Review* 45, no. 2 (Spring 2012): 25–43. https://doi.org/10.1353/ltr.2012.0008.

Cruz-Malavé, Arnaldo. "Teaching Puerto Rican Authors: Identity and Modernization in Nuyorican Texts." *ADE Bulletin* 91 (Winter 1988): 45–51.

———. "'What a Tangled Web!' Masculinity, Abjection, and the Foundations of Puerto Rican Literature in the United States." *Differences* 8, no. 1 (Spring 1996): 132–151.

———. "'What a Tangled Web . . . !': Masculinidad, abyección y la fundación de la literatura puertorriqueña en los Estados Unidos." *Revista de Crítica Literaria Latinoamericana Año* 23, no. 45 (January 1997): 327–340.

Cullen, Deborah. "Aequilibrium." In *The (S) Files 2002: The Selected Files*, curated by Deborah Cullen and Victoria Noorthoorn. New York: El Museo del Barrio, 2002.

———, ed. *Arte ≠ Vida: Actions by Artists of the Americas, 1960–2000*. New York: El Museo del Barrio, 2008.

Cullen, Deborah, and Victoria Noorthoorn. *The (S) Files 2002: The Selected Files*. New York: El Museo del Barrio, 2002. Published in conjunction with an exhibition of the same title, organized by and presented at El Museo del Barrio, October 24, 2002–February 16, 2003.

Cvetkovich, Ann. *Depression: A Public Feeling*. Durham, NC: Duke University Press, 2012.

Dávila, Arlene. "Latinizing Culture: Art, Museums, and the Politics of U.S. Multicultural Encompassment." *Cultural Anthropology* 14 (1999): 180–202.

Debord, Guy. *The Society of the Spectacle*. Detroit: Black and Red, 1967.

De Kesel, Marc. *Eros and Ethics: Reading Jacques Lacan's Seminar VII*. Albany: State University of New York Press, 2010.

De La Roche, Elisa. *Teatro Hispano!* New York: Taylor & Francis, 1995.

Denis, Nelson A. *War Against All Puerto Ricans: Death and Terror in America's Colony*. New York: Nation Books, 2015.

Derrida, Jacques. *The Gift of Death*. Translated by David Wills. Chicago: University of Chicago Press, 1995.

Descartes, René. *A Discourse on Method*. London: J.M. Dent, 1994.

———. *Meditations on First Philosophy: With Selections from the Objections and Replies*. Translated by John Cottingham. Cambridge: Cambridge University Press, 1996.

Dibblin, Jane. *Day of Two Suns: U.S. Nuclear Testing and the Pacific Islanders*. London: Virago Press, 1988.

"Digital Mural Project: Papo Colo." Galería de la Raza. www.galeriadelaraza.org.

Douglass, Frederick. *Narrative of the Life of Frederick Douglass*. Irvine, CA: Xist, 2015.

Doyle, Jennifer. *Hold It Against Me: Difficulty and Emotion in Contemporary Art*. Durham, NC: Duke University Press, 2013.

Duany, Jorge. *The Puerto Rican Nation on the Move: Identities on the Island and in the United States*. Chapel Hill: University of North Carolina Press, 2002.

Du Bois, W. E. B. *The Souls of Black Folk*. Edited with an introduction and notes by Brent Hayes Edwards. Oxford: Oxford University Press, 2007.

Durkheim, Émile. *Suicide: A Study in Sociology*. Translated by John A. Spaulding and George Simpson. Edited with an introduction by George Simpson. New York: Simon & Schuster, 1979.

Einstein, Albert. *Relativity: The Special and General Theory*. Victoria, BC, Canada: Emporium Books, 2013.

El Museo del Barrio. *The (S) Files 2002: The Selected Files*. New York: El Museo del Barrio, 2002.

Estrin, James. "Puerto Rican Identity, In and Out of Focus." *New York Times*, August 28, 2012. https://lens.blogs.nytimes.com.

Fanon, Frantz. *Black Skin, White Masks*. Translated by Charles Lam Markmann. New York: Grove Press, 1967.

———. *A Dying Colonialism*. Translated by Haakon Chevalier. Introduction by Adolfo Gilly. New York: Grove Press, 1965.

———. *The Wretched of the Earth*. Translated by Constance Farrington. Preface by Jean-Paul Sartre. New York: Grove Press, 1963.

Felski, Rita. *The Gender of Modernity*. Cambridge, MA: Harvard University Press, 1995.

Ferguson, Roderick A. *Aberrations in Black: Toward a Queer of Color Critique*. Minneapolis: University of Minnesota Press, 2003.

Fernández, Ronald. *Prisoners of Colonialism: The Struggle for Justice in Puerto Rico*. Monroe, ME: Common Courage Press, 1994.

Ferreira da Silva, Denise. *Toward a Global Idea of Race*. Minneapolis: University of Minnesota Press, 2007.

Fink, Bruce. *The Lacanian Subject*. Princeton, NJ: Princeton University Press, 1995.

Fiol-Matta, Licia. "Forget '98: An Introduction." *Social Text* 17, no. 2 (Summer 1999): 99–104.

———. *The Great Woman Singer: Gender and Voice in Puerto Rican Music*. Durham, NC: Duke University Press, 2017.

Flores, Juan. *From Bomba to Hip-Hop: Puerto Rican Culture and Latino Identity*. New York: Columbia University Press, 2000.

Foucault, Michel. *Discipline and Punish: The Birth of the Prison*. New York: Vintage Books, 1995.

———. *The History of Sexuality*. Vol. 1. New York: Vintage Books, 1990.

———. *Politics, Philosophy, Culture: Interviews and Other Writings, 1977–1984*. New York: Routledge, 1988.

Freeman, Elizabeth. *Time Binds: Queer Temporalities, Queer Histories*. Durham, NC: Duke University Press, 2010.

Freud, Sigmund. "Mourning and Melancholia." In *The Standard Edition of the Complete Psychological Works of Sigmund Freud, Volume XIV (1914–1916): On the History of the Psycho-Analytic Movement, Papers of Metapsychology and Other Works*, trans. James Strachey. London: Hogarth Press, 1957.

Friedman, Andrea. *Citizenship in Cold War America: The National Security State and the Possibilities of Dissent*. Amherst: University of Massachusetts Press, 2014.

Gherovici, Patricia. *The Puerto Rican Syndrome*. New York: Other Press, 2003.

Goffman, Erving. *The Presentation of Self in Everyday Life.* New York: Anchor, 1959.

Goldberg, RoseLee. *Performa: New Visual Art Performance.* New York: Performa, 2007.

Gonzalez, David. "Pedro Pietri, 59, Poet Who Chronicled Nuyorican Life." *New York Times,* March 6, 2004.

Gonzalez Rice, Karen. *Long Suffering: American Endurance Art as Prophetic Witness.* Ann Arbor: University of Michigan Press, 2016.

González-Torres, Félix. *"Untitled" (Portrait of Ross in L.A.).* Art Institute of Chicago. www.artic.edu.

Gordon, Lewis R. *Existentia Africana: Understanding Africana Existential Thought.* New York: Routledge, 2000.

———. "Introduction: Black Existential Philosophy." In *Existence in Black: An Anthology of Black Existentialism,* edited by Lewis R. Gordon. New York: Routledge, 1997.

Grosfoguel, Ramón, Frances Negrón-Muntaner, and Chloe S. Georas. "Introduction." In *Puerto Rican Jam: Rethinking Colonialism and Nationalism,* edited by Frances Negrón-Muntaner and Ramón Grosfoguel. Minneapolis: University of Minnesota Press, 1997.

Halberstam, Jack. *In a Queer Time and Place: Transgender Bodies, Subcultural Lives.* New York: New York University Press, 2005.

Heathfield, Adrian. "Durational Aesthetics." In *Cultures of the Curatorial 2: Timing: On the Temporal Dimension of Exhibiting,* edited by Beatrice von Bismarck et al. Berlin: Sternberg Press, 2014.

Hegel, Georg Wilhelm Fredrich. *Hegel's Science of Logic.* Translated by A. V. Miller. Amherst, NY: Prometheus Books, 1989.

———. *The Phenomenology of Spirit.* Translated by A. V. Miller. Oxford: Oxford University Press, 1977.

Heidegger, Martin. *Being and Time.* Translated by Joan Stambaugh. Albany: State University of New York Press, 1996.

———. *The Concept of Time.* Translated by William McNeill. Cambridge, MA: Blackwell, 1992.

Henry, Paget. "Africana Phenomenology: Its Philosophical Implications." In "Postcontinental Philosophy," coordinated by Nelson Maldonado-Torres, special issue of *Worlds & Knowledges Otherwise* 1, dossier 3 (October 1, 2006). Durham, NC: Duke University Center for Global Studies and the Humanities. http://globalstudies.trinity.duke.edu.

Hernández, Carmen Dolores. *Puerto Rican Voices in English: Interviews with Writers.* Westport, CT: Greenwood, 1997.

Hulen, Bertram. "Attack on Winship Raises an Inquiry." *New York Times,* July 31, 1956, 58.

Hull, Harwood. "Freedom Bill Splits Puerto Rico." *New York Times,* May 3, 1936, E6.

———. "Trial for Sedition Stirs Puerto Rico." *New York Times,* July 26, 1936, E7.

"Ickes Warns Puerto Rico to Shun Terrorism; Says U.S. Won't Tolerate Action of 'Fanatics.'" *New York Times,* March 11, 1936, 11.

Jackson, Jhoni. "Powerful Photo Series 'Puerto Ricans Underwater' Is a Biting Metaphor for an Island Drowning in Debt." *Remezcla,* November 28, 2016. http://remezcla.com.

Jiménez de Wagenheim, Olga. *Nationalist Heroines: Puerto Rican Women History Forgot, 1930s–1950s*. Princeton, NJ: Markus Wiener, 2017.

———. *Puerto Rico's Revolt for Independence: El Grito de Lares*. Princeton, NJ: Markus Weiner, 1993.

Jones, Amelia. *Body Art / Performing the Subject*. Minneapolis: University of Minnesota Press, 1988.

Khanna, Ranjana. *Dark Continents: Psychoanalysis and Colonialism*. Durham, NC: Duke University Press, 2003.

Kihss, Peter. "Sublime Heroism Cited in Shooting." *New York Times*, March 3, 1954, 14.

Killian, Kevin, and David Brazil. *The Kenning Anthology of Poets Theater: 1945–1985*. Berkeley, CA: Kenning Editions, 2010.

Klein, Melanie. "A Contribution to the Psychogenesis of Manic-Depressive States." In *The Selected Melanie Klein*, edited by Juliet Mitchell. New York: Free Press, 1986.

Kristeva, Julia. *Powers of Horror: An Essay on Abjection*. Translated by Leon S. Roudiez. New York: Columbia University Press, 1982.

Krogstad, Jens Manuel. "Historic Population Losses Continue across Puerto Rico." Pew Research Center, March 24, 2016. www.pewresearch.org.

Lacan, Jaques. *Ecrits*. New York: Norton, 2002.

———. *The Seminar of Jacques Lacan, Book XVII: The Other Side of Psychoanalysis*. Translated by Russell Grigg. New York: Norton, 2007.

La Fountain-Stokes, Lawrence. "Puerto Rican *Rasanblaj*: Freddie Mercado's Gender Disruption." *e-misférica* 12, no. 1 (2015). http://hemisphericinstitute.org.

———. *Queer Ricans: Sexualities and Cultures in the Diaspora*. Minneapolis: University of Minnesota Press, 2009.

La Operación. Directed by Ana María García. 1982. Brooklyn, NY: Cinema Guild, 2007. DVD.

Laing, R. D. *The Politics of Experience*. New York: Pantheon Books, 1967.

Lebrón, Dolores. *Antología de la Poesía Cósmica de Lolita Lebrón*. Edited by Fredo Arias de la Canal. Mexico: Frente de Afirmación Hispanista, 2000.

Lederer, Susan E. "'Porto Ricochet': Joking about Germs, Cancer, and Race Extermination in the 1930s." *American Literary History* 14, vol. 4 (2002): 720–746.

Lee, Denny. "A 'Museo' Moves Away from Its Barrio Image." *New York Times*, July 21, 2002.

Lee, Pamela M. *Chronophobia: On Time in the Art of the 1960s*. Cambridge, MA: MIT Press, 2004.

Lepecki, André. *Exhausting Dance: Performance and the Politics of Movement*. New York: Routledge, 2006.

———. "Stumble Dance." *Women & Performance* 14, no. 1 (2004): 47–61.

"Loisaida Figures." *Centro Voices*, February 1, 2017. http://centroweb.hunter.cuny.edu.

Lopez, Iris. "An Ethnography of the Medicalization of Puerto Rican Women's Reproduction." In *Pragmatic Women and Body Politics*, edited by Margaret Lock and Patricia A. Kaufert. New York: Cambridge University Press, 1998.

Luciano, Dana. *Arranging Grief: Sacred Time and the Body in Nineteenth-Century America*. New York: New York University Press, 2007.

Maldonado-Torres, Nelson. *Against War: Views from the Underside of Modernity*. Durham, NC: Duke University Press, 2008.

Márquez, Roberto, ed., trans. *Puerto Rican Poetry: An Anthology from Aboriginal to Contemporary Times*. Amherst: University of Massachusetts Press, 2006.

Marx, Karl. *The 18th Brumaire of Louis Bonaparte*. New York: International, 1969.

———. *Capital: A Critique of Political Economy*. Translated by Ben Fowkes. London: Penguin, 1990.

Matilla Rivas, Alfredo. "Algunos Aspectos Del Teatro De Pedro Pietri." *Confluencia* 5, no. 1 (Fall 1989): 91–97.

———. "Forward." In *Illusions of a Revolving Door: Plays/Teatro*, edited by Alfredo Matilla Rivas. Rio Piedras, PR: Editorial de la Universidad de Puerto Rico, 1992.

Mbembé, Achille. "Necropolitics." Translated by Libby Meintjes. *Public Culture* 15, no. 1 (Winter 2003): 11–40.

———. *On the Postcolony*. Translated by A. M. Berrett, Janet Roitman, Murray Last, and Steven Rendall. Berkeley: University of California Press, 2001.

McCann, Joseph T. *Terrorism on American Soil: A Concise History of Plots and Perpetrators from the Famous to the Forgotten*. Boulder, CO: Sentient, 2006.

Merleau-Ponty, Maurice. *Phenomenology of Perception*. Translated by Colin Smith. New York: Routledge, 2002.

Miklowitz, Paul S. *Metaphysics to Metafictions: Hegel, Nietzsche, and the End of Philosophy*. Albany: State University of New York Press, 1998.

Miller, Toby, and George Yúdice. *Cultural Policy*. London: SAGE, 2002.

Morales Carrión, Arturo. *Puerto Rico: A Political and Cultural History*. New York: Norton, 1984.

Moten, Fred. *In the Break: The Aesthetics of the Black Radical Tradition*. Minneapolis: University of Minnesota Press, 2003.

Muñiz-Argüelles, Luis. "The Status of Languages in Puerto Rico." In *Language and Law: Proceedings of the First Conference of the International Institute of Comparative Linguistic Law*, edited by Paul Pupier and José Woehrling. Montreal: Wilson and Lafleur, 1989. www.muniz-arguelles.com.

Muñoz, José Esteban. "'Chico, What Does It Feel Like to Be a Problem?' The Transmission of Brownness." In *A Companion to Latino/a Studies*, edited by Juan Flores and Renato Rosaldo. Oxford: Blackwell, 2007.

———. *Cruising Utopia: The Then and There of Queer Futurity*. New York: New York University Press, 2009.

———. *Disidentifications: Queers of Color and the Performance of Politics*. Minneapolis: University of Minnesota Press, 1999.

———. "Ephemera as Evidence: Introductory Notes to Queer Acts." *Women & Performance* 8, no. 2 (1996): 5–18.

———. "Feeling Brown: Ethnicity and Affect in Ricardo Bracho's *The Sweetest Hangover (and Other STDs)*." *Theatre Journal* 52, no. 1 (March 2000): 67–79.

———. "Feeling Brown, Feeling Down: Latina Affect, the Performativity of Race, and the Depressive Position." In *The Routledge Queer Studies Reader*, edited by Donald E. Hall and Annamarie Jagose, with Andrea Bebell and Susan Potter. New York: Routledge, 2012.

———. "Vitalism's After-Burn: The Sense of Ana Mendieta." *Women & Performance* 21, no. 2 (July 2011): 191–198.

Nabokov, Vladimir. *Lolita.* New York: Random House, 1989.

Nancy, Jean-Luc. *Being Singular Plural.* Translated by Robert D. Richardson and Anne E. O'Byrne. Stanford, CA: Stanford University Press, 2000.

"The Nation." *New York Times*, March 7, 1954, E1.

"Nation: Four Go Free." *Time*, September 17, 1979.

"Nationalism Made Puerto Rico Issue." *New York Times*, March 1, 1936, E5.

Negrón-Muntaner, Frances. *Boricua Pop: Puerto Ricans and the Latinization of Culture.* New York: New York University Press, 2004.

———. "Introduction." In *None of the Above: Puerto Ricans in the Global Era*, edited by Frances Negrón-Muntaner. New York: Palgrave Macmillan, 2007.

Nelson, Anne. "Lolita Lebron Would Rather Die in Prison." *Nation*, August 11–18, 1979.

Ngai, Sianne. *Ugly Feelings.* Cambridge, MA: Harvard University Press, 2005.

Nietzsche, Friedrich. *The Gay Science: With a Prelude in Rhymes and an Appendix of Songs.* Translated by Walter Kaufmann. New York: Random House, 1974.

———. *On the Genealogy of Morals.* Translated by Douglas Smith. Oxford: Oxford Paperbacks, 2009.

———. *Thus Spoke Zarathustra.* Cambridge: Cambridge University Press, 2006.

Noel, Urayoán. *In Visible Movement: Nuyorican Poetry from Sixties to Slam.* Iowa City: University of Iowa Press, 2014.

———. "On *Out of Focus Nuyoricans, Noricuas*, and Performance Identities." *Liminalities* 10, nos. 3/4 (2014). http://liminalities.net.

Nyong'o, Tavia. *The Amalgamation Waltz: Race, Performance, and the Ruses of Memory.* Minneapolis: University of Minnesota Press, 2009.

———. "Little Monsters: Race, Sovereignty, and Queer Inhumanism in *Beasts of the Southern Wild*." *GLQ* 21, nos. 2–3 (2015): 249–272.

Ortega, Mariana. *In-Between: Latina Feminist Phenomenology, Multiplicity, and the Self.* Albany: State University of New York Press, 2016.

Otto Gatell, Frank. "Independence Rejected: Puerto Rico and the Tydings Bill of 1936." *Hispanic American Historical Review* 38 (1958): 25–44.

"Papo Colo." MoMA PS1. Published online in conjunction with an exhibition of the same title, organized by and presented at MoMA PS1, May 22–August 28, 2016. http://momaps1.org.

———. Museo de Arte de Ponce. Published online in conjunction with an exhibition of the same title, organized by and presented at Museo de Arte de Ponce, October 29, 2016–January 30, 2017. www.museoarteponce.org.

Pasquini, Stefano. "One Last Word on Puerto Rico: Stefano Pasquini in Conversation with Papo Colo." www.stefpasquini.com.

"Pedro Pietri." *Playbill.* www.playbillvault.com.

Pérez, Emma. *The Decolonial Imaginary: Writing Chicanas into History.* Bloomington: Indiana University Press, 1999.

Pietri, Pedro. "In His Own Words." In *The Outlaw Bible of American Poetry,* edited by Alan Kaufman. New York: Thunder's Mouth Press, 1999.

———. *The Masses Are Asses.* Los Angeles: Green Integer Books, 2003.

———. *Pedro Pietri: Selected Poetry.* Edited by Juan Flores and Pedro López Adorno. San Francisco: City Lights Books, 2015.

———. "There Was Never No Tomorrow, Nuyorican Pedro Pietri in His Own Words." Edited by Raymond R. Beltrán. February 6, 2004. www.laprensa-sandiego.org.

Plato. *The Republic.* Translated by G. M. A. Grube. Revised by C. D. C. Reeve. Indianapolis: Hackett, 1992.

"Porto Ricochet." *Time,* February 15, 1932, 32–33.

"Puerto Rican Assails 'Yankee Despotism.'" *New York Times,* April 17, 1936, 13.

"Puerto Rico Celebrates." *New York Times,* July 26, 1935, 9.

Quiles, Daniel R. "Bearing Witness." *Art in America,* June/July 2008, 112.

Ramírez, Yasmín. "Passing on *Latinidad*: An Analysis of Critical Responses to El Museo del Barrio's Pan-Latino Mission Statements." Presentation at the Interpretation and Representation of Latino Cultures: Research and Museums Conference, Smithsonian Institute, Washington, DC, November 20–23, 2002. http://latino.si.edu.

Ramos-Zayas, Ana Y. *National Performances: The Politics of Class, Race, and Space in Puerto Rican Chicago.* Chicago: University of Chicago Press, 2003.

Ricœur, Paul. *Living Up to Death.* Translated by David Pellauer. Chicago: University of Chicago Press, 2009.

Rivera, Ryan. "Identity Crisis." BFA thesis, School of Visual Arts, 2002.

Rivera-Servera, Ramón H. *Performing Queer Latinidad: Dance, Sexuality, Politics.* Ann Arbor: University of Michigan Press, 2012.

Rodríguez, Juana María. *Sexual Futures, Queer Gestures, and Other Latina Longings.* New York: New York University Press, 2014.

Rodríguez-Fraticelli, Carlos. "Pedro Albizu Campos: Strategies of Struggle and Strategic Struggles." *Centro Journal* 4 (1992): 24–33.

Roig-Franzia, Manuel. "A Terrorist in the House." *Washington Post Magazine,* February 22, 2004, W12.

Roseman, Marina. "The New Rican Village: Artists in Control of the Image-Making, Machinery." *Latin American Music Review / Revista de Música Latinoamericana* 4, no. 1 (Spring–Summer 1983): 132–167.

Rossini, Jon D. *Contemporary Latina/o Theater.* Carbondale: Southern Illinois University Press, 2008.

Ruiz, Vicki L., and Virginia Sánchez Korrol. "Lebrón, Dolores 'Lolita' (1910–)." In *Latinas in the United States: A Historical Encyclopedia.* Bloomington: Indiana University Press, 2006.

Saldaña-Portillo, María Josefina. *The Revolutionary Imagination in the Americas and the Age of Development.* Durham, NC: Duke University Press, 2003.

Santiago, Leyla, Catherine E. Shoichet, and Jason Kravarik. "Puerto Rico's New Hurricane Maria Death Toll Is 46 Times Higher Than the Government's Previous Count." *CNN*, August 28, 2018. www.cnn.com.

Sartre, Jean-Paul. *Nausea*. Translated by Lloyd Alexander. Introduction by Richard Howard. New York: New Directions, 2007.

Schechner, Richard. *Performance Theory*. New York: Routledge, 1988.

Schwartz, Tony. "2 Freed Puerto Rican Nationalists Say They Can't Rule Out Violence." *New York Times*, September 12, 1979, 1.

Sewell, Bevan. *Encyclopedia of U.S. Military Interventions in Latin America*. Santa Barbara, CA: ABC-CLIO, 2013.

Shakur, Assata. *Assata: An Autobiography*. Chicago: Chicago Review Press, 1987.

Shimizu, Yuko. *My Friend Ryan*. September 21, 2010. http://yukoart.com.

Shuster, Alvin. "Shooting Blasted Day of Routine." *New York Times*, March 2, 1954, 18.

Silliman, Jael, Marlene Gerber Fried, Loretta Ross, and Elena Gutiérrez. *Undivided Rights: Women of Color Organize for Reproductive Justice*. Cambridge, MA: South End Press, 2004.

Soto-Crespo, Ramón. *Mainland Passage: The Cultural Anomaly of Puerto Rico*. Minneapolis: University of Minnesota Press, 2009.

Spivak, Gayatri Chakravorty. *In Other Worlds: Essays in Cultural Politics*. New York: Routledge, 1987.

———. "Subaltern Studies: Deconstructing Historiography." In *Selected Subaltern Studies*, edited by Ranajit Guha and Gayatri Chakravorty Spivak. Delhi: Oxford University Press, 1988.

———. "Time and Timing: Law and History." In *Chronotypes: The Construction of Time*, edited by John Bender and David E. Wellbery. Stanford, CA: Stanford University Press, 1991.

Stern, Roger. *Superman: Sunday Classics: 1939–1943*. New York: DC Comics, 2006.

Stoler, Ann Laura. *Carnal Knowledge and Imperial Power: Race and the Intimate in Colonial Rules*. Berkeley: University of California Press, 2002.

Striff, Erin. "Introduction: Locating Performance Studies." In *Performance Studies*, edited by Erin Striff. New York: Palgrave Macmillan, 2003.

Sweeny, Robert W. "'This Performance Art Is for the Birds': 'Jackass,' 'Extreme' Sports, and the De(con)struction of Gender." *Studies in Art Education* 49, no. 2 (2008): 142.

Thompson, Chris. "Afterbirth of a Nation: William Pope.L's Great White Way." *Women & Performance* 14.1, no. 27 (2004): 67.

Thomson, Iain. "Can I Die? Derrida on Heidegger on Death." *Philosophy Today* 43, no. 1 (1999): 29–42.

Tovar, Federico Ribes. *Albizu Campos: Puerto Rican Revolutionary*. New York: Plus Ultra Educational, 1971.

Trias Monge, José. *Puerto Rico: The Trials of the Oldest Colony in the World*. New Haven, CT: Yale University Press, 1999.

Trussell, C. P. "Witness Describes Shooting, Capture: Reporter Sees Firing in House." *New York Times*, March 2, 1954, 1.

Turner, Lou. "Fanon Reading (W)right, the (W)right Reading of Fanon: Race, Modernity, and the Fate of Humanism." In *Race and Racism in Continental Philosophy*, edited by Robert Bernasconi with Sybol Cook. Bloomington: Indiana University Press, 2003.

Uszerowicz, Monica. "'I Am an Invented Character': A Performance Artist on Living in His Utopia." *Hyperallergic*, August 24, 2016. http://hyperallergic.com.

Vargas, Deborah. *Dissonant Divas in Chicana Music: The Limits of La Onda*. Minneapolis: University of Minnesota Press, 2012.

Vicens, A. J. "Puerto Rico Files for Bankruptcy the Day after Trump Admin Brags about Blocking Funds." *Mother Jones*, May 3, 2017. www.motherjones.com.

Viego, Antonio. *Dead Subjects: Toward a Politics of Loss in Latino Studies*. Durham, NC: Duke University Press, 2007.

———. "The Unconscious of Latino/a Studies." *Latino Studies* 1, no. 2 (July 2003): 333–336. https://doi.org/10.1057/palgrave.lst.8600035.

Vilar, Irene. *The Ladies' Gallery: A Memoir of Family Secrets*. Translated by Gregory Rabassa. New York: Other Press, 2009.

Virilio, Paul. *The Aesthetics of Disappearance*. Translated by Philip Beitchman. Los Angeles: Semiotext[e], 2009.

Warr, Tracey, with Amelia Jones, eds. *The Artist's Body*. New York: Phaidon Press, 2012.

West-Durán, Alan. "Puerto Rico: The Pleasures and Traumas of Race." *Centro Journal* 17 (2005): 46–69.

Wilson, Martha, and Papo Colo, "'Oh Colo How You Perform Contradiction? Let We Count the Ways': Martha Wilson in Conversation with Papo Colo." In *Will, Power & Desire: Painting, Sculpture, Drawing, Performance: 1976–1986*. New York: Rosa Esman Gallery/Exit Art, 1986.

"Win Puerto Rican Trial." *New York Times*, June 24, 1932, 10.

INDEX

ADÁL, 24–25, 33, 183n10; and *Puerto Ricans Underwater/Los ahogados*, 5–13, 172–173, 183n13, 188n89; and Reverend Juan Pedro Pietri, 5–6, 183n14, 203n39

aesthetics, Brown: "brown bowel aesthetic," 119–125; critiquing machismo, 30, 79, 159; and drag performance, 206n13; and queerness in González-Torres's work, 151–152, 207n35; and queerness in Rivera's work, 141–143, 150–154, 159–161, 206n13, 207n35

aesthetics, durational, 11–14, 135, 137, 148, 152–153. *See also* duration; endurance; endurance art; movement

aesthetics, gendered: critiquing machismo, 30, 79, 159; depicting gender violence, 119–125; and drag performance, 206n13; exhausted hypermasculinity, 33, 85–86, 93–94; and impotence, 1, 8–9, 33–34, 83, 94; and modernity, 197n103; resisting masculinist temporality, 14, 39, 62–63, 123; revolutionary femme, 30–33, 37–41, 57–63, 65, 194n52, 197n100

aesthetics, queer, 187n88; and Brownness in González-Torres's work, 151–152, 207n35; and Brownness in Rivera's work, 141–143, 150–154, 159–161, 206n13, 207n35; and drag performance, 206n13

Ahmed, Sara, 28

Albizu Campos, Pedro, 43, 45–46, 182n9, 190n4, 191n21

Althusser, Louis, 47–48, 58–61, 72

Aparicio, Frances R., 26–27

ataque de nervios, 26, 52–55, 194n57

authenticity, 10, 82–83, 150–152, 157; and *Da-sein*, 20–21, 86, 145–148, 158, 194n52

Barthes, Roland, 8, 63, 142, 154–157, 161, 196n93

Bash (Rivera), 142, 152, 156–157. See also *Body/Psyche*

becoming, 19, 22, 37, 81, 87, 126. *See also* Being; *Da-sein*; incompleteness

Being: and abjection, 120; and Black existentialism, 15–17, 48, 206n6; Lebrón's recitation for, 31, 50, 71; philosophical question of, 86–87, 193n51; and Ricanness as critique of philosophical tradition, 17–24, 31–32, 85–86, 148, 173, 198n19. See also *Da-sein*

being-in-the-world, 19, 22, 28, 61, 137, 147

being-toward-death, 19, 23–24, 147

being-with, 19, 28, 129, 145–147, 151–152, 163, 207n36

Bennett, Tony, 95–96

Bergson, Henri, 105, 114–118, 123, 126–127, 149, 156, 204n49

Bhabha, Homi K., 77, 198n19

biopolitics, 24, 50, 193n49

Black existentialism, 15–17, 85, 137, 186n74, 206n6

Blackness, 15–17, 74, 85, 137, 161

Body/Psyche (Rivera), 137, 138, 142, 206n14; *Bash*, 142, 152, 156–157; *Breath Piece*, 142, 163–164; *Goodbye Piece*, 142, 159–162; *Hand Play*, 142, 148–149, 152; *Reflex*, 142, 165–166

ABOUT THE AUTHOR

Sandra Ruiz is Assistant Professor of Latina/Latino Studies and English at the University of Illinois at Urbana-Champaign and an affiliate faculty member of the Center for Latin American and Caribbean Studies; the Program in Comparative and World Literature; the Program in Holocaust, Genocide, and Memory Studies; and the Unit for Criticism and Interpretive Theory. She is the Co-founder of the Brown Theatre Collective.